THE GUTENBERG REVOLUTION

A HISTORY OF PRINT CULTURE

The Gutenberg Revolution
A History of Print Culture

Richard Abel

Transaction Publishers
New Brunswick (U.S.A.) and London (U.K.)

Copyright © 2011 by Transaction Publishers, New Brunswick, New Jersey.

All rights reserved under International and Pan-American Copyright Conventions. No part of this book may be reproduced or transmitted in any form or by any means, electronic or mechanical, including photocopy, recording, or any information storage and retrieval system, without prior permission in writing from the publisher. All inquiries should be addressed to Transaction Publishers, Rutgers-The State University of New Jersey, 35 Berrue Circle, Piscataway, New Jersey 08854-8042. www.transactionpub.com

This book is printed on acid-free paper that meets the American National Standard for Permanence of Paper for Printed Library Materials.

Library of Congress Catalog Number: 2010045632
ISBN: 978-1-4128-1857-5
Printed in the United States of America

Library of Congress Cataloging-in-Publication Data

Abel, Richard, 1925–
   The Gutenberg revolution : history of print culture / Richard Abel.
     pages cm.
   Includes bibliographical references and index.
   ISBN 978-1-4128-1857-5 (acid-free paper)   1. Printing—Europe—History—Origin and antecedents.   2. Printing—Europe—History—16th century.   3. Printing—Europe—History—17th century.
4. Printing—Western countries—History.   5. Europe—Intellectual life.
6. Civilization, Western—History.   I. Title.
   Z124.A519   2011
   002.094—dc22
                                                        2010045632

This book is dedicated to the three ladies in my life.

Contents

Introduction		ix
1	A Brief Account of the History of the Culture of the West to 1450	1
2	Gutenberg's Printing Revolution and the Cultural Revolution of the Last Half of the Fifteenth Century	23
3	The Spread of Printing and Its Consequences in the Sixteenth Century	75
4	The Cultural Triumph of the Seventeenth Century and the Role of Print Therein	127
5	Epilogue: Closing Remarks and Summary	161
Bibliography		171
Index		185

Introduction

Books are not absolutely dead things but doe contain a potencie of life in them to be as active as the soule was whose progeny they are: nay they do preserve in a violl of the purest efficacie and extraction of that living intellect that bred them.
—John Milton, *The Areopagitica*

Never since the sun has stood in the firmament and the planets revolved around him had it been perceived that man's existence centers in his head, i.e. in Thought, inspired by which he builds up the world of reality.
—Georg W.F. Hegel, *The Philosophy of History*

One of the most puzzling lapses in the historical accounts of the rise of the West from a state of relative backwardness in the near millennium following the decline of the Western Roman Empire in the fourth to fifth AD period to that of a remarkably robust cultural achievement by the fifteenth to sixteenth century is the casual way in which historians have dealt the grave epistemological problem in the West and Gutenberg's invention of printing. The cultural achievement which was in the centuries following the fifteenth century came to be the cultural configuration of not just the West but of much of the rest of the world is an unimaginable absent Gutenberg's gift and its subsequent widespread adoption across most of the world. By the fourth or fifth century, the major implications of the new religious order of Christianity had been debated and resolved. So the cultural vitality inherent in the required intellectual effort had been largely exhausted. But no substantial body of new ideas had been introduced to foster further explorations dedicated to the search for the good and the true. It was only with the coming of the printed book and the resultant wide dissemination of an advanced ideational hypothesis that the idea generation in the West took wings.

Virtually, every historian of any stature writing of the Renaissance and/or the centuries following merely mentions the printed book in passing as one of the three notable inventions of the fifteenth century. The printed codex is simply lumped with the two other major fifteenth-century inventions of the compass (actually the invention of the compass card providing minute directional headings) and gunpowder. Galileo so lumped these three innovations together. Since then, historians and history of ideas writers have almost universally repeated Galileo's formulation. The blind Milton, in his defense of the freedom of the press at the time of the English Revolution, was one of only a few to recognize the crucial importance of the immense and powerful knowledge engine of cultural generation that Gutenberg brought into being.

It almost would seem that the advent of the first examples of the cultural power of multiple identical copies of the same book text made possible by the introduction of the integrated technology of type, the press, and the printing on vellum, parchment, or paper coupled with the widespread dissemination thereof would offer a "red flag" achievement to historians. The historians who so blithely whisk by this radical improvement in the means of hammering out and passing knowledge from one mind to a number of other minds, by contrast, have almost universally commented upon the continuing intellectual and cultural distortions engendered by the errors in and a variety of other linguistic and orthographic eccentricities common to handwritten manuscripts. A significant number of these historians have dwelt in greater or lesser length upon the often-marked differences in the texts of the manuscript copies of the principal texts used across Europe for a millennium and a half—the Bible, Psalters, or the divergent conduct of the mass throughout Christendom resulting from scribal error in their copying. Yet it seems that Milton was one of the few prepared to give the cultural impact of the stable content of the printed book its due in correcting these shortcomings and in accelerating cultural accumulation. Nicholas of Cusa, one of the leading intellects of the mid-fifteenth century, a cardinal, and the papal legate for the transalpine churches, was much aware of these differences of meaning in the liturgical literature and the resultant departures from a common understanding arising out of the multiple errors of transcription and was likely a keen proponent of Gutenberg's invention.

In the same way, students of the Middle Ages all draw attention to the slow, spasmodic evolution of thought and practice in the period from the fifth to the fifteenth century. They also address the paucity of manuscripts and the meager collections of manuscript books in the monastic libraries and those of a few of the kings or occasional noblemen—five hundred to perhaps more than two thousand in the Vatican library at its best. The medievalists frequently comment, some at length, on the repetitive or arid character of most of the intellectual writings of this near millennium. All also expiate on the obstacles to passing the cultural inheritance on

Introduction

with so few texts and all of them more or less flawed. But few, if any, note the sudden introduction of printed books in multiple copies marking the latter half of the fifteenth century and the "sudden" upsurge in the generation and testing of ideas in these comparatively few years of this and the following century.

The first serious historian to note and comment upon the cultural nodal point of the fifteenth century and its remarkable transition was Elizabeth Eisenstein in her genuinely magisterial book, *The Printing Press as an Agent of Change* (1980). In this massive study, Eisenstein traces this sudden acceleration in the generation and exchange of ideas and some of the many consequences flowing therefrom. But in the standard exercise of academic modesty, she characterizes the invention of printing simply as a historical change agent, not as a technological invention that radically transformed the evolution of the culture of the West—more radically perhaps than did the invention of the steam engine or other technological innovations of the nineteenth century repeatedly but rightly celebrated by historians and writers on the history of ideas and technology. The technological invention and cultural impact of printing warrant a higher place and greater celebration in the history of the West and in the history of ideas than simply as an agent of change. It was surely the latter, but it was of much greater import in the history of Western and world cultural history than simply a change agent. It was a radical resolution of the epistemological problem that had dogged the West for a millennium. It marked not the opening of a new chapter but the opening of an entirely new volume in the history of first the West and later the world. Now this new cultural volume must realistically be viewed in its opening chapters as the third volume in the cultural history of the West, the first volume being the history of the founding and growth of the Judeo-Christian religious tradition and the second being the Greek and Roman classical traditions and practices. These two major cultural traditions did not dry up and blow away but remained as fundamental lineaments of the culture of the West to be augmented, in time, by the cultural accumulations generated in the late medieval times and sharply accelerated from the mid-fifteenth forward.

So the aim of this volume is simply to endeavor to clearly delineate the mechanism undergirding the epistemological revolution wrought by the fifteenth-century invention of printing and to trace the resultant rapid reorientation and acceleration of the evolution of the culture of the West. So extensive and vast were the cultural consequences of Gutenberg's gift that only the principal lineaments thereof can be identified in this writing.

Further, there are effects that have not yet played themselves out so are not yet sufficiently evident to assess. In a genuine sense, this writing is but a prologue to what the writer hopes will be a growing concern with and investigation of the cultural consequences of the printing revolution and their evolution.

The author is manifestly indebted to Elizabeth Eisenstein for opening so wide the view of the place of printing in the history of the West and the history of ideas. Absent her remarkable historical insight, this writing could hardly be. In something of the same sense, the violls of John Milton noted above were of greater insight and understanding than were the appraisals of other early commentators who saw fit to merely lump the invention of printing with the invention of the compass and gunpowder.

It is necessary to briefly limn out the background formed in earlier centuries to clearly understand the radical cultural impact of the fifteenth-century printing revolution. The eighth-century Carolingian Renascence and the Twelfth-Century Renascence gave notice of the viability of the new Christian/classical culture of the West. However, both renascences proved too culturally fragile in the face of adversity to endure in a sustained way. The cultural salvagers of those two renascences preserved much of the extant classical substance together with that of the Bible and the writings of the church fathers. But the ideational infrastructure needed to support a vital cultural evolution could little withstand the mishaps and misfortunes ever present in the human condition. The picture of those two renascences and their collapse are dealt with in broad strokes in the first chapter. The cultural upsurge of the Renaissance, resulting in part from Gutenberg's invention, occupies the remaining chapters.

Shortly after completing the manuscript for this book, directed to tracing the cultural renewal of the West fostered by Gutenberg's invention of printing and the printed book, one of the leading scholarly publishers in the United States published a series of essays reflecting upon the dilemmas and difficulties faced by today's serious publisher seeking to maintain the best in book publishing. *This book is a useful reminder by a contemporary publisher of the realities faced by modern publishers of books of substance in advancing the ongoing cultural odyssey of advancing the search for truth and good.

---

*See Irving Louis Horowitz, *Publishing as a Vocation*, Transaction Publishers, 2010.

1

A Brief Account of the History of the Culture of the West to 1450

Ideas never die: they are ageless and always ready to revive in the minds which need them, just as ancient seeds can germinate when they find a fertile soil.
—Etienne Gilson, *History of Christian Philosophy in the Middle Ages*

The period in Europe from no later than the end of the reign of Justinian the Great in the sixth century, the Roman Empire in the West came to its end. It was brought down by the various wandering tribes from the North and the East that overrode most of the continent as well as North Africa despite the empire's growingly desperate two-century struggle to survive. The fall of the Roman Empire was a genuine cultural cataclysm in the West. How could have such a millennial-old power encompassing most of the world known to Europe been brought to its knees? Of even more acute disquiet was the parallel loss of the quite impressive cultural structure that had been constructed by the Greeks and preserved/embellished by the Romans. Yet much of this structure was lost or massively corrupted within not more than two centuries. This debacle lent substantial credence to the observation that it is always harder and more time-consuming to create than to destroy. Further, the slow creation of viable ideas and their implementation can only arise when there is a body of ideas that other minds can employ as the flints of thought against which the iron of creativity can be struck to create the sparks of new ideas. This immense body of interrelated ideas—in short knowledge, which required over ten centuries, a millennium, or more, to create and implement—was gravely imperiled.

Such a hard-won accumulation and integration of ideas into a meaningful and coherent whole unique to each one of the four great civilizational complexes of the modern world has come in recent times to be referred to as a "culture." This culture is a vast matrix of intellectual concepts and ethical precepts. This complex of ideas is encompassed within the subsidiary bodies of more specialized concepts and precepts such as language, theology, philosophy, history, economics, law, education, governance, etc. All of these identifiably discrete sectors of a culture are embodied in a considerable variety of social institutions—churches, agriculture, manufacture and distribution of goods and services (markets), courts, schools, governments, etc. It is these frictions or problems forever inherent in and between these complexes that lead to the constantly changing historical kaleidoscope of these four cultures.

So the extreme dismay with which a handful of observers watched the collapse of the classical culture can be well appreciated. The culture—the critical inertial force of intellectual concepts and ethical precepts, which kept the culture vital and resilient against unending assault and contradictions—was mortally imperiled. What was to become of the traditional ways of life which had given the people a sense of an assured, stable, and more or less comfortable way of life?

Further, such an idea-rich, highly integrated body of beliefs and intellectual concepts and ethical precepts is incorporated not simply in the *weltanschauung* of the natives of a culture, but most of the institutions thereof are integrally interwoven into this matrix. In short, within broad measure, all the natives therein more or less share a common set of beliefs and hypotheses and live within a society whose institutions are largely supportive of this particular complex body of ideas. Culture from this perspective may usefully be viewed as the glue that holds the allegiance and moves the evolution of the society in a roughly coherent fashion over the centuries.

But by sometime in the fourth or fifth centuries, there was the unpalatable and inescapable fact of the growing collapse of the Roman Empire and the associated classical culture. The dependable classical culture was in manifest and apparently inescapable decline. Its death throes were agonizingly prolonged. This extended progressive decay presented to a handful of thoughtful people the opportunity to endeavor to implement means aimed at the preservation of the shape and content of a world absent the towering Roman Empire and all the treasures of classical thought and practice that had been created and housed in it for the millennium of the life of Greece and Rome. What might be done to assure the safeguarding of at least some fraction of this vast treasure for subsequent use whatever might be the dimensions and character of that future? What remnants of the classical culture might be preserved to, if not prevent, at least mitigate a descent into the barbarism that was pressing the Graeco-Roman world from all sides? Where was to be found the flint of thought against which the iron of creativity could be struck to create the sparks of new ideas from which could fire for the creation of those ideas/hypotheses crucial to the continuing vitality of a viable cultural tradition? The same congery of concerns and anxieties hovered over the small but burgeoning clusters of Christians—Catholic, Orthodox, and Arian.

It is the West's very good fortune that a diverse handful of individuals, widely scattered across the heartlands of the empire, cognizant of the impending failure of the classical/Christian cultural nexus, undertook the daunting task of seeking to save some of the cultural knowledge and related bodies of ideas that had painfully been created along the Mediterranean. These hoarders preserved some of the records that embodied culture with the avowed intention of passing them along as the materials that might be used in the construction of whatever unknown culture succeeded that of the culture they knew, treasured, and guided their ways of conceiving of and acting in the mysteries of the world.

The Hoarders

This meager and scattered few, possessed of some vision of what the future might have in store, undertook this preservation work involving as much of the accumulated classical learning as they were able. In the main, they carried this work out in remote locations and within spaces they thought might preserve the manuscripts written on papyrus—hardly the most durable of writing materials in the humid environments of Europe. These few hoarders, however vague and uncertain the outcomes of their efforts and however shaky their grounds of selection of which violls of the purest efficacy were to save, passed along to a later and more settled Europe much of the classical learning upon which the present-day culture of the West was erected.

A parallel preservation effort had to be mounted to save the Judeo-Christian literature in which all the learning and thought undergirding that fragile new religious belief still faced the long-established and preponderant pagan beliefs involving a familiar pantheon of gods. These relatively recent and novel writings were considered by some of the hoarders among the most central of these writings to be saved. The hope was that these Judeo-Christian writings would in time win the day for the religious beliefs and would provide the foundations of a universal church. Among these critical texts were the Old and New Testaments of the Bible and the commentaries thereon by the church fathers and the rabbinical literature. The Bible had been passed along in its early days in several versions before being settled in the version known as the Vulgate translated by St. Jerome in the fourth century. Of almost equal importance was the exegetical writings of the early church fathers elucidating and formulating the major doctrines of the new faith derived in part from the Bible.

The work of these theologians and writers was one of the world's major and most compelling exercises of intellectual syncretism and synthesis ever undertaken. They had more or less successfully and comfortably melded and integrated the Judaism of the Old Testament, the Greek philosophy of Neoplatonism, and the teachings of the new religion of Christianity contained in the New Testament. This remarkable intellectual synthesis was to provide the foundations and the organizing axis of the extraordinary cultural edifice of the West, even up to the present day.

The recently founded Christian church was a remarkable hierarchical and geographic institution, modeled in part upon the Roman Imperial structure. It was composed of a hierarchy of religious officials headed by the pope under whom served a phalanx of bishops. The geographic area each bishop served was termed a diocese. Within each diocese were a large number of geographically local priests serving single congregations, largely in villages. Parallel to this structure was another structure not found in the Roman model, but unique to the Christian church, a band of ascetics gathered together in a reserved location, the monastery. The number of these discrete orders and the membership thereof grew over the succeeding centuries with the extension of the reach of the church.

A number of the major church dioceses, together with the nascent monastic orders, preserved the writings of most of the church fathers. Many more possessed the Bible in one of the several versions—the original languages in which the Bible was written as well as early translations into several ethnic languages thereof. Of course, the Vulgate version translated by St. Jerome was widely held, but in copies, most of them varied more or less markedly due to the often idiosyncratic scripts used or the remarkably varied abbreviations devised by the several scribes copying them. Further, all of these copies departed in a greater or lesser degree from their originals due to inevitable copying errors or scribal inattention or failures of scribal understanding. The Vatican Library was to be for some centuries the largest library in the West—in the early centuries under review here holding perhaps nine hundred to one thousand manuscripts, quite meager as compared to the estimated number of manuscripts of distinct classical writings. Given the limited number of texts in the principal library of the church, the paucity of texts, however poorly transcribed, in most of the few other libraries can be imagined. Of these religious manuscripts in various church libraries, the preponderance was in the newly fashioned codex format rather than rolled scrolls of papyrus. The codex format, which continues in near-universal use today for books and which was first widely used by the Christian sects, was written on parchment or vellum.

Of utmost importance were in the early the writings of St. Augustine, which not only laid the substantial elements of the foundations of subsequent doctrine but also, by virtue of the Hellenistic tradition in which Augustine was educated, preserved crucial aspects of Hellenistic Neoplatonic learning. As a major contender in the early church councils, which resolved the meanings of many of the Christian doctrinal tenets, Augustine's writings were a crucial element. It should be noted in passing that several of these doctrinal debates also led to the disagreements between and ultimate separation of the Eastern Orthodox church from the Western Catholic church.

One of the greatest of the hoarders was St. Benedict of Nursia, who established, in the early sixth century, an order of monks, which was to flourish for centuries in the form of Benedictine monasteries throughout the West. Benedict's rule for these monasteries included one requiring the monks to read at least one book a year. The consequence of this rule was, of course, that every Benedictine establishment had to form, for that day, a generous library of minimally fifty or so books. To supply the nearly endless library needs of a burgeoning number of monastic houses, another rule required each monk to perform some work for the monastery among which were a stipulated number of hours every day to the work of copying book manuscripts. Much of this monastically produced religious literature was dispersed across Christendom by this means.

The violls of secular learning, while of secondary importance in the Christian worldview, were also of substantial concern to the hoarders. Because Latin was the language in use, and likely projected to remain viable, most of the texts saved by the hoarders of this treasure were those written in Latin. Consequently, little of the Greek corpus was stored for the future by the Western hoarders. As good fortune would have it, much of the Greek trove was preserved in the Arab world, Constantinople, and the historical Greek purlieus. This body of Greek ideas was not to enter the West in substantial proportions until the twelfth century and the fifteenth century.

Of perhaps primary importance in making the Latin writings accessible was the provision of the key for unlocking the chest containing the violls preserving the "living intellect" of the writers. The lock and key of every body of cultural learning remains that of the language. So grammars and dictionaries of Latin were absolutely necessary to opening the lock on much of the Judeo-Christian literature and the entirety of the preserved Latin literature. The surviving basic Latin language textbooks were the two sections of Donatus's *Ars Grammatica Grammatica*, the *Ars Minor*, and the *Ars Major*. These basic texts were composed about AD 350 and handed down until well into the sixteenth century. The more advanced textbook of the Latin language was that of Priscian *Institutes* composed about AD 515, which also remained in use into the sixteenth century.

One of the most important of the hoarders was Boethius (AD 480–525), who translated not only the basic texts of Aristotle's *Organon* (the *Categories* and *On Interpretation*) but also Porphyry's *Isagoge* (an explanation of Aristotle's *Introduction to the Categories of Aristotle*). These works, together with Plato's *Timaeus*, translated by an unknown Roman formed the basic Greek tools, other than the Bible, upon which most of the intellectual and ethical edifice of the West was constructed by the church fathers. (P. Shorey, the historian of medieval philosophy commented, "The shortest cut to the philosophy of the Middle Ages is to commit the *Timaeus* to memory.")

Perhaps of equally paramount importance was the writings of Cassidorus, the scion of a wealthy family of Roman notables. He became convinced that the Roman Empire was living its final days, so turned to the life of a Christian monk. He established a monastery on family lands in the south of Italy, which housed a small band of like-minded men and a sizable library of the works Cassidorus considered most important. Cassidorus himself wrote the *Institutiones* (late sixth century), which provided much of the structure and content of the seven liberal arts, the standard guide to formal education in Europe through the length of the Middle Ages. From the monastery library, he assembled not only the guidelines for the curriculum of the trivium (grammar, rhetoric, and dialectic) and the quadrivium (arithmetic, geometry, astronomy, and music) but also the extensive bibliographies of each together with summaries of the learning encapsulated in each.

Prior to the work of Cassidorus, a stilted allegory set in a party of the gods attending the marriage of Mercury to Philology, by Martianus Capella about AD 420, *De Nuptiis Mercurii Et Philologiae* was preserved. The plot and dialog record the gods speaking of the seven liberal arts, so providing another source for the organization and content of the curriculum of medieval monastery and church schools.

Several related reference works of the greatest importance for roughly a millennium were composed in the early seventh century by Isidore, bishop of Seville, a florilegium (a miscellany of intellectual concepts and ethical precepts assembled by the author; a form of literature founded by Isidore and extensively employed through the Middle Ages that evolved into the modern daybook) widely referred to in the Middle Ages. He also compiled a compendium of the then most authoritative interpretations and explanations of the Bible, *De viris illustribus*. But his most widely known and prized work was the *Etymologies* in twenty long sections. The *Etymologies* consisted of detailed entries encapsulating much of the known bodies of knowledge organized by subject matter. This massive project, containing much error in light of latter accumulations of knowledge, might be likened to the standard encyclopedia of the Middle Ages and early Renaissance.

Additionally, the texts of approximately 150 other titles, largely from the Roman literature, were saved by a variety of unknown hoarders, most in monasteries or churches, and frequently brought to light only centuries later—well into the sixteenth century.

The Salvagers of the Carolingian Renascence

The effort of discovering and copying this miniscule collection of the intellectual and ethical treasures of the classical and Judeo-Christian worlds was undertaken in about the fourth and fifth centuries not only by the Benedictine order but also by the clan monasteries, which had by an unusual chain of historical events been established in Ireland. The Irish monks ventured into the outlying islands of the western Mediterranean, where they encountered bands of religious who had hoarded not only some of the Latin works but the Greek as well. The Irish monks later also ventured into England and subsequently to the fringes of Northern Europe bent on establishing small enclaves of monks for the purpose of missionizing. They manifestly carried small collections of the books they thought most important for understanding their quiet faith, which in turn formed the basis of some of the most significant Medieval libraries of the region. The most famous of these monastic libraries were Iona off the west coast of Scotland and, of even greater consequence, Lindesfarne on the east coast of England, just north of North Umbria.

These two Irish monasteries formed the springboard for the remarkable revival of learning in North Umbria. It was from this latter tradition that the great Bede emerged, a polymath who ornamented the great library at Yarrow formed by the Bishop Biscop (628–90). This bishop, dedicated to learning and education, traveled widely in his search for books to add to his library, assiduously commissioning copyists at Lindesfarne as well as Rome and other continental monasteries to supply him with the books. It was from this few hundred books (secular and religious) collected by the bishop that the Venerable Bede (673–735) became perhaps the most learned man in the West, writing a history of England that became the model for subsequent history writing and producing an Old English translation of the Bible.

The Yarrow library was the model upon which Egbert, the archbishop of York, modeled his cathedral school and library. The archbishop, like the earlier bishop to the north, was very much concerned with establishing another school and library in York. Egbert particularly mined the libraries of the churches and monasteries, founded in the seventh century by Catholic missionaries, along the Pilgrims' Way through Flanders, along the Rhine to St. Gall and Lake Constance in Switzerland, and then over the Alps to Rome borrowing for copying or having copied (manuscripts were scarce and precious, so many holders refused to subject them to the hazards of travel) for his library. His efforts led to the great library of York, perceived at the time "… as the best library in Europe." Here it was that the child Alcuin (735–804) was entered into the cathedral school to become a priest. He soon set a mark as an assiduous student possessed of a brilliant mind, following the footsteps of Bede. At York, Alcuin not only mastered the standard religious learning but also became acquainted with the surviving remnants of the work of Pliny, Lucian, Terence, Horace, Ovid, and others of the hoarded Latin writers.

At about the same time, the towering wheelhorse of a new age, the remarkable son of the house of Martel, Charlemagne (742–814) entered into history. Carl der Grosse was not only an indomitable warrior, enormously expanding the limits of the Holy Roman Empire, but also possessed an acute mind interested in, and thoroughly understanding, the knowledge that lay at the base of the emerging Western culture. Carl was almost viscerally aware that if his work and the continued viability of Western culture and his Holy Roman Empire was to live on, he had to not only educate the children of the cadre of his chief lieutenants but also create an educational model to that end in his imperial city, Aachen. By so doing, he sought to rally the allegiance of the numerous isolated and self-focused warlords of the localities, which he had incorporated into his domains to these twin objectives. So complimenting his annual summer campaigns of conquest, the inclement months of the year were spent in recruiting and associating with some of the leading scholars of the age. For establishing this school and a domestic college, he enlisted Alcuin of York.

His plans for this remarkable scholar went well beyond stimulating good winter conversation at court. Charlemagne had in mind the formation of an outstanding library and a court school in which the children of the empire's leading families might be well educated. But his thinking went beyond simply teaching/learning at Aachen. He sought to have a number of the key monasteries in the empire upgraded to become not only leading centers of education and loci for the training of religious or imperial officials (the clergy provided the standard pool from which government officialdom was recruited for centuries) but also nuclei for the dissemination of books and cultural learning to the larger end of forming a coherent culture and body of widely accepted beliefs and knowledge. The school at Charlemagne's court provided the model as well as the catalog of the books to be copied for the cathedral and monastic schools decreed by the emperor as well in many cases of elements of the teaching staffs and manuscripts for copying in these remote locales.

To make a long and intriguing story short, Charlemagne, however nebulously, had in mind a reformulated and renewed integrated culture modeled along the lines of the Roman Empire but which had evolved in the subsequent three or four centuries but incorporating the new realities of a Christian culture recognized not simply along the shores of the Mediterranean but also throughout the north and east regions of what came to be known as Europe. Alcuin was to be the cultural engine revising and driving this new Carolingian-inspired Western culture. So the age can rightfully be labeled the Carolingian Renascence.

The Decline and Erosion of the Carolingian Renascence

Despite this far-seeing and valiant effort, much of the fruit, but not all, was left to rot, thanks to the division of the realm among Charlemagne's less competent sons and the repeated invasions of the Vikings in the West and the Hungarians in the East. Charlemagne's weak successors were unable to cope with these external depredations leading to the progressive decay of institutions in less knowledgeable and forceful hands than those of the emperor's and those of Alcuin.

Accompanying these erosions of military strength and political vision was perhaps the most serious shortcoming of the thin mantle of Christian culture, which Charlemagne and some of his Merovingian predecessors had succeeded in spreading across Northern Europe. The sense of a common cultural identity and worth to resist these assorted destructive incursions was too feeble to fuel a genuine sense of resistance in a common enterprise. Rather the common sense answer was to fall back to a tribal or primitive feudal body of allegiances.

Charlemagne's empire was to crumble back into a congery of small isolated warring loci controlled by a self-identified band of warlords, not simply at the hands of his feckless offspring but also bands of competing warriors and their gangs of followers. These bands, sometimes simply raiders like the Norsemen but more frequently self-anointed local strongmen, created a crazy quilt of local dominances deigning themselves kings, barons, princes, dukes, etc. The Carolingian vision of a renewed common culture was beggared across the continent. Cultural decay rapidly became evident on every hand. It would be roughly four hundred years before a comparable inflorescence would reappear in the West.

Elements of the church, most notably some from the monastic orders or the church, together with the occasional brilliant secular leader—from among the dynasties of the Ottonians, Hohenstaufens, Capetians, Plantagenets, and others—maintained or palely imitated some measure of the culture slowly reassembled in the nexus of the Carolingian Renascence. The meager cultural treasure of Europe had emerged from the scanty and harsh rigors of the Dark Ages but remained a still culturally weak and primitive outlier of the cultures of the Euro-Asian continent. The remnants of the Roman Empire in the East, the Byzantine Empire, far outshone its Western relative, while the trajectory of the Islamic Empire in the Middle East, North Africa, and Spain not only had led to enormous geographic expansion, thanks to the religious injunction to convert the world to Islam by the sword if necessary (*jihad*), but also had become the naturalized province of much of Greek Hellenistic learning.

It was the latter's transmission of much of the Greek learning to the West that massively contributed to the second revitalization of cultural learning and creation in the West, which emerged in the Twelfth-Century Renascence.

The Twelfth-Century Efflorescence and Renascence

This major historical cultural upsurge was stimulated in part by a burst of creativity in the West, one of those historical events difficult to fully untangle. The leading lineaments in this cultural resurgence included, first, a rise in organized instruction at a higher level conducted by a cadre of learned clerics outside the monastic or church school setting in which such instruction had previously been carried on. In due time, these congeries of itinerant scholars came to be called by the name of universities. Here young men, still largely in clerical orders, came to learn from leading figures in the teaching of one or another of the seven liberal arts. These teachers soon came to be identified as professors. So the passing of the cultural tradition came to possess another new and highly specific channel. The same may be said of the elaboration and augmentation of that culture fostered by these new institutions.

However, save for Charlemagne's unfinished salvage efforts of learning centered initially on the group of learned men he had gathered at his court, such work was carried on subsequently in only an exceedingly fragmentary and highly diffused way in various monasteries scattered about across the West. In these circumstances, such learning and instruction might very well die in particular monasteries with the death of the one or two monks so involved. But under even the best of circumstances, such learning and cultural innovation could diffuse only slowly and in a haphazard way incorporated, as it was in the mind of a young monk who might travel and reside in another monastery. Or such ideas and thought might be recorded in a couple of manuscripts—often riddled with errors, many recorded not in the serviceable letterform of Carolingian miniscule but in a script employed by only a few readers, and lacking any punctuation and other guides to readers as to the way meaning was to be construed. Altogether, the reader can readily appreciate that two readers using two different copies of a presumably common text could, like ships passing in the night, argue in intense contradiction, thanks to differing texts. To provide a bleak summary, the cultural inheritance of the West was itself not only sited in isolated places in diverse monastic locations but also frequently quite unreliable after but a couple of error-laden previously copied versions. The universities, therefore, provided the principal conduits of the transmission of the still fragile and evolving thinly distributed Western culture.

Of equal or greater adverse import was the relative absence of a network of thinkers/writers who were advancing hypotheses that other thinkers/writers could use to critique such hypotheses or alternatively employ as intellectual springboards to create and disseminate more inclusive and compelling hypotheses. Small wonder that the period between the eighth and twelfth centuries seemed to move in slow motion. The formation of the initially de facto congeries of learned men subsequently organized into universities constituted an enormous advance in the organized structuring of cultural learning and evolution in the West. Students from across Europe and a few from Byzantium attended the lectures delivered by the professors and the seminars in which two or several professors faced off to argue, often furiously, the merits of the thought/writings of one another—powerful settings for hypothesis creation, criticism, and alternative hypothesis creation. With the formation of universities, it might be assumed that the future safety of the Western cultural legacy and its future advancement were now better embodied in a more formal and perhaps enduring institutional form.

In parallel with the advent of the university, the reorganization of the church and the beginnings of the dynastic state together with the accompanying practice of lawmaking and law courts prepared the ground for the subsequent upwelling in the shaping of the primary structures of the culture in the Twelfth-Century Renascence. This body of ideas relative to the secondary structures of church and governance organization led to not only substantial changes in the institutional character of these organizations but also the role they played in the evolution of the culture of the West.

In both cases of lawmaking, law courts and the profession of the lawyer had their beginnings in the discovery, in the late eleventh century, of a single manuscript of the Roman Emperor Justinian's *Corpus Juris Civilis*, the legal code of Roman law codified by a select body of legal scholars in Justinian's capitol of Constantinople in the seventh century. This surviving manuscript quickly led to the formation of the West's most important law school at the University of Bologna. The Roman law code found a ready acceptance by both the church, in Gratian's recasting of Canon law, and the monarchs of the dynastic states in its base assumption that the emperor (read pope or king) was the fount of all law and that justice was to be found only in the law courts thereof. Suddenly a total integrated body of law, which in turn led to a growing number of lawyers trained in its uses, was available to replace the multitude of traditional, largely ad hoc legal codes of church and state and practiced by a kind of master/apprentice practice in the employment of these diverse codes.

In the case of the church, the twelfth-century reorganizations and restructuring began with a burst of religious reform. The beginnings of this reform movement have been traced to the Benedictine Abbey in Cluny. This Cluniac reform took the form not simply by intensifying belief and renewing dedication to the strict rules laid down by St. Benedict but also by imparting a new, dramatic grandeur to the conduct of the liturgical services mounted throughout the day. This reform movement swept through the church and infused many of its congregants with a heightened religious devotion and more demanding code of personal ethical conduct. This same arousal of religious thinking and feeling inevitably led to an increased claim of authority in both religious and secular settings.

In parallel with the Cluniac reform, innovations in agricultural technology proved to be able to support an increased population. These innovations included the substitution of the horse for oxen thereby increasing the acreage that any single village might successfully crop, the introduction of the three-field system of crop rotation to produce a larger total harvest over the period of the rotation, and the successful conversion/addition of acreage due to the diking/drainage of marshlands. All led to increasingly successful tillage of not only long-cultivated fields but former wastelands and forests as well. In a basically subsistence agricultural economy, such increased output could supply a subsistence diet to a larger number of people. So a larger population also marked the twelfth century.

Increased population led, in turn, to an increase in the numbers of people who could find employment only in the newly emergent free towns. A growing urban bourgeoisie of traders and craftsmen proved a more effective means of supplying the needs of a larger population as well as providing an increase in total social wealth. This increased wealth found its way widely, however gradually, throughout the society, leading to both further investment in the improving of the capitalization of agriculture and crafts manufacture and advancing of a wider trading system capable of furnishing more cheaply desirable commodities—salt, spices, fabric, tools, etc.—to an increased number of local communities. The same growth of capitalistic trading not only vastly improved the movement of food from crop surplus areas to areas of poor crops, substantially reducing famine which was formerly a familiar curse across the land, but also provided amenities hitherto foreclosed to much of the rural society.

The nascent dynastic states in the meantime were beginning to take shape. In every case, such nascent dynastic states consolidated the governance and control of numerous local and quarreling warlords. This firming up of the state was supported by the uneven and ragged fixing of distinct, regional vernacular languages. Further, a more widely understood language enabled the kings, dukes, princes, etc., who could lay some claim to authority in these particular linguistic and geographic regions, to advance the establishment of greater control over the inhabitants. This control was exerted primarily through the apparatus of the feudal system, which also provided these dynasties with a mounted corps of trained military nobility able to fight the dynastic wars that pervaded the next several centuries. The authority of the dynastic courts was further augmented by the employment in increasing numbers of learned clerks, graduates of the burgeoning law schools modeled after Bologna.

These mutually supportive developments of universities, in religious belief and practice, and in state-building of the eleventh century, provided a fertile seedbed for the fecund, twelfth-century cultural renascence. Ironically, much of that new seed was to be derived through the culture of the avowed adversary of Christendom—the Arab and Persian Islamic culture, which controlled by this time all but a small fragment of the Byzantine Empire and much of the Iberian Peninsula.

Arguably, the primary motive force of the cultural upsurge of the twelfth century resulted from the infusion of another avalanche of classical texts. In this case, a large number of the major Greek texts injected a great trove of new ideas into the vital stream of the evolving formulation of an ever-more powerful and inclusive Western body of intellectual concepts and ethical precepts. This stream originated largely in the Umayyad Caliphate of Muslim Spain, where the reception and employment of Greek learning was still being cultivated, having been largely choked off by the Abbasid Caliphate in the eastern Muslim world. This treasure included Plato's *Dialogues* (translated but little used until the fourteenth century when another stream of Greek learning was introduced into the West from failing and ultimately vanquished Constantinople). Of greater utility in the twelfth century and succeeding centuries were the works of Galen on medicine, Ptolemy on natural science, Euclid on geometry, Archimedes on engineering, Proclus on Neoplatonic philosophy, Dioscorides on botany and pharmacy, other lesser Greek thinkers and writers, additional exegetical works of the Orthodox Greek fathers, and above all, the extant canon of Aristotle. In addition, the work of Arabic thinkers based on the Greek inheritance, whether commentaries on Greek texts or original writings by Arabic thinkers based upon the Greek texts, became available.

It is well to pause here to highlight one of the distinguishing and astounding characteristics distinguishing and delineating the Christian culture of the West relative to the other major cultural traditions. This remarkable difference is exemplified by this eager reception in the West of foreign or semi-foreign ideas native to other cultural formulations. In this case, the West can be described as a vortex sucking into its orbit many of the ideas/hypotheses created elsewhere that might come its way. This twelfth-century reception repeated that of the Judaic and Greek ideas into the emerging Christian culture and, in turn, was to be repeated several times, as the West progressively opened and revealed for the first time the full extent of the peoples and cultures occupying this planet.

The first problem facing the West in the twelfth-century reception was translating these works from Arabic into Latin. This work was carried out largely in Christian monasteries located in the north of Spain. The most notable of these translators were all clerics: Domingo Gonzalez, John of Spain, and Gerard of Cremona, etc. But translating was hardly enough for the question of accuracy and authenticity remained as all these texts had made the desperate copying voyage from Greek to Hebrew or Aramaic to Arabic or Syriac to Latin. All the hazards incurred in the translation and the copying manuscript tradition of nodding off, misunderstanding, the use of uncommon alphabets, the inclusion of glosses by translators or copyists, and the absence of any punctuation (so the reader had only a long string of words, usually lacking any word spacing) beclouded the distribution of these writings across Europe. All these difficulties repeatedly beset this extended stream. Such authentication could only be conducted after the fact by knowledgeable readers of both Latin and the original manuscript language comparing and emending the text of several different copies—a long and tedious exercise at best, which also requires the good fortune of possessing, in a single library collection, translations or copies of the same work rendered by several translators or copyists.

Whatever these textual and linguistic difficulties, the even larger question was that of once again incorporating a coherent body of philosophical ideas from a dissimilar tradition into that of a body of ideas centering upon and cohering to the Christian revelation. The latter was by the twelfth century an already elaborate theological/philosophical structure answering the cultural intellectual and ethical needs of the then culture of the West. The task of integrating this body of Greek–Islamic culture was largely undertaken by Dominican and Franciscan monks. The workshops in which this enormous ideational remodeling and cultural expansion project was undertaken was carried forward in the new universities as well. The towering mind in this extraordinary integration of distinct and unique bodies of ideas was that of Thomas Aquinas. Aquinas was a Dominican, who worked first in Cologne with the learned Albertus Magnus and then in Paris to conceive and write the monumental *Summas*, which not only set the theology of the Roman Catholic Church up to the present but also proved to be a body of thought that has had to be conjured with by all succeeding theologians and philosophers.

Unfortunately, this avalanche of Greek texts carried with it a generous tincture of fraudulent baggage including astrological treatises, hermetic writings, alchemical tracts, Gnostic formulas, and suchlike. These bodies of bizarre fantasy were to periodically disfigure the thought of many and to pester genuine thought and understanding in the West right up to the present—another but later age of excessive expectations.

By way of relief from the contemplation of such illusory imaginings as these, the twelfth century was a period of intense and profitable technological innovation. These advances included the following: the invention of the crank converting rotary motion to reciprocal motion and vice versa; letters of credit facilitating long-distance trade; wind- and watermills, needed innovations in humankind's ever-lasting search for additional and more potent energy sources; spinning wheels and treadle looms, providing vastly improved means for the production of fabrics for a growing population; the primitive compass aiding navigation, etc. The Twelfth-Century Renascence technological achievements parallel that upsurge of technological invention associated with the eighteenth and nineteenth centuries.

In closing this brief recount of that remarkable renascence of the twelfth century, it is appropriate to sum up by picturing that period as a giant fermentation chamber effervescing with ideas. This heady concoction resulted in the creation of vast bodies of newly brewed intellectual concepts and ethical precepts pregnant with future possibility—an enormous, new fabrication of enduring cultural concepts undergirding the growth of the unique civilization of the West. Yes, this renascence complex of ideas and knowledge was beleaguered by contradictions; harboring numerous but unrealized unintended consequences; and the pursuit of the futile wish fulfillment of astrology, alchemy, Gnostic delusions, etc. But for all these shortcomings, the twelfth century remains a massive leap forward in the evolution of and an enormous addition to the cultural capital of the West. And so well did the Twelfth-Century Renascence writers and innovators do their job that much of the trove of cultural capital amassed by them remains a vital force in the ideational structuring of the society of the present and a reserve account of intellectual and ethical capital on which the world draws daily.

The Decline and Erosion of the Twelfth-Century Renascence

The late thirteenth and fourteenth centuries provided the setting for the striking subtitle of Barbara Tuchman's best-selling book, *A Distant Mirror: The Calamitous 14th Century*. It was indeed a calamitous century with the addition of two or three more decades in the fifteenth century. All manner of unforeseen and unintended religious and political consequences coalesced with major natural events to make this one of the most difficult periods the West had endured since the barbarian invasions of the Roman Empire nearly a millennium earlier.

One of the most painful and likely most culturally devastating outcomes of this period of tribulations was the loss of a significant fraction of the received knowledge so patiently and painfully hoarded and salvaged and then so laboriously incorporated into the total body of knowledge available to those in the West. This loss was made graphic by the numbers of monasteries and their libraries scattered in substantial numbers across the West, which had been utterly abandoned by the early fifteenth century. Those historic trends and happenings can best be recounted under three heads: those centering upon the church and the religious life, those relating to the bloody and continuing formation of dynastic states, and lastly, the severe dislocations resulting from the onset of a little ice age and the arrival of the black death.

Several distinct but related threads in the evolution of religious thinking, practice, and structure entwined and were to lead to a radically different shape of religion in the West in a couple of centuries following the great Thomistic synthesis. While each of these intertwined threads can best be delineated separately, the reader must keep in mind their mutual interplay. The first thread derives from the tedious turn the university Schoolmen took in the century following the magisterial work of Albertus Magnus and Aquinas in synthesizing Christian theology and Aristotelian and interpolated Islamic philosophical reason. The succeeding Schoolmen became preoccupied in dialectic chopping of fine points of logic and epistemology—leading to the satirical characterization of their debate—"How many angels can dance on the head of a pin?" Forgotten seemed to be the human meaning of the Christian message of the creation, the fall, redemption, the resurrection, and salvation, which had been the substance of the teachings of the earlier priests and monks when they were virtually the only educators. This withering of the message of personal salvation led to early reform movements in religion—John Wyclif and his translation of the Bible into English and the subsequent underground Lollard movement. The latter, in turn, seems to have triggered John Hus in Bohemia in the founding of the Hussite sect.

In parallel, the administrative structure of the church had, as the result of the profound renewal of piety and Christian belief that had been initiated in the twelfth century, led the papacy and the church hierarchy to reassert a claim for political and secular authority superior to that of the dynastic monarchs, which had been a periodically recurring bone of contention in the West since the fourth century. In so doing, the pope and the religious establishment succeeded only in stimulating a countermovement by the nascent monarchial dynasties with their own interests in controlling the role of the church and the clerisy in managing secular affairs. All of this wrangling for power and authority fostered one of the great church scandals—the Babylonian Captivity, which involved the removal of the papacy from its long-time seat in Rome to Avignon in France in 1309. This move occurred as a power play by the French engineered by a substantial body of French cardinals on the Curia in a struggle with Pope Boniface VIII.

But this scandal did not stop here. The Curia returned to Rome in 1377, seeking to salve the indignation of the powerful Roman aristocracy. The cardinals thereupon elected Urban VI, a seemingly docile and pliable choice, but who on ascension undertook a vigorous attack on churchly corruption and clerical luxurious prodigality. Thereupon many of the French cardinals, fearing a loss of income and sumptuous living, returned to Avignon, where they elected another pope, Clement VII. Now the church had two popes and two Curiae issuing frequently contradictory edicts. These joint scandals at the highest levels of the church hierarchy led to the revival of the notion of a governing council composed of lay and clerical delegates—a practice that had been discarded by the Western Church centuries earlier. The growing chorus of demands for a councillor form of church governance led to the calling of a council: first the Councils of Pisa (1409), then Constance (1414) followed by that of Basle.

The church had, in substantial measure, lost its way and the allegiance of many believers. The failures of the theologians in supporting meaningful doctrine, the scandals surrounding the hierarchy, the emergence of remarkably viable movements of reformation, and the increasing resort to astrology, alchemy, and other Gnostic forms of magic simply augmented the confusion and uncertainty besetting the cultural substance sustaining the populace.

This cultural pessimism and confusion was further deepened by the continuing warfare resulting from the dynastic ambitions of the monarchs dominating the Western scene. Particularly grievous was the Hundred Years' War fought largely between France and England together with the Spanish crown or that of the Holy Roman Emperor as an occasional ally on one side or the other. This conflict arose out of the differing claims of the French and English crowns to substantial areas in France. In Italy, the wars between the papacy and the empire seemed interminable. Other extended dynastic confrontations occurred spottily across Europe. The periods of warfare in these wars lasted well beyond the terms to which the various kings' knightly feudatories had agreed (usually forty days), so monarchs resorted to employing mercenary warriors in growing numbers, usually younger sons of the nobility as cavalry and the most wretched of the society as foot soldiers. Typically, the warring dynasts did little to provision these mercenary armies, which were, therefore, reduced to commandeering the crops, animals, and stored feedstuffs of the populace surrounding the battlegrounds, so devastating the people in the wide swathes of the countryside through which the armies passed or battled.

The resort to mercenary foot troops increased over time as the longbows of the English first and later the Swiss peasants as massed lancers put an end to the might of the "shock troops" of mounted, armored knights. Meanwhile, the masses of mercenary, common foot soldiers were unemployed for extended periods in the winter, so simply resorted to forming raiding bands preying further upon the peasants to obtain food, lodging, clothing, and other necessaries creating other vast areas of economic devastation. As can be imagined, the collective loss of accumulated wealth across the West attributable to these dynastic ambitions was enormous and would take several generations to restore when finally the egos of the governing dynastic families had been satisfied.

In the meantime, the Turkish tribes, first the Seljuk tribe and then its offshoot the Ottoman tribe, had begun their sustained assault on the remnants of the Eastern Roman Empire of Byzantium. The Turks soon overran the Middle East and the Balkans, closing the noose around Constantinople. There was a genuine concern by those paying any heed to developments in the east of Christendom that the West, or at least substantial portions of it, might be swallowed by the Turks. So to further complicate matters for the West, its very existence and identity seemed gravely threatened by an Islamic *jihad* once again.

But the calamity of the fourteenth century did not stop just with the erosion of faith, the continuing devastations of war, and the Turkish onslaught. The weather cycles inherent to the planet turned colder and eventually into a new ice age. Wheat formerly grown in such abundance in Greenland as to permit exportation of the surplus to Denmark could by the fourteenth century no longer be grown on that island. Comparable crop failures occurred across Europe, leading to widespread hardship if not outright famine. A population which had increased up to the twelfth century and sustained by an enhanced subsistence economy now began to shrink for want of sufficient food crops. Wandering bands of famished peasants became a common sight on the roads and around other, often distant, villages. Entire villages were abandoned. The lingering question harbored by people unfamiliar with the ever-changing global climate was as follows: Have we sinned and is this punishment meted out for so doing? (Again, a currently fashionable formulation.)

The new ice age was not the only unfamiliar phenomenon assailing the seemingly assured perceptions of the populace. A strange and previously unknown malady, soon labeled the black death, swept from Sicily north across Europe in only a few years. The disease was endemic to the great steppe grasslands of Central Asia. It had appeared in Byzantium and Eastern Europe in the third and fourth centuries, but memory of it had been lost in the largely illiterate intervening period. Early in the fourteenth century, a Genoese trading ship from the Black Sea arrived in Sicily, carrying a boatload of sailors either dead or dying of the Black Death. In the succeeding two-thirds of a century, it is estimated that 40 percent of the population of Europe died as victims of the plague. Again the answer to the question of the plague reiterated that respecting the meaning of the ice age famine: Have we sinned and is this the punishment meted out for so doing? (It would not be until the nineteenth century that the nature of the plague was to be fully deciphered.)

The populace of the West in the fourteenth century seemed to be under attack from all quarters—the Four Horsemen of the Apocalypse seemed to be running widely across Europe. And the church had forfeited much of the cultural explanatory power it once possessed. The growing assertiveness and acquisitiveness of the dynastic families led to increasing distrust of governing power and the loss of incredible wealth. Small wonder that much of the cultural capital of the West was destroyed together with much of the population and the material capital so laboriously created and accumulated.

The still fragile cultural integrity of the West was again faced with a loss of meaning. This loss of intellectual and ethical cultural coherence was not as far advanced as that which led to the collapse of the classical cultural edifice, but this former debacle was still a compelling memory. These memories coupled with the *weltanschauung* of the Christian faith fueled a plethora of gloomy millennial speculations. Only in a few isolated enclaves, most notably Florence, Venice, Genoa among the

A Brief Account of the History of the Culture of the West to 1450

foremost, was the flame of the evolving Western culture still burning brightly. However, in the main, the West was sunk in a sea of gloom.

But still unknown to the devastated West, a genuine and enduring Renaissance lay just ahead. The creative genius of the West was about to be rekindled and the horrors of the fourteenth century assuaged at least in some small measure—life always being an uncertain thing.

2

Gutenberg's Printing Revolution and the Cultural Revolution of the Last Half of the Fifteenth Century

Diffused knowledge immortalizes itself.—Sir James MacKintosh

All history is the history of thought.—Benedetto Croce

The Fifteenth Century: A Time of Tension

Here the observation must be made that the ideational vitality engendered by the twelfth-century reception of the Greek texts had exhausted itself in the ensuing century and a half. This exhaustion was massively augmented by the continuing dynastic wars together with the meteorological adversities of the Little Cold Age coupled with the outbreak of that baffling epidemic—the black plague—and the Turkish *jihad,* which had overwhelmed most of Eastern Europe. However, the intellectual fatigue marking the fourteenth century and the early fifteenth century arose as had the previous episodes of cultural fatigue following the collapse of the Roman Empire and that of the Carolingian Renascence by virtue of the drying up of the generative impetus of different/innovative ideas.

Think for a moment of the very few copies of virtually all of the limited texts that might provide seeds for the flowering of further thought and exploration of the complex material world and the even more complex world of the living including human society—no more than two thousand in the largest library and fifty to one hundred in a few dozen other locations. This limited inventory of texts was for the most part scattered across Europe in monastic libraries or in a few royal/noble libraries. In the case of many texts, only three or four copies were available across the entire continent. Then compound this scarcity of springboards to the further ideational exploration of the human situation by the rampant copying errors in virtually every one of this limited number of texts. In such a sea of ignorance, due to the limited number and wide diffusion of extant copies of a text, coupled with the utter confusion resulting from the differences in the text of the extant copies, it is small wonder that the springs of idea hypothesizing were virtually dried up—that sterile debates centering on the number of angels that could dance on the head of a pin, as the tale would have it, occupied the debates of the late fourteenth and fifteenth centuries. By the end of the thirteenth century, the astute, gifted minds of the church doctors had thoroughly mined and exploited the intellectual and ethical ore provided by this circumscribed body of received ideas. Virtually all of the reasonably defensible hypotheses aimed at extending the West's understanding of human nature and the human condition, which might reasonably be derived from these meager veins of thought, had been derived and were in circulation through the network of the doctors and their universities.

But something happened in the fifteenth century, which in a brief stretch of time, radically changed the state of the culture from one of sterile, near-empty pessimism to that intellectually charged period historians have labeled the Renaissance. Historians hold widely differing views regarding the fountains of this cultural upsurge centered upon one of a variety of combinations of events. One focuses upon the receipt of the Greek language acquired by a handful of the interested in Italy from a few immigrants fleeing Constantinople. Another centers on the revival of Greek learning in Constantinople and its subsequent reflection in the West. Yet another has it that the opening of the flood gates of Greek literature occasioned by the Turkish capture of the remaining Christian enclave in Asia releasing a torrent of classical manuscripts previously unknown in the West. Yet others of an aesthetic persuasion seek the explanation of the Renaissance in a revived interest in and appreciation of the multitudinous remains of Greek and Roman classical architecture, statuary, and painting. Some have it that the dawning of the idea of Europe as unique among the cultures of his world distinguished the Renaissance from the earlier renascences. Whatever, all such explanations seem to share to a greater or lesser degree the sense that *mirabile dictu* this explosion of thought and enterprise sprang into being full-blown upon the West in the fifteenth century, akin to Athena's emergence from the head of Zeus.

The crucial element that is missing from these various views is the dispersed and subterranean nature of the incipient late fourteenth- and early fifteenth-century renascence and how poorly "the dots were connected" in what appears at first glance to be a repeat of the eighth- and twelfth-century renascences. Only a few locales, mainly, but not exclusively in Italy, were collecting the Greek manuscript "violls," flooding in from the Middle East. Florence, Rome, and Venice were the principal towns of entry and the sites involved in the deliberate collection of these writings.

Nor were the Italians in these several centers the only collectors of Greek manuscripts from the East or Latin manuscripts again being discovered in ignored or forgotten collections in Central Europe. Others, most notably in the German-speaking lands, were involved in the same intellectual enterprise. They recognized as surely as the Italian collectors and translators the cultural riches contained in these "violls" and were equally eager to integrate them into the increasingly complex and mushrooming European cultural amalgam. The Northerners were more inclined to acquire manuscripts dealing with the subject matters of religion, philosophy, and ethics, the Italians, writings devoted to or exemplary of rhetoric, literature, grammar, etc. Any significant knowledge of Greek was confined to a handful of people in these various centers—some immigrants from Constantinople, the larger number composed of their pupils, both in Italy and elsewhere in Europe. The fourteenth- and fifteenth-century renascences were largely the possession of a few in dispersed locales, the preponderance in Italy and the German-speaking lands.

But the manuscripts underlying this fifteenth-century renascence were, like their handwritten predecessors, few in number and laden with the usual copyists' errors. Further, the sudden blossoming of a newly formulated crop of idea/hypotheses derived therefrom was documented in but a handful of manuscripts which were circulated only among a tight little circle of the like-minded. From a broad historical perspective, nothing had changed. New hypotheses and ideas seeking to understand and depict human nature and the human condition remained the intellectual and ethical wealth of a tiny body of colleagues and enjoyed little culture-augmenting force in the larger culture.

The institutional structures at this time were quite unlike the earlier renascences of the eighth and twelfth centuries. In those earlier eras, the movement of manuscripts and associated ideas shared in well-identified, visible establishments had long since been intimately linked by regular circuits of travel. Thus the Carolingian Renascence was centered in a chain of monasteries stretching across most of Western

Europe. The monasteries constituting this chain were closely associated with and strongly controlled by the Carolingian court, the crucial center on which this renewal turned. Monastics, most particularly abbots, routinely traveled throughout this network of monasteries ranging from England to Italy, and from the north of Germany to the south of France. The acquisition of copies of or the copying of a manuscript held in a particular house or manuscripts to be borrowed and copied in the home house constituted a major motive and objective of this continuing travel. In short, the monastic centers and the people participating in this Latin salvage and revival were comparatively well-known to all in the network and involved most of Europe. All were in regular communication and routinely involved in the exchange of manuscripts and monk/scholars.

The renascence of the twelfth century was the product of the recently emerged universities and fueled by the spate of translations from the Greek and Arabic following upon the partial conquest of Muslim Spain. These institutions, like the monasteries of the eighth century, were highly visible to the fraternity of the learned responsible for the burst of cultural renewal marking those centuries. And as was the case with the monastic network, both masters and students traveled the university network to optimize their careers routinely carrying ideas, manuscripts, news, and gossips between these university centers. So the masters and students of all the universities were more or less fully acquainted with the ideational content, the dominating interests, and the assessments of the respective faculties of each university at any given time.

In both cases, one can say of these earlier renascences that they were driven by "communal" forces or alternatively were small, more or less, self-contained societies—the monasteries in the first instance and the universities in the second. Both shared the further characteristic of being manuscript-based with all the shortcomings incident to that configuration of "violls": varied formats, scribal copying errors, the gathering of the writings of several different authors in a single binding variously identified on the binding, and scribal interpolations. The consequence was that the few participants in either renascence were not infrequently thinking and were occasionally engaged in debates, which went right past one another because they were arguing from divergent textual bases. Further, the library resources upon which they had to depend were pitifully small by comparison with those that were forming by the late fifteenth century. The earlier monastery or church collections seldom contained more than fifty to hundred volumes. Twelfth- and thirteenth-century professors possessed but a handful of books. City, cathedral, and university libraries of the twelfth century typically held only a few hundred titles, virtually all church-related. Perhaps the largest library in the German language region was that of King Matthias Corvinus of Hungary (1440–1490) numbering not more than one thousand books and manuscripts.[1] At its greatest extent in 1369, the catalog of the Papal library at Avignon numbered twenty-one hundred entries. (The collection was subsequently reduced, probably principally by theft, to about sixteen hundred volumes.)[2] In short, the textual resource base still remained very dispersed and small, thereby effectively throttling any rapid cultural evolution. This restricted base of manuscript sources continued to provide the bulk of the thinkers and scholars with virtually the entirety of the intellectual resources they had at their disposal to satisfy their intellectual objectives up to the time of the late fourteenth century. Only in the fifteenth century following the flight from Constantinople was the inventory of discrete book titles augmented in any significant way. It is slight wonder that, in such limited and constrained circumstances, the range of intellectual interests and frames of reference were so narrow and constricted relative to the broader and more numerous hypotheses, which began to emerge when the Renaissance had begun to mature in the sixteenth century.

Quite different from the medieval and university communal models were the qualities marking the people, institutions, and the situation of those involved in the making of the late fourteenth/early fifteenth-century renascence and the subsequent fifteenth/sixteenth-century Renaissance. The first difference to note is that the great preponderance of the leading Renaissance figures was citizens moving freely in a civil society relatively independent of any established institution—though some formed civilian institutions, such as Ficino's Platonic Academy in Florence. A great many were, of course, associated with religious foundations or educational institutions and some were lesser ecclesiastics. But their field of endeavor was chiefly undertaken in the larger civil society. Marsilio Ficino of Florence in the early fifteenth century and Desiderius Erasmus of Northern Europe in the early sixteenth century might well be singled out as emblematic of the "independent civil" role of the thinkers and writers in the Renaissance world of letters and ideas. Both were nearly entirely independent of any established institution, despite their formal clerical affiliations.

A second distinguishing characteristic was that these independent writers/scholars were scattered about Europe in geographically dispersed locations. They largely looked to small, relatively discrete groups of confreres in close geographic proximity. Their writings, in manuscript form, were in substantial measure circulated within these constrained, like-minded assemblages. There is no question that at some minimal level constant exchanges of people and manuscripts took place across Europe. But all the new/different civil groups dealing with new ideas and revised bodies of knowledge were still too novel to have put into place the established linkages and exchanges of the monasteries and/or the universities. Here was English Lollardy with its outlier in Hussite Bohemia. There was the triumvirate of Dante, Petrarch, and Boccaccio in Florence and soon, thereafter, the Platonic Academy of Ficino. In the north, there were the Brethren of the Common Life and their mystic spokesman, Thomas à Kempis and his book, *Imitatio Christi*. In Venice, a growing state-sponsored Greek translation/printing enterprise was vigorously conducted despite the city's continuing preoccupation of dealing with the Turkish invasions of the Eastern Mediterranean. Aristotle remained as the sole footing for university study of natural philosophy in most universities all the while Aristotelian physics was being falsified by a few in Paris and Cambridge.

One could go on identifying these new, different, conflicting, and contrary intellectual formulations in their dispersed habitats and local foci, but the point is clear: Europe was awash with not only its medieval heritage but a mass of newly valued, classical, intellectual, and ethical ideas and bodies of knowledge as well. These numerous, conflicting, emergent hypotheses made profound demands on scholars to come to some defensible understanding of these ideas and bodies of knowledge, of how they related to each other, and of how they might be integrated into/with the existing intellectual and ethical regimens. Sometimes simultaneously, more usually following a greater or lesser delay, the evolving European cultural landscape was, on the one hand, randomly littered with falsifications of various received ideas or bodies of knowledge. And on the other hand, it was awash with partial or new formulations of ideas and their yet rough integration into existing bodies of knowledge. It was by the middle of the fifteenth century that all a hotchpotch of rapidly fermenting and diverse problems and ideas still lacking any efficient cultural means of broadly, rapidly, and more or less accurately disseminating either the new understandings/falsifications/creations of ideas or the relation of the classical manuscript material flooded in from the Middle East to the inherited traditional bodies of knowledge.

Gutenberg's Impact

Gutenberg's invention thus completely and radically restructured the trade in intellectual products and thereby, even more radically, enlisted a vastly increased number of minds recruited to the challenge of formulating more and better solutions to the ever-constant problems arising in human society. This new army of minds forever altered the tempo and directional evolution of the culture of the West. The entire infrastructure of cultural debate with its necessary falsifications of received hypotheses and creations of new, more powerful hypotheses was massively reconstructed—and much of this within a century or two depending upon how the impact of this radical reorganization of the means of cultural formation is assessed. Within a matter of a couple of decades, the pace of cultural formation in the West was enormously accelerated—textually identical printed books in quantity could be quickly disseminated to all of Europe and particularly to the key cultural centers.

Further, the bodies of knowledge contained in these new, widely dispersed "Gutenberg violls" were better able to survive the vicissitudes of fire, war, neglect, and all the other enemies of manuscripts/printed books by virtue of this wide dissemination. Debate, now founded on identical, if still largely unauthenticated, texts became more efficient and incisive, as the contending voices were no longer speaking/writing past one another by virtue of being based on variant texts.

Much more importantly, by virtue of the wider distribution of the identical text, the number of commentators, critics, innovators, and others qualified to debate these matters of more or less grave cultural significance contained therein was increased by orders of magnitude. A much greater mass of thinkers—and as always fakirs—could address and debate identical, intellectual content. And a text was, almost overnight, exposed to a much larger array of alternative points of view, other bodies of knowledge, and other evidence leading to more rapid and encompassing means of falsification—or incorporation into extant bodies of knowledge. It might be said that the critical mass of those minds in a position to critique, falsify, or support any hypothesis circulated in printed form had, within a brief period of time, increased by orders of magnitude, while the time intervals required for assessment and judgment were decreased by orders of magnitude. It bears repeating here that the texts printed by Gutenberg were of careful and scholarly editorial quality and as such offer early evidence of the active intellectual role publisher/printers performed in the succeeding ideational ferment.

But this sanguine prospect lay some distance yet in the future for the generality of the literate. The most commonly printed books remained the standard fare of the medieval manuscript tradition. The fulfillment of the Gutenberg revolution was to be largely limited for the best part of two generations to the traditional thin layer of clericals and university scholars still uncertain about the intellectual and cultural value of the flood of translations and new ideas emanating from a few centers of "advanced" thought, the truth of the ideas and bodies of knowledge contained therein, and how any valuable cultural goods located in these new "violls" might be compounded with existing bodies of knowledge. This thin layer melded to some degree with an even thinner layer of humanists and a scattering of more adventurous individuals intent on outside-the-box intellectual explorations, who did much to validate the cultural significance of Gutenberg's work. Of the latter, as is common to the human lot, the large preponderance of the speculation advanced by these unconventional thinkers/writers would prove to be mere exercises in fantastical, utopian, or irrelevant cerebration. Only a small remainder of these intellectual ventures would prove to be the legitimate offspring of the revolution set into motion by the sudden release of the Greek cultural treasures archived in Constantinople and the new, more efficient print knowledge transfer infrastructure—the new knowledge-generating engine.

There were a number of reasons for this technological/cultural lag. Of these, there were two which played major roles. The first, of course, is the common human inability to rapidly both learn to trust and come to understand the potential of and appreciate the radically new. This inability should not be construed as some kind of a disability, for all new ideas are best met with considerable skepticism because over the course of the centuries, most have proved ill-founded and advanced by those with an axe to grind or been found to be the playthings of "activists" and other cranks. The society at any given time has every historical reason to treat new ideas with caution and deliberation.

The second was the long, dark shadows still being cast by repeated outbreaks of the plague and other diseases as well as the continuing and ever closer threat of the Ottoman Turk *jihad*. The plague and other highly contagious diseases, such as smallpox, etc., continued to flare up without any premonitory signals in precisely the same way every new disease behaves with a disease-innocent population lacking any prior immunological experience with it. A constant dread hung over Europe for the next several centuries, a dread routinely reconfirmed by repeated outbreaks.

The latter Islamic threat hovered closely over the Italian Peninsula and the European Balkans. Constantinople, the West's principal intellectual and trade entrepôt and link to the East, was lost to Christendom in 1453. The Turks made a successful, though brief, landing at Otranto, Italy, in 1480 after having overrun most of what we now know as the Balkans from Greece north to Hungary. The Venetian trade entrepôts in the Black Sea and the Mediterranean were captured, and the loss of the trade formerly originated in those centers badly compromised the European economy. In short, a successful, implacable, and avowedly militarily motivated religious enemy was not simply at the gates but within the walls—certainly ample grounds to compound the ever-present fear and gloom, which had overhung Europe for the best part of two centuries. The turning point of its subsidence only occurred following the failure of the Turkish siege of Vienna in 1683.

To compound the prevailing sense of pessimism and uncertainty was the continuing economic decline, which had marked the West since the last half of the previous century. The agricultural sector was by and large badly affected, the consequence of repeated crop failures due to global cooling. Peasants fled to the towns in increasing numbers, but the towns were little able to deal with such onslaughts. Extensive poverty was widespread. This economic malaise marked most of the fifteenth century.

In the meantime, following the termination of the Hundred Years' War—the dynastic opponents financially and militarily exhausted and now increasingly dependent upon their respective parliamentary institutions and extensive borrowings from the German and Italian bankers for financial succor—the kings of the principal nations of Europe turned inward to consolidate their regimes. The displaced citizenry offered a ready opportunity to employ standing, mercenary armies to achieve dynastic ambitions. Simultaneously, royalty commonly resorted to strategic marriages to augment their territories.

A parallel sense of falling back and consolidating after the high drama and tensions of the Babylonian Captivity of the papacy; the councils of Constance and Basel besetting the church, the Conciliar movement having been successfully neutralized by the Vatican; the emergence of the *via moderna* and the *devotio moderna*; and the uncertainty engendered by the new religious learning flowing out of Constantinople marked much of the cultural ambience from the time of Gutenberg to close to the end of the fifteenth century. It was as if the pall of the fourteenth century augmented by these additional difficulties still overhung the continent but in darker hues. Despite the genuine ideational ferment evident in specific centers, the last half of the fifteenth century remained a time of uncertainty and cultural introspection but more importantly a time of enormous confusion.

A renewed interest in the idea of the monastic life, away from the uncertainties of the secular world, was broadly evident throughout Europe. This renewal of monasticism, of course, brought in its train the more positive note of the renewal of the monastic interest in learning and in rehabilitating or regenerating monastic libraries. This initiative was stimulated by the recovery of a number of classic writings discovered in neglected monastic libraries by Petrarch, Boccaccio, and their humanist associates, of both Italy and Germany, bent upon recovering as many of the "violls" of classical learning as they could. Not only were new monastic scriptoria established but also the advent of printing suddenly made many of the standard religious texts readily available free of all the former constraints and difficulties of locating an acceptable text and copying it.

Another notable aspect of the ambiguity and uncertainty overhanging much of the West was the remarkable upsurge in ecstatic and mystical forms of religious experience and worship. The precedents of the Lowland's Windesheim Congregation and its related Brethren of the Common Life in formulating this style of religious understanding and practice soon spread from the lay society to the monastic foundations pioneered by the Benedictine monastery of Melk in Austria—the Melk Observation. All of this was powerfully stimulated by that seminal figure who appears and reappears in a variety of roles throughout the middle of the fifteenth century, Nicholas of Cusa. Cusanus was perhaps the foremost philosopher of that era and a committed Neoplatonic mystic. This powerful spiritual stream was to influence much of the thought and intellection of this and the succeeding two centuries.

The growing body of mystical belief and practice was notably enhanced by the reception of much numinous and magical speculation entering the West in some of the "violls" of late classical and Arabic thought arriving from Constantinople and Sicily. Perhaps the most notable of these "violls" of esoteric doctrine was the *Liber de potestate et sapientia Dei* of the spurious Hermes Trismegistus translated into Latin by Ficino and then more widely translated into various leading European vernaculars. (It needs to be noted in this connection that Cosimo de' Medici of Florence had Ficino put aside his work on translating Plato to translate Hermes.) But the Hermes Trismegistus was only one of the occult books, which were received among the numerous Hermetic "violls." Other similar late Neoplatonic magical and occult tracts floated in on the tide of Greek "violls" entering the West. These esoteric and occult bodies of ideas exerted a considerable influence on the culture of the West for several centuries—and remnants of this fascination remain evident today in various peripheral "spiritual" circles. Pico Della Mirandola, Ficino's successor in the Platonic Academy, was committed to "natural magic" and endeavored to associate the mystical Jewish Kabala with the burgeoning Hermetic tradition. Perhaps the foremost proponent of humanism, the budding natural sciences (he was a vocal supporter of Galileo), and the Hermetic Tradition was the sixteenth- or seventeenth-century Giordano Bruno, burnt at the stake not for supporting Galileo, as is often asserted, but rather for his heretical Hermetic ideas.[3] In this connection, the manuals of the time identify Bruno as one of the principal "pansophists," that mixed body of humanistic plus mystical theological plus early scientific thought, which informed much of sixteenth- and seventeenth-century speculations.[4]

The judicious assessment and sorting out of the mysticism growing out of an ecstatic worship of the Christian God and the new, competing, mystical visions of the order of the universe carried into the West with the deluge of Greek manuscripts would require at least three centuries to sort out—Newton, after all, was still pursuing alchemy and related magical pursuits in the seventeenth century. This observation highlights the enormous intellectual effort, which was required to simply comprehend the nature and intrinsic validity of this flood of new ideas. Once this enormously complex and uncertain intellectual work was accomplished, the even more difficult work of falsifying elements of these enormous bodies of knowledge, then creating new and more powerful hypotheses, and finally integrating all of these newly formulated hypotheses into the received, and presumably more trustworthy, bodies of knowledge had to be undertaken. These Herculean and lengthy intellectual efforts are the clearest proof of the sheer difficulty involved in the tedious and painful process of more closely approaching the truth and the good—the demonstration of which is one of the implicit objectives of this writing. The creation of a culture worth putting into place is neither an easy nor a quickly accomplished job.

In parallel with the growth of the new monastic libraries was the founding of more or less public libraries in the new centers of classical learning. Perhaps the first were the Medician libraries of Florence that were the rich legacy of the Florentine primacy in the advancement of humanism. They contained not only the de Medici collection of scarce manuscript sources both Latin and Greek but also the translations into Latin of many of the key Greek authors—Aristotle, Plato, and the Neoplatonist as well as the Hermetic literature. Shortly thereafter, the now exceptional Vatican Library was given a major impetus by the noted humanist and manuscript collector, Aeneas Sylvius Piccolomini, who was elected Pope Pius II in 1458.

Venice was not far behind, the city having been given the extraordinary personal library of Greek manuscripts of Cardinal Bessarion, a leading Orthodox cleric and convert to Roman Catholicism, who had not only played key roles in the effort to reunite the Eastern and Western churches but also, as a migrant to Italy, among a substantial band of refugees, did much to advance the study/learning of the Greek language in the West. He was a leading intermediary in facilitating the flood of Greek "violls," coming from Constantinople and the East.

A parallel growth in notable court libraries occurred in Vienna at the Imperial Library and the Budapest library of Matthias Corvinus, noted above. Several of the major cities along the Rhine also boasted large and growing collections. Like the Italian libraries, the holdings of these Northern Renaissance libraries were principally manuscripts, the format most prized by their aristocratic founders as tokens of superior taste and aesthetic sensibility. Only slowly did printed books encroach upon the status of the former. The libraries north of the Alps tended to focus upon the Latin and Patristic writings but contained a goodly collection of Greek writings.

By present-day collection standards, these notable libraries were scarcely larger than that of any number of today's private libraries. Despite this seeming spareness, they provided much of the fuel, which powered the culture-building work of the growing body of scholars, writers, and academics.[5] The rapid increase in the number of libraries, some available only to the members of an institution, others available to all or significant numbers of the public, was the necessary accompaniment to the radical growth in numbers of the intellectually trained and involved.

Transitions: The Economy

All of these extremely consequential cultural developments were played out in a Europe that was largely at peace. The minor flickering wars of the last half of the fifteenth century did not consume so great a number of soldiers' lives or proportion of the accumulated wealth of the continent as had been the case in the previous century and a half. The happy consequence of this re-accumulation of wealth was that substantial investments could be made in manufactures, trade, transportation, and communication infrastructure, and other forms of private investment that would massively augment Europe's capacity to provide for its growing populations and for future growth. This burgeoning of trade and commercial infrastructure reflected not only the maturing or practical playing out of over two centuries of ideas respecting the effective creation and employment of economic principles but also how the material condition of at least the bourgeoisie and urban craftsmen might be improved. The economic burst of the late fifteenth century, in turn, led to the creation of a plentitude of new ideas about how this vigor might be maintained. Printed books devoted to the spread of these new ideas about how commerce and trading should be conducted proliferated. For example, the introduction and rapid spread of the body of ideas instructing in the theory and use of scientific (double entry) bookkeeping (needed to make a rational assessment of the economic condition of a trader or a kingly court) depended upon the publication and distribution of books.[6] The subsequent cultural developments of the late fifteenth century are virtually incomprehensible in the absence of a clear appreciation of the gathering force and strength of the economic engine brought into being by the huge output of the knowledge, which early capitalism had developed by that time.[7]

Precisely, the same observations may be made with respect to the rapidly accumulating bundles of ideas that resulted in the bodies of knowledge identified by the terms of "banking," the "corporation" and the "joint-stock company," and "insurance." The long-term consequence of these several conjoined bodies of knowledge facilitated the employment of this re-accumulation of wealth to be turned to more productive social and cultural purposes than the West had previously been able to pursue in the absence of such a comprehensive understanding of economic and business principles.

This economic engine (at base, then and always, the organization of the work and exchange necessary for individuals to "keep body and soul together") was an extraordinary development in the history of humankind, for it was, even in the late fifteenth century, becoming unique among the four great cultures. It possessed a not yet fully comprehended but inherent potency that was to provide the West and latterly much of the rest of the world with a heretofore unimagined degree of freedom to pursue alternative cultural goals. No longer would the manifold benefits of economic culture be restricted to all but a handful but to the relief to the larger population of the constant dread and the obsessive calculation and the financial weaving and ducking imposed by an uncaring and often adverse and always obdurate nature—variable soils, unpredictable variations in annual rainfall and temperatures, planetary warming and cooling, insect infestations, waves of human and plant disease, and on and on. Burgeoning economic well-being released a gradually increasing increment of human time and ingenuity, some of which could be devoted to the creation of other cultural structures/artifacts offering humankind desirable alternatives to the often harsh mercies of the indifferent natural state.

It should be noted in passing that once the body of ideas concerned with the more efficient production and exchange of goods and services was sufficiently advanced to do a reasonable job of providing the well-being of some significant fraction of the population, the greatest enemy of the unrestrained employment of these ideas and their further ideational development has almost invariably been the imprudent employment of political power, whether secular or sacred. The mere possession of the capacity to co-opt the wealth of the citizenry, deprive them of their freedom and even life—thanks to the state's monopoly of physical force in society—has historically been in the forefront of the impediments to the ever-wider disbursement of the fruits of the Western economic engine. Yet the proper development of this powerful economic engine requires the state only as the protector of the legal conditions necessary to its most effective operation.[8]

A number of historians have resorted to the astonishing human and humane value of the Western economic system to formulate hypotheses aimed at explaining the modern cultural preeminence of the West or simply the historical evolution of the West. All such explanations invariably fail in bearing so heavy a load of explanation. At best, and it is a needful "best," the complex and interrelated body of ideas dealing with the exchange of goods and services designated as "economics" is one of the critical social and cultural foundational elements or underpinnings or inputs of the larger cultural undertaking involved in meeting the needs/desires of humankind. As such, the Western body of knowledge in economics has been one of the essential contributors to the cultural strength of the West.

Transitions: Intellectual

Another much-to-be-wished-for outcome of the relative peace of the last half of the fifteenth century was that this period provided a comparatively salubrious environment in which the enormous intellectual undertakings arising out of the need to deal with the rush of "violls" of Greek knowledge coming into the West could be carried forward. The remarkable economic engine being developed in parallel provided the means to dedicate greater amounts of time and effort to this cultural work.

The first great intellectual hurdle to be overcome was the matter of training a wider body of people in the ability to read Greek in an adequate fashion. And then to deepen the understanding of that foreign language to the point that moderately satisfactory translations could be made into the other European "foreign" language employed at the time, Latin.

Then followed, as noted above, the formidable intellectual task of coming to some relatively comprehensive and informed understandings of the cultural wealth contained in the almost overwhelming array of these "violls." While significant elements of Neoplatonic thought had been melded into Christian thinking and doctrine by the early church fathers, the total *weltanschauung* of the classical Greek ways of understanding and dealing with the world, humankind, and humankind's place in that world was in goodly measure *terra incognita* to the Europe of the fifteenth century. This huge, complex and largely cultural topography compelled a wide-ranging yet thorough job of first, exploration, and then of mapping before it might be converted to and integrated into an already viable and quite elaborate received cultural nexus.

With this necessary cultural survey and the resulting map reasonably well in hand, the two-century-long scholarly processes of purifying the often confused and partial texts received could be commenced and initially carried out with minimal distractions caused by invading armies and marauding bands of mercenaries. While a handful of the principles of philology had been worked out earlier in order to come to grips with some of the problems of the transliteration, translation, and emendation of the Bible and the Roman texts which had come down to the later West, the bulk of the work of establishing the body of ideas/ knowledge subsumed under the head of philology had to be undertaken by Renaissance scholars. Certainly, one of the crowning achievements of Renaissance scholarship was the initial working out of the principles of dealing rationally with the complexities and irrationalities embedded in the exotic orthography and copying inaccuracies of the texts. The Carolingian scholars had endeavored to identify and expunge the errors of transcription and the interpolations of earlier copyists but this work was of the most elementary kind and not up to the demands placed on the fifteenth- and sixteenth-century classicists in the reception of not only the "violls" of Greek knowledge but the "viols" of the saved Latin writings collected anew by Petrarch, Boccaccio, and their Italian and Northern European successors. At the end of the day, this work of "cleaning up" the later West's inheritance of classical texts was largely accomplished by the end of the seventeenth century but the knottier problems of producing "authentic" texts remain with us today.

Given the fragility of the infrastructure supporting the maintenance, transmission, creation, and integration of knowledge and learning in the early decades of the Renaissance, the sixty-year reign of relative peace in the late fifteenth century coupled with the enormous growth of wealth permitted as culturally worthwhile a re-accumulation of cultural goods as it did for the re-accumulation of economic goods.

Transitions: Medieval to Renaissance

As William Faulkner perceptually noted, "The dead past is not only not dead but not even past." With this observation one other matter of the utmost importance deserves reiteration here: That is the continuity of the received medieval cultural tradition in the Renaissance. Many historians, following the cue of some of the most fervent of the fifteenth- and sixteenth-century proponents, would have it that the Renaissance marked a radical shift from the dull, dark, rude society and culture which preceded it. The Renaissance, in this view, was all a "new thing" advanced by "new men" or better yet, a fresh and vital renewal after a dark and inhumane millennium. Much was made of the purer Ciceronian form, of Latin used by humanists in the fourteenth and subsequent centuries—the presumed outward and visible sign of the alleged new-found superiority of the new culture—as compared to the Latin used by the medieval writers and Schoolmen.

Intimately coupled with this emphasis upon a closer approximation of Latin to that of classical Rome was an intense preoccupation with the cultivation of rhetoric—a practical form of swaying audiences to a particular proposition or point-of-view. This preoccupation with rhetoric, Virgilian/Ciceronian Latin, and humane studies seems to have grown out of the traditional educational practices of the Italian schoolteachers who retained some residual notions of the schooling practices of their Roman predecessors. With the opening of the floodgates of classical "violls" from Constantinople the traditional schoolmasters' concerns for rhetoric and "correct" Latin were given an enormous boost, which catapulted the studies of the trivium to a renewed major cultural eminence.[9] The humanists lauded the superiority of classical rhetoric to the medieval dialectic both in terms of transmitting learning and in advancing the accumulation of knowledge—or to use the methodological terms employed in this work, rhetoric was perceived as better able to falsify and create new hypotheses than was the older logico/dialectical approach.

Skillful use of rhetoric involved among other things a facile capacity to bring up all manner of fluent turns of phrase or quotations from classical writings on the spur of the moment apposite to the subject matter touched on in conversation and debate. The method of acquiring these quotes involved the dedicated maintenance of two or more notebooks. In one of which memorable turns of phrase, striking idiomatic expressions, etc., were recorded and regularly consulted to fix them in the memory. The second was used for the recording of arresting moral examples, illustrative historical incidents, etc. Other notebooks might be kept devoted to sub-groups of these more universal memory aids—compilations devoted to epithets, etc. Of course, the contents of all these "cribs" were to be faithfully memorized. These notebooks acquired the name of "commonplace books" in English. The commonplace books were, in essence, elaborate versions of the medieval florilegium but in the Renaissance case devoted to rhetorical uses. Early in the sixteenth century, Erasmus offered a concrete endorsement of this practice, which had been a continuing and common humanist practice, with the several editions of his compilations, the *Adagia* and *Apophthegmata*.[10]

As Ong has pointed out, these commonplace books, like the preceding florilegia, were in practice a great reservoir of the accepted learning of the time. They were the wheat separated from the chafe of the writings in which they had first appeared. They were an epitome or index of the store of knowledge built up in centuries of writings.[11] Like the elaborate symbolism of classical themes employed in Renaissance painting and sculpture one could not understand the allusions employed in Renaissance literature absent a substantial familiarity with the classical literature. So these commonplace books not only provided the ground for literary and rhetorical writings but also served to unlock the received meanings of imitative contemporaneous writings.

Typical of the present-day insistence on the crucial cultural difference between the medieval and Renaissance is that of one of the leading historians of the Renaissance who contended, about a generation ago, that Aquinas simply employed the newly introduced translations of Aristotle to make his theological case without seeking to understand the vast gulf of difference between Aristotle's classical culture and that of the Christian high Middle Ages. By contrast this historian asserted that, Marsilio Ficino in his *Theologia Platonica* sought to reconcile Christian theology with Platonic philosophy (actually the Neoplatonism of Proclus and Dionysius the Areopagite).[12] But this comparison fails to note that the problem Aquinas set himself was the reconciliation of reason and revelation not the reconciliation sought by the Platonic Academy of fifteenth-century Florence with Ficino's perception of the cultural setting of Plato's Athenian Academy in the fifth century BC. On the contrary, the decisive element in such a comparison of a leading thirteenth- and a fifteenth-century European thinker is the keenly felt need of both to reconcile the contents of newly discovered "violls" of an esteemed predecessor from the classical world with the hard-won theology of about a millennium of intense theological and philosophical effort. In both cases the fundamental ground with which the translations from both of the newly acquired group of "violls" of classical thought had to be conformed was the Judeo-Christian religious tradition and doctrine. The fundamental character and cultural supremacy of the religious tradition remained the same in both cases. The classic formulations of the Doctors and Ockham remained the vital and lived beliefs of most of the Renaissance intelligentsia. And, at base, the intellectual foundations of the Renaissance remained firmly rooted in Aristotelianism.[13]

In the case of one of the two figures whom this history has identified as iconic of the Renaissance, Erasmus, it has been said that in his late writings of the early sixteenth century he put into place the final formulation of Christian Humanism, a project which had occupied the humanists for the best part of the fifteenth century. Many of the humanists had included in their study the works of the church fathers as late examples of the classical tradition.[14] Erasmus himself not only translated and oversaw the publication of the Bible anew but also edited and prepared for publication the extant works of a number of the church fathers, including St. Ambrose, St. Augustine, St. Jerome, and St. Chrysostom. Prior to the appearance of these new, critical printed editions, adepts of the Northern *devotio moderna* had renewed study of the church fathers in Northern Europe. From Petrarch on, the Italian humanists sought to marry eloquence, learning, and a holy life, the latter including the study of the Patristic and the later formulations of the doctors' literature. In short, the Renaissance remained well within the cultural tradition of medieval Christendom.

Transitions: The Printing Revolution: Printed Books and Publishers

The best illustration of this continuity of thought is found in the 40,000 incunabula still extant. Assuming an average edition size of 200 copies, 8,000,000 books were published in the first fifty years. This number exceeds by orders of magnitude the entire production of copies handwritten from the eighth to the fifteenth century.

Such immense numbers provide a startling confirmation of the intellectual continuity binding the Middle Ages and the Renaissance, for the vast bulk of them were derived from the mostly religious manuscript holdings of the monastic and cathedral libraries. It was not until the sixteenth century that the publication of the flood of Greek literature began to appear, that in both Greek and Latin. Likewise, the original writings of the humanists only began to appear in print in any considerable measure in the sixteenth century.

So what was published in the last half of the fifteenth century? It hardly needs pointing out that arriving at any precise quantity of the numbers of books published in the incunable period by subject, even in broadly defined classificatory categories, is laden with traps of ignorance and snares of uncertainty. For what follows resort has been made to the calculations of Robert Steel[15] and Rudolph Hirsch.[16] The numeric conclusions of both men are so close that only a single proportion is provided here. Employing the same broad subject categories of these two investigators, the following proportions emerge:

Theology	45%
Literature (including philosophy)	36%
Law	11%
Science (including medicine as well as the pseudoscience of astrology, alchemy, etc.)	8%

As Hirsch points out, historians have widely assumed that the use of books was confined to a small fraction of the populace, the number who were competent in Latin. But this is not a valid conclusion, for a review of extant incunable holdings turns up a large number of heavily illustrated xylographic books and other books of a popular nature. Popular books are scattered throughout the above categories—thus, romances are included in literature and books of Mariology in theology. He endeavors to break these popular books out of the above tabulations and arrives at the following:

Romances, tales, and facetiae	3.81%[17]
Poetry	4.30%
Plays, orations, letters	4.12%
History, biography (popular history, lives of saints, etc.)	3.36%
Virgin Mary	1.44%
Calendars	0.73%
Witchcraft	0.27%
Occult	0.94%
Total	18.97%

It should be evident to any reader that printers/publishers sought to serve first the needs of the clergy—a large percentage of the early print era were Bibles, missals, and other service books; Patristic literature; Scholastic theology; contemporary theological writings; religious education books for both school and university students; and volumes intended to serve the clergy such as homilies, etc.

The second largest category, literature, includes a broad miscellany of distinct classes of books. The leading class was that of classics for both university faculty and students as well as preuniversity students. Of the classics, the then extant writings of Cicero occupy a predominant place. His writings on morality occupied pride of place in Northern Europe while his letters and writings on oratory were more popular in Italy. Cicero's use of the Latin language was a model across Europe and, particularly, in Italy. The vast preponderance of the fifteenth-century printed classics derived from the Latin, books of the Greek writers/thinkers grew gradually in numbers only in the last decades of the fifteenth century. The classics represent roughly one-third of the titles classed here. The works of Dante, Petrarch, and the early humanists as well as some of the classics in vernacular languages together with the standard grammars, dictionaries, etc., occupy second place. The almost immediate and prominent place, which romances, fables, tales, and related facetiae played in the book trade, gives clear evidence of the human appetite for fictions of all kinds and presages the growth of the novel when levels of literacy increased so enormously in the eighteenth century. The final class encompasses the writings of contemporary authors dealing with all the above subject classes.

Publications in the categories of law and science were clearly oriented to the then current needs of professionals in these fields and dealt with the then knowledge and practice in the various subfields of both categories. Law books were published to serve not simply the growing number of lawyers and judges required by an increasingly complex political, economic, and social order but also the swelling bodies of bureaucrats required by the crystallizing autocratic states. Law books had to be tailored to three broad categories of the law: canon law for church courts and bureaucracies, Roman law for the secular courts and the nascent autocratic–dynastic bureaucracies, and local law of which the most notable were the common law reports of England as well as that of some "free cities" enjoying a more reasonable and responsive code than the widely used Roman law. Mercantile law, governing commercial transactions throughout Europe, the Mediterranean, and the Middle Eastern trading zones, was a creature of the merchants and traders and largely codified in the practices of the market. Mercantile law was substantially formulated and administered independently of any political organization.

Science book publishing was heavily tinctured with books dealing with astrology, magic, alchemy, and other apocryphal forms of explanation and divination. Only a small number of the pre-1500 books in science were devoted to the classical authors, a larger percentage dealt with the work of contemporary investigators in either the physical or the biological sciences.[18] Books dealing with the biological sciences included the classical medical books of Hippocrates and Galen, the standard works used in the medical schools of Sicily, Bologna, Paris, etc., as well as reprints of Dioscorides's *Materia Medica* and the botanical writings of Albertus Magnus. Aristotle's writings on natural philosophy and the work at Paris and Oxford stimulated thereby were brought into print. Mathematics was not heavily represented in the offerings of the fifteenth-century printers/publishers despite the fact that a goodly number of classical mathematics manuscripts were collected and placed in various libraries.[19]

Not specifically singled out for mention in these classifications of incunable book publishing is the publication of books of musical scores. The invention of the means to print musical notation was made by Ulrich Hahn of Ingolstadt in 1476. His first score printed using his system of "double printing" was a complete missal printed in Rome. Other printers in Germany and Italy quickly followed up his invention, leading to a vast proliferation and dissemination of scores and interests in composition. Music has been an omnipresent art for as long as we possess any dependable historical/archeological evidence and was one of the four subjects of the quadrivium, closely related to mathematics. So the ability to print, rather than memorize or painfully copy, scores facilitated the expansion of the universe of music in the West, in terms of both geographic spread/imitation and complexity/interest in compositional technique, precisely in the same way that printed books facilitated the distribution and acceleration of the cultural evolution in other fields. All this opening of the world of music was put into place just in time for the full realization of the transition to polyphony and the proliferation of religious music at the hands of the reformers and counterreformers.[20]

At this point, the printers/publishers who produced and marketed these eight million books in a period of roughly forty-eight years must be brought into focus. It was they who were the catalysts of this avalanche of books, some of the highest merit, some utter rubbish, a number for simple, fictive entertainment but virtually all, save books of entertainment, judged at the time to possess some larger cultural value that would serve one or another sector of the larger world more or less well. Yes, by and large, they were compelled to "make a profit" (and to recover their capital and operational costs) as almost every writer on the period of the incunables feels compelled to point out with a faint air of denigration to one of outright condemnation. But material wealth was far from the sole motivation, which brought two centuries of learned men into the profession of printing/publishing. Most possessed a dedication to learning, its advancement, and the making of significant contributions to the contents of man-made culture. This commitment was, in most cases, as firm as that of the then academics to the academy. Every reader can be certain that those academics were as concerned with their material well-being as both their printer/publishers and their modern counterparts who provide these gratuitous, inferential judgments were/are.

Most of the Renaissance printers/publishers of serious books sought scholarly advice about the titles they should publish from scholars conversant with the then standards of intellectual concepts and ethical precepts as widely as the primitive fifteenth-century communication infrastructure allowed.

The first, and most critical, function of publishing is the building of the list. That is the publishing, over the years, of a body books that are reckoned as contributions to the bodies of knowledge the publishers seeks to enhance. Building a list largely involves not only identifying and contacting authors known to be writing a book advancing creditable falsifications, new hypotheses, or integrations of these hypotheses into existing bodies of knowledge. The authentic publisher is compelled to also seek out recognized scholars/writers who might be induced, as a consequence of the publisher's identification of a cultural need, to write a defensible account of the falsifying/creating/integrating of one or more ideas into an existing body of knowledge.

Immediately associated with the growth of lists, whether of converting "standard" works (mostly religious oriented) or new contributions to the world of knowledge, was the necessary and growing demand for the textual accuracy and completeness of printed books. This requirement, in turn, imposed the necessity of augmenting the publisher's mechanical staff with a staff of knowledgeable textual editors and copyreaders. This body of redactors became the initial body of jurors to which the critical mass of successive groups looked for passing judgment on the worth of the contents of books considered for publication. The iconic examples of this critical oversight of the printing/publishing of books probably are Cardinal Bessarion in Venice and Erasmus at Froben's establishment in Basel.

The publisher and his/her editorial staff were themselves usually possessed of considerable cultural knowledge and were commonly well-trained therein. They were able to be active participants in the generation as well as propagation of new cultural ideas—as active parties in the functioning of the knowledge-generating engine, which had the printed book at and as its base.

But as every publisher knows, just as critical as building a good list is the successful dissemination of the finished copies of each book. Again, an intelligent and well-conceived marketing program aimed at selling as many copies of a title as widely as possible must be conducted not solely in the interest of the publisher's profit, as often airily and spitefully pointed out by many academic commentators, but out of the decent discharge of the implicit expectations and understandings between author and publisher. The author had and has every reason to seek as wide a circulation of his ideas as reasonably possible. And beyond these specific commitments and covenants between author and publisher, a title must be sold widely to serve readers concerned with the advancement of knowledge and with the responsible discharge of the obligation to the building of the culture.

The incunabula printers/publishers, in substantial measure, recognized and endeavored to observe these publishing imperatives of editorial soundness and widespread dissemination, as they sought to inject into the cultural treasure of the West printed editions encompassing a large measure of the writings, which have defined and shaped the culture of the West. Virtually all of these printed versions, in contrast to copies made by scribes, can be found, even if only a single copy, in one library or another. The ability and willingness to produce large numbers of identical copies and distribute them widely meant that the loss of cultural work, which marked the millennia from the writing of manuscripts to the invention of printing, was radically reduced. The consequence, of course, has been that these "violls" of knowledge have remained culturally useful, even if the contents of many were subsequently falsified. The latter is a certain proof that a handful of people in every generation are able to learn from their predecessors' mistakes. The hand of these cultural gatekeepers in the printing/publishing establishments is evident in all the other large-scale developments of the last half of the fifteenth century, discussion of which follows.

Undoubtedly, the foremost matter of cultural concern in the fifteenth century was the continuing decline of the leadership of and respect for the church. Note was made earlier of the wave of mystical spirituality that had washed over much of Europe and to the pursuit of which a formal church organization was unnecessary. The initial stages of a Christian humanism were widely evident. The French crown had advanced its control of the church, converting it to a virtually national Gallic church. In a parallel devolution, the pope ceded the appointment of the clergy to the Habsburg emperor. The reunited crowns of Spain (Aragon and Castile) established the notorious Spanish Inquisition, enforcing a particularly strict body of doctrine and practice, which was imposed upon the Muslims and Jews. Savonarola sought to establish a strict theocracy in Florence and attempted to depose the pope. Charles VIII of France invaded Italy leading to conflict with the papacy over control of the extensive Papal States. The Vatican turned its attention and revenues to the worldly humanist pursuits of grandeur and the reconstruction of Rome, seeking to make it the equal of Florence. But above all, these singular and overt signs of a growing dereliction of its religious mission were the widening undercurrents of demand for reform and a return to the simple and primitive church of its founding.

Although it was a dangerous game, sympathetic printers/publishers produced implicitly or explicitly antipapal tracts. The Lollards, followers of Wyclif, retained and kept alive his English translation of the Bible. The Hussite movement in Bohemia (named for its notable proponent, John Hus) employed much of the Lollard doctrine. Both protesting sects remained alive, even if underground, until well into sixteenth century. These covert religious churches remained a continuing fount of antipapal and reformist tracts and books.

In the meantime, as previously noted, printers/publishers were busily transmuting into print or, in due time, reprinting all the vast body of accumulated "viols," which had provided the church with not only its intellectual and ethical structure but its vital lifeblood as well. To make a long story short, the infant book trade was successfully working both sides of the religious divide—and by so doing made relatively plainly obvious the public square, formerly enshrouded in the fogs of a near monolithic society, and highlighted the often contentious but deeply held dialogues that on occasion could be carried on therein. But such continuing, open, and passionate controversy about so profoundly critical and central a cultural platform and as culturally elemental as religion is was at the very least profoundly unsettling. This uncertainty could, as numerous commentators pointed out, serve, at best, as the harbinger of grave social and cultural uncertainty and confusion and at worst the harbinger of a terminal cultural wasting away.

"Artificial writing," the master key that seemed to offer such a cultural elixir and had produced such a quantum leap in the economic production of cultural goods and their widespread dissemination, had burst upon a society used to far less rapid and far more limited debate of contentious issues. That culture had not had the time or experience to adjust to and master the consequences of such radical departure in the ways of cultural falsification and formation. Only at a later date were substantial segments of the culture-forming classes able to comfortably deal with such a fact. The same heightening of uncertainty and confusion by the appearance of the printed book will be seen in other cultural arenas of lesser but notwithstanding important cultural import.

Transitions: Ethical Understandings

As previously pointed out, the Renaissance should be seen as largely as a continuation of or successor to many of the principal concerns animating the Middle Ages and the heir of most of the cultural goods developed in the earlier periods. One of the most telling illustrations of this continuity of thought and judgment can be found in the preoccupation with the immense body of received ethical concerns, moral teachings, and ethical precepts. The foundational Christian maxim, "In everything do to others as you would have them do to you," remained much alive. But this general and fundamental ethical imperative had been vastly augmented, and the derived moral tenets greatly multiplied in numbers in the intervening centuries. All were addressed to the regulation and judging of a multitude of social interactions and exchanges between people by Christian thinkers in the succeeding millennium and a half. The monks of the Carolingian Renascence had extracted from the salvaged Latin "violls" much of the best of Roman ethical precepts and subsequently integrated this body of ethical knowledge with the received body of Christian ethical knowledge. Here it should be noted that the "violls" containing some of the ethical writings of Cicero were particularly prized and broadly employed in the continuing augmentation of the Western body of ethical knowledge.

The twelfth-century reception of the "violls" of much of the Aristotelian corpus together with those of the Muslim and Jewish writers introduced another enormous body of ethical reflection and moral guidance into the West. Again over the succeeding two-century timespan, these new bodies of knowledge had to be integrated into the received and traditional body of ethical knowledge.

The fifteenth-century recovery of the "violls" of the Greek writers led to another efflorescence of ethical reflection and the further augmentation and refinement of the operational body of received ethical knowledge. Nearly all the extant ethical reasoning and precepts of the classical and Christian worlds were now at the disposal of Renaissance thinkers and writers and given enduring form in printed books. The "new men" of the Renaissance particularly prized the subject matters dealt with in the trivium—grammar, rhetoric, and dialectic or logic. By virtue of the usages of prior centuries, the trivium was construed to include ethical knowledge and reflection. The Renaissance thinkers and writers readily adopted this construction, locating ethics in the broadened category of rhetoric.

Second only to the received moral instruction of the Bible and the church, the thinkers and writers of the Renaissance looked to the writings of Cicero. In this high regard for Cicero, essentially a Stoic, the Renaissance simply followed the lead of the medieval churchmen and university doctors, most of whom saw Cicero as a forerunner of the best of Christian ethical thought. However, the fifteenth-century writers enjoyed a more extensive corpus of Cicero's work, for in their earnest manuscript-collecting campaigns conducted in old monasteries and churches, particularly in the North, they turned up a large number of medieval manuscripts, "violls," of Cicero's works, which had simply sunk out of sight for centuries for want of widespread dissemination.

Further enriching this range of ethical precepts and moral principles were the first translations and retranslations of the Neoplatonist corpus, most notably Plotinus and Proclus.

This vast array of ethical knowledge precepts and standards derived from several quite diverse traditions and sources also presented a major intellectual challenge to the thinkers and writers of the fifteenth century. The most immediate problem was, of course, to endeavor to come to a relatively clear and settled understanding of classical ideas that had been recorded and what the governing principles implicit in these writings were. As the history of ethical thought makes obvious, this task of understanding what earlier thinkers/writers had concluded and the reasons and logic underlying these conclusions is by no means a simple intellectual undertaking. These very issues remain alive and vigorously debated right up to the present day.

But the intellectual difficulties involved did not stop here. Despite their acceptance at one time or another in the past, the next obvious question was as follows: What of these precepts and principles remain valid in the contemporaneous setting—and by what criteria is their validity/invalidity to be judged? These questions, which preoccupied the Renaissance mind, remain not entirely resolved matters today. In short, the falsification of selected elements of this vast body of precepts and principles posed a major and enduring problem. As did the creation of alternative more encompassing ethical and moral hypotheses.

The work of culture makers is never-ending! For beyond all the work of understanding and assessment detailed above lay the work of eliminating falsified principles and the integration of new hypotheses into the then current body of operative ethical knowledge.

Again it was the printers/publishers as the gatekeepers of and the dealers and traders in cultural ideas/knowledge who were intimately yet wide-rangingly involved in all these culture-making undertakings. And again, their efforts of dissemination of differing and often conflicting writings and the risks involved therein in a very genuine sense contributed greatly to generating that fog of uncertainty and, hence, confusion that enveloped the last decades of the fifteenth century.

Transitions: The Visual Arts

Virtually every early history of or narrative dealing with and seeking to define and explain the Renaissance, beginning with the accounts of Leon Battista Alberti's (1404–1472) *De re aedificatoria* (1485) and contemporaries and continuing through the centuries, particularly in Jacob Burckhardt's (1818–1897) notable *The Culture of the Renaissance in Italy* (1860) and the work of subsequent historians following his lead, has intensively focused upon the art and artists of the fifteenth and sixteenth centuries as a key explanatory tool, typically employing painting and sculpture as key diagnostic evidentiary examples.

From this narrow aesthetic focus, a number of writers have sought to derive the remarkable evolution of the more complex religious, philosophical, economic, technological, institutional, political, and other cultural factors of the period. Such an approach to explaining so remarkable a transition as the Renaissance is simply unsustainable. The present account does not look to the visual arts of the Renaissance as particularly helpful in describing the cultural evolution of the West but rather simply as one of the outcomes of the broad resurgence of a mass of new ideas or knowledge unleashed in the West. It is worthy of note that the "revival" of artistic techniques and forms construed to be classical Greek were being explored about a generation earlier in Constantinople and so may have provided the impetus for the Western interest.

The visual arts have until quite recent times been employed for a limited number of social purposes. They were most notably not only employed to communicate culturally important messages to overwhelmingly illiterate populaces but also served the literate as illustrations of the textual materials from which they had been instructed or read. In the course of most of the history of the West, until the introduction of photography, painting and sculpture have been used for compelling illustrative purposes, to provide memorable images of culturally significant persons or events or beliefs, or to stimulate a sense of loyalty and bolster allegiance to persons or institutions.

But the noteworthy character of all these representations is that they convey ideas and meanings previously elaborated, most commonly in great detail, in linguistic/textual terms. The painters and sculptors put into material, visual forms, and hence more readily comprehended images, the ideas previously worked out by thinkers and writers. This work of shaping bodies of ideas in sufficient detail and to a level of clarity that they might be rendered into visual form has, as has been noted previously, commonly required extended periods of time and repeated falsifications and the creation of repeated new hypotheses to reach their then fullest articulation.

So for these reasons, the visual representations of the Renaissance are here viewed only as elements to characterize the cultural evolution of the West in the fifteenth and sixteenth centuries. They merely reflect in visual form the ideas worked out earlier in textual form and the changed means of depiction thought to be the revival of classical forms. The concern of this book is the evolution of the ideas and knowledge, which created the culture of the West not with the derivative visual outliers of that culture.

Transitions: Science

In the earlier discussion of the inventory of books printed in the fifteenth century, mention was made of the printing of a small number of classical and medieval writings in science. The centrality of science in the historical outcomes of the present-day West compels a brief return to these bodies of knowledge, for the foundations of Western science were largely in place by the end of the fifteenth century. As Kelley concludes, "… modern science was not a revolutionary break but the climax of a long tradition extending back to the devout and unheroic scholastic philosophers of the fourteenth century."[21] This inherited medieval foundation demonstrates in another aspect not only the profound continuity into the Renaissance period of the learning developed in the medieval period but also the even more powerful inheritance from the classical world on which these medieval foundations were mounted—and upon which the further development of Renaissance science depended. Mathematics and astronomy were the leading subject matters of interest from the quadrivium in the late fifteenth century.

Much of the Greek mathematical knowledge received from the East was collected in manuscript form by a few Renaissance figures. But only a small fraction of this work was brought into print in the fifteenth century. Even the Pythagorean notion of the harmony of the spheres referring to the regular, predictable circuit of the objects, which the naked eye could see in the night sky and which put men fascinated by such astral phenomena of the regularities in the mind of the lawful music of a metaphysical creator, had little currency before the sixteenth century. Euclid's *Elements* was first translated in the thirteenth century but not brought into print until the fifteenth century. A handful of contemporary mathematics texts of an elementary kind and a handful of classical texts were also brought into print in the fifteenth century.

Ptolemy's *Almagest*, encapsulating the then-definitive-body of Western astronomical knowledge, had first been translated in the twelfth century from an Arabic manuscript in Spain and from a Greek manuscript in Sicily, although it was the version from Spain, which dominated Western thought for several centuries. A new translation from the Greek was made in 1451 and printed shortly thereafter.[22] More popular than the *Almagest* was Ptolemy's *Cosmographia*, which was reprinted seven times before 1500 and which became a standard geography in the Renaissance.[23] The *Almagest*, when read in connection with Aristotle's *On the Heavens*, was creating a number of logical problems for not only astronomers but also physicists concerned with the fundamental elements making up the universe and navigators seeking to make sense of what they were learning as they sought to press farther out into the Atlantic Ocean.[24] The problem turned upon reconciling the Aristotelian idea of the four elements being arranged as concentric spheres—the first sphere the earth, topped by water, followed by fire, and lastly air as the outermost sphere—with the idea of the sea as a lake in the earth. But the Aristotelian idea was not what the explorers were finding—leading to great uncertainty and confusion with respect to the constitution of the very earth itself.

Complicating the orderly and rational understanding and integration of astronomy, one of the first of the investigations of the material world and the forces impelling it in the West and the incorporation of those findings into the knowledge accumulated by humankind and preserved in writings in libraries and in artifacts preserved in museums was the closely associated body of ideas classed as astrology. And to further complicate and befuddle more profoundly the fifteenth-century mental environment were the notions of alchemy, witchcraft, magic, and distinguishing black from white magic. All these diversionary and elaborate mystical explanations were attributed to "wisdom of Babylonia and Egypt," and more generally to the East. All of which implicitly posited the assumption that humankind could ward off illness, bad luck, and other of the misfortunes, which remain the human lot by prophesying the future and so avoiding predicted misadventure. (The fallacy of prediction remains a potent force for error in the modern age—planning and such related nonsense.) Given the vast uncertainty which has forever surrounded humankind and which was particularly aggravated the intellectual problems faced by humankind in the early Renaissance period in assessing and understanding such a flood of new ideas and then falsifying both received and new ideas simultaneously is simply staggering to contemplate, even at a distance of half a millennium.

To add to this burden, the creation of new and more powerful, inclusive hypotheses to replace the falsified ideas and then integrating these new hypotheses into the extant but growing bodies of knowledge had still to be undertaken. This work was, in the event, to consume some of the most brilliant minds of the next three centuries. Much of what the West of the previous millennium-and-a-half thought it knew about the universe in which it lived had to be reassessed in light of the newly received "violls" and the subsequent work stimulated by the reopening of those "violls." The reader can well imagine the immense intellectual difficulties in ascertaining the truth of these imported notions by simply recalling all the difficulties in arriving at a fairly defensible understanding of the history of the Soviet experience in pursuing the utopian vision of socialist society or of establishing the probabilism of quantum physics, with all the current documentary and experimental evidence available to the making of such assessments. That it took several centuries to convince the generality of thinkers that the occult beliefs and practices imported into Europe in the twelfth to fifteenth centuries were without substance is a testimonial to both the inherent difficulties in arriving at any trustworthy conclusions with respect to the true and the good and the sheer dogged determination and persistence of humankind in the inherent human will and drive to understand the nature of the world and humankind and to locate a firm base for the derived intellectual and ethical judgments to be lodged in bodies of accepted knowledge. (The reader may accuse the author of reiterating the grave epistemological problems facing and the means of their solution employed by the thinkers of the millennium plus dealt with in this writing as overkill to the point of tedium. This theme has been repeatedly hammered on only to seek to emphatically drive home the point of the enormous and time-consuming effort required of countless well-equipped minds in the shaping of the still only partially completed quest for an intellectually defensible *vade mecum* to the true and the good.)

Some from the community of printers/publishers were substantially involved in the fifteenth-century advances in mathematics and astronomy. Most notable of these printers was Regiomontanus of Nürnberg, who calculated and published the *Ephemerides* calculated by him and the *Theoricae planetarum novae* calculated by him and Georg von Purbach. Other printers/publishers, nonmathematical types, printed/published other mathematical and scientific books. But as pointed out in connection with other bodies of knowledge described earlier, the rapid and widespread dissemination of the same texts made possible by printing not uncommonly led to increased uncertainty and confusion in the vast threshing out of sound grain from the enormous burden of indefensible chaff.

Transitions: Music

Related to the study of astronomy was the making of music, the fourth component of the quadrivium. Making music seems to have been a constant in the mental and cultural life of humankind for as long as we have any notion of the human living of life. It appears to be yet another fundamental means of communication and expression akin to the symbol systems of language and mathematics. The fact that the grammar and lexicon of the practice of music has not yet been ferreted out places it squarely among the inscrutable mysteries associated with the foundations of language and number systems—but a system of greater and subtler connotation. Note has already been taken of the invention of music printing in the last quarter of the fifteenth century. Just as in the other domains of knowledge and culture, the insertion of the extraordinary invention of printing led to a more rapid evolution of the bodies of knowledge underlying the techniques of musical composition and performance. Most notable was the swift dissemination of the polyphonic mode of composition and presentation in the fifteenth century in contrast to the six centuries it took to develop the technique.

This same explosion in the widespread availability of identical music scores led to the equally significant and rapid evolution of a common canon of the musical language and music notation. This new ability to more firmly and authentically ground composer intent and to ground performance throughout Europe was a major contributor to the evolution of music in the West.

The rapid dissemination and adoption of polyphony laid the groundwork for the explosion of music making and listening in the sixteenth and subsequent centuries. Again the key to the laying of cultural foundations is to be found in the increased falsification/creation/integration of ideas about music beginning in the late fifteenth century facilitated by printers/publishers.

Transitions: Medical

Sharing some of the confusing characteristics of the influx of classical astronomical writings were the printed books dealing with medicine. Translations of Hippocrates and Galen were joined by translations of the Arabic writers, Avicenna's *Canon* and Maimonides's *Aphorismi*, and the Latin medieval Vincent de Beauvais's *Speculum maius*. Not simply confusing but contradictory descriptions of disease states and their treatment pocked all of these texts. These standard texts not infrequently advanced cures as diverse as employing magical practices or urged the use of plants and minerals sharing concocted symbolic imagery with the human body part afflicted. The principal accomplishment of the Renaissance medical men was to bring some order and stability to the names and symptoms of disease and illness. The leading physicians of the Renaissance were largely dealing with these received texts as grist for philosophical speculation or more commonly as exercises in philological analysis/correction—"... it was humanistic with a vengeance."[25] Small wonder that the practice of medicine, like that of the other sciences, was such a hard-won undertaking. One closing observation made by Sarton bears repeating in this context, "... the very high proportion of worthless publications among [scientific] incunabula is appalling ... mediocre publications would swamp the others ... for the simple reason that mediocre authors are always more numerous than distinguished ones."[26] Here a truism growing out of reflections on fifteenth-century scientific literature remains as valid for 75 percent of today's scientific literature. There are few grounds to fasten this observation exclusively upon comparisons of the writings in the sciences, for writings in other subject fields share at the very least similar comparative proportions.

Printers/publishers, despite their critical and intimate role in culture-making are, as a class, far from exemplary in their willingness to forego publishing "trash." As is true of most vocations, only a small minority of first-rate, authentic printer/publishers in every generation confined themselves to making genuine cultural contributions and upholds the traditional and accepted honor of the "trade."

Associated with the Renaissance receipt and study of classical and Muslim medicine was that of the plant sciences. This for the reason that a knowledge of plants as medicines was intrinsic to the medical concepts of Hippocrates, and so on. Here the works and names of Theophrastus, Aristotle's successor as head of the Academy; Dioscorides, whose *Materia medica* growing out of his work as a Greek physician to Roman Legions; and Pliny the Elder, whose Latin *Historia naturalis* was preserved in its entirety throughout the intervening centuries were dominant. To this inherited body of botanical learning, the significant additions of several medieval figures should be added: most notably Albertus Magnus, Aquinas's teacher, and strikingly Hildegard of Bingen, the remarkable prioress and mystic of the twelfth century. The botanists and physicians of the fifteenth century were more concerned with the recovery of classical texts and the philosophical analysis of these matters than with the fieldwork incident to relating the plants to their environment and the descriptions in the classical texts. In short, the botanists of the fifteenth century behaved in much the same way as the physicians with whom they were associated.

Much the same thing can be said of those with an interest in animals, minerals, and other aspects of natural history.

While there can be no question about a widespread and growing interest in the sciences in the early Renaissance, the primary focus of activity was the recovery of the classical texts. A kind of intellectual hiatus seems to have beset the Renaissance mind in the course of this undertaking. Many of the classical texts were translated and thanks to Gutenberg's revolution achieved a substantial distribution throughout Europe. Despite, or more reasonably due to, this sudden flood of new material and its heretofore unknown, rapid, and widespread dissemination, the necessity to understand it and undertake even preliminary analyses of it largely stifled any aggressive falsification/creation of new hypotheses/integration of it. Those cultural exercises remained for future centuries to undertake. And even the translation, emendation, and printing of the complete corpus of classical learning would have to be carried out by later scholars. The sheer volume of work to be accomplished simply outstripped the human resources available for the job. And to multiply these difficulties, the utter confusion engendered by conflicting texts and the significant disconnects between the newly received texts and the still dominant cultural constructions of the Middle Ages remained to be resolved. But the fifteenth century did add immeasurably to the available classical intellectual stock, which they well understood was a necessary gathering of substantive bodies of knowledge needed to advance the project of understanding the rules and principles, which the Creator had employed at the beginning.

Transitions: Techne

While technological invention and evolution shared virtually no common ideas with the sciences until late in the nineteenth century, both were concerned with understanding or employing factors in the physical objective world to realize human intellectual or practical ends.[27] Technology in the Renaissance, as in the Middle Ages, depended entirely upon the "cut and try" methods, and "cobbling together" means of fabrication employed by craftsmen and other manual workers. Just as the twelfth and thirteenth centuries had been an era of intense technological innovation, so the late fifteenth century was an era of even greater technological creativity. In this book in which Gutenberg is a leading figure, the inventions incident to introduction of printing deserve mention here as the greatest technological and cultural advance of the period.

Among other technological successes, the fifteenth-century improvement in the uses of gunpowder was of substantial cultural import. Indeed, several historians have used this innovation as a key historical analytic tool. These uses extended to the improvement of roads through blasting; the facilitation of construction, again by blasting for foundations and the construction of other below grade-level structures; and powerful weapons. Of even more fundamental importance, gunpowder engendered the demise of the medieval castle, which could be readily destroyed by undermining and sapping and all that implied in terms of the demise of the feudal system of governance followed by the withering of the manorial system of structuring the economy. This sequence of factors led, of course, to the forming of a capitalist economy and the modern nation-state.

Perhaps of even greater cultural importance was the rapid development in the use of firearms employing gunpowder—including not only handheld guns but land-based and naval artillery. The body of ideas built up around the technology of gunpowder, including the demise of the horse-mounted knight and archer serving only limited tours of duty, in favor of the paid rifleman and artilleryman serving full time in a standing army, was quite remarkable. Equally remarkable was the new naval ship designed to destroy from a distance with cannon replacing galleys designed for ramming and boarding of enemy vessels. All of these changes, in turn, necessarily dictated the creation of new ideas of ways to think about and to devise new bodies of strategic and tactical military and naval doctrine.[28] The latter was yet another example of an advance in technological knowledge contributing to the emergence of the modern nation-state.

Renaissance commentators and successors in virtually every subsequent generation, when reflecting upon and marveling at the technological advances of their/that age, not uncommonly have grouped printing, gunpowder, and the compass together as having forever shifted the course of the culture into a radically new trajectory. Coupled with Euclid's geometry, the compass provided a more accurate means for land surveying and the setting of property boundaries.

Of at least equivalent importance, the making of the compass not only made possible the setting and maintenance of a desired course for a navigator out of sight of land but also fueled, together with the making of firearms, the ever-finer and more sophisticated processes of manufacture. Such devices demanded ever-greater precision in their manufacture and operation to meet the understandable needs of their varied users.

The techniques of manufacture of other goods were enormously enhanced by the application of the ideas and knowledge accumulated by the instrument and firearms makers. These advances paved the way to the improvement, by geometric factors over the following generations of the tools, instruments, engines, devices, processes, etc., requisite to the technological achievements of the West.

Of the multitude of technological innovations put into place in the fifteenth century, three others demand brief comment. The first is mining and metallurgy. Continuing demand for increasing quantities of metals of all kinds throughout the fifteenth century—for weaponry, firearms, traditional swords, daggers, pikes, etc.; for construction purposes; for hardware of all kinds, including naval fittings; and for wagons, carriages, etc., particularly tires, axles, and similar demanding functions, vastly stimulated the search for, mining of, refining of, and manufacturing with metals. Shallow mining, employing hand-powered winches, fire to soften the ore, and hand tools yielding minimal amounts of metal, had been pursued for centuries. But increased demand dictated deeper mines, which were, in substantial measure, made possible by the harnessing of waterpower for lifting men and ore as well as ventilating and dewatering the workings and gunpowder for breaking the ore and driving the vein face forward. All of the rapidly developing ideas impelling these advances in mining were incorporated into a great and growing body of knowledge relating to the means of obtaining the metals necessary to the building of increasingly complex technological and cultural structures. Absent such enormous improvements in the extraction of ores and their subsequent reduction to usable metals, the radically innovative culture of the West would have been, if not stunted, forced into culturally less fruitful avenues.

But before any mined metal can be converted to purposeful use, the ore must be refined by extracting the surrounding rock as well as other minerals mixed with the element or compound being sought. The further mastery of the knowledge of waterpower greatly improved the above-ground breaking, grinding, and final extraction processing. Final processing commonly involved chemical processes; some quite sophisticated and developed by happy happenstance not from any underlying body of knowledge, for the science of chemistry lay some distance in the future. Rather, these serendipitous discoveries emerged from the "trial and error" undertakings of those entrepreneurs who entered or acquired "works" in the shadowy and dangerous underground world of "gnomes" and others who toiled and delved in the nether regions of the earth. These "lucky" or inadvertent discoveries of specific processes, techniques, and reactions were not an uncommon occurrence in a culture still lacking firm, nearly fully falsified bodies of knowledge related to such processes, etc. These kinds of discoveries were the work of observant practitioners prepared to accept the reality of repeated examples of such phenomena and then incorporate these observations into the geographically localized bodies of trade secrets, which would in time be incorporated into larger, more inclusive bodies of knowledge—and memorialized in books.

Another of the great technological innovations of the last half of the fifteenth century was the rapid improvement of the sailing ship. This advance had to do in the first instance with the rigging of sailing vessels to improve sailing to windward, an absolute necessity in a ship far from any land in the Atlantic Ocean and its frequent, vicious storms. At roughly the same time in the fifteenth century, the stern post-mounted rudder was developed. This innovation was a marked improvement over the steering oar and again augmented control over a craft in turbulent seas and strong and unpredictable winds. The final innovation in the building of ships capable of doing the open-ocean voyaging, which opened the fifteenth-century age of exploration, was "... the widespread adoption of carvel (flush plank) building with caulk filled seams ... [this] permitted the construction of large and generally watertight craft throughout Western Europe thereafter."[29]

The final topic of the fifteenth-century technological innovation to be dealt with here far from exhausts the technological revolution that marked the fifteenth and subsequent centuries in the West. This is because the aim here is not to trace the history of techne in the West but to focus on the broad outlines of the development of bodies of knowledge and the enormous clusters of related ideas that are implied by each and the role of the fostering of these ideas in books.

This last example is that of the production of textiles. Textiles loomed as the largest commodity in trade, both internationally and within Europe during the Middle Ages and the Renaissance. The dominance in this trade, which the technological innovations of the West facilitated, was a critical element in increasing wealth as well as general enrichment of not only the West, in general, but also of specific regions within Europe—Italy, Flanders, etc. The cultural consequences of the net accumulation of wealth manifestly not only contributed to the gradual economic and financial advance of the West but also helped fuel further cultural expansion.

The manufacture of a piece of cloth requires a number of sequential steps. All were at one time performed entirely manually. But in the West, an increasing number of the steps were mechanized. Mechanization itself involved the development of a large number of ideas over time and their successful integration into devices thus circumventing dependency on weak and easily fatigued human energy and power. In the case of textiles, this new power was mainly derived from waterpower—progressively applied to cleaning (fulling) the wool, cotton, or silk to the operation of ever larger treadle looms capable of weaving increasingly complex fabrics and kinds of textiles in increasing dimensions and volumes. Thus, by the fifteenth century, Europe had exchanged its role as a net importer of textiles from the Levant to that of a net exporter of not only the coarser and bulkier textiles but also even the finer fabrics of light cotton and silk.[30]

It must be noted here that because much of this technological innovation was the product of individual entrepreneurial masters/artisans, and in the case of crafts trades by craftsmen often organized in guilds, much of this knowledge was accumulated and falsified, new practices were created, integrated into the respective bodies of knowledge held in substantial trade secrecy, and passed on in practice or master/apprenticeship arrangements. Despite this more hands-on mode of knowledge dissemination, a modest but continuing output of trade and crafts books was consistently available in these centuries. Few examples survive, for like children' books, books dealing with practice and the doing of practical activities are commonly simply worn out or when superseded thrown away.

These early examples of the "T" in STM (science, technology, and medical) publishing were notably concerned not simply with the specifics of one trade or another but also with generalized engineering knowledge dealing with wheels, levers, gearings, eccentrics, cogs, pulleys, shafts, etc., and their various ratios and integrations for performing all manner of specific manufacturing processes—or alternatively, the making of jewelry, coinage, textiles, and artisan products. The consequence was that the understandings derived by readers were readily adapted to quite different and often novel manufacturing and fabrication processes. Technological knowledge proceeded, in great measure, by applying the underlying principles of practical mechanics to new and heretofore unimagined manufacturing applications. As the ideas relating to techne were evolved, that growing knowledge was conveyed in books.

An able school of historians has sought to track and explain the pre-eminence of the West by the continuing technological innovations of the West. They note that gunpowder was developed in China but used simply for fireworks and other spectacular displays. The Orient never sought to extend the employ of this apparent plaything to the augmentation of controllable power as in explosives for construction, mining, or small and large firearms. Similar was with the compass at the root of which lay the lodestone first discovered in China but treated there as a fascinating natural phenomenon. The Chinese employed it neither for land surveying to better depict the features of the landscape nor in the haven-finding art. Only after years of exposure to and denigration of the West did that remarkable culture adopt the Western conversion of such assets to practical measures improving, in most cases, some aspects of the human lot. But technology, as has been pointed out in several connections earlier in this text, is not about things but about ideas of how to think about, conceive, make, and employ humanly fabricated devices and practices. The West, and the rest of the world in recent times, owes much to the Western tradition of technology. But it owes more to the ever-questing nature of Western curiosity; highly developed sense of creativity; active willingness to try ideas out (experimentation); willingness to set aside traditional institutions, practices, and tools when better alternatives are created; and an openness to whatever ideas created in other cultures that may have some modicum of utility in its own. In short, the explanation for Western preeminence lies not in the physical embodiments of fabricated things, institutions, and practices but in a mind-set geared to a willingness and openness to "cut and try"—an enthusiasm to receive/falsify/create/integrate new ideas into existing bodies of knowledge. All of this inventive innovation was at base a continuing effort to augment the energy/power available to the society and to relieve humankind from the dull drudgery of providing that power.

Transitions: Antiquities and History

The Renaissance humanists were not only avid collectors and translators of classical writings but equally avid collectors, categorizers, and expositors of classical antiquities—coins, medals, pottery, architectural details, statuary, painted vases, inscriptions, etc. This pursuit is now styled archeology, epigraphy, etc. But in the fifteenth century, it was carried on under the appellation *antiquitas*. These antiquarians defined their activities and investigations as systematic collections and expositions of discrete aspects/functions of the past, paying little attention to the relationships between those of immediate antiquarian concern and other aspects/functions of the past. Thus, a close and well-researched book on the coins of the Roman Republic in that era paid no heed to inscriptions, save as some were unusual.

These collectors did not see themselves as historians, for the latter were nearly unanimously assumed confined to those classical authors who dealt with a chronological account of some past episode or period involving the tracking of multiple developments—Thucydides, Herodotus, Livy, Tacitus, and so on. The *antiquitas* might comment on a passage taken from these historians or advert to the writings of one of them to round out their artifactual collections but they never styled themselves as "historians." Yet as Momigliano points out, they laid the groundwork of research among artifacts and literary sources as well as research methodologies for historians who did not begin to write chronological accounts relating various aspects of the past until the eighteenth century.[31]

In short, the study of the past was transmuted from simple medieval chronicles to a dedicated pursuit of discrete artifactual elements, both material and literary, about the past. This Renaissance reorienting of the medieval practice of the writing of chronicles to the acquisition of factual materials provided the grist for the much later writing of histories.

Consequently, the Renaissance simply lacked explanations of past human undertakings as a sovereign means not simply of understanding how it was that the culture had arrived at where it was at the time but also of limning out human nature and the ideas underlying the social forces and institutions created to serve and reflect human qualities, both good and evil. The West had not yet developed one of the most powerful tools of human understanding—history. This powerful tool, over time, grew out of the intellectual working-through of the examples provided by the classical historians and the further development of the intense curiosity, which had driven the *antiquitas* to sift out, collect, categorize, and explain the relics and remnants of the past. The works of both the *antiquitas* and their successor historians are powerful examples of the avidity with which Western culture fastened upon the acquisition and subsequent extension of new and previously unknown or unexplored ideas. But the enormous explanatory powers of history lay yet some centuries in the future. The Renaissance remained preoccupied with the recovery of antiquity, not with the creation of new understandings of and ideas about that heritage. The absence of the means demanded for coming to reasonably certain grips with the past remained one more factor in creating the uncertainty and confusion, which was one of the hallmarks of the Renaissance.

Transitions: Government and Governance

Large numbers of Western historians, perhaps the preponderance, have sought to explain the evolution of cultures, and particularly Western culture, in terms of tracing the evolution of one or another cultural institution. The most common of the institutions employed for developing historical explanations is the social institution of the state. Hardly less popular, in the last century and a half, have been explanations based upon the economic organization of the society. Less commonly, some have looked to the development and employment of science/technology as the key to understanding the evolution of cultures. The cultural and explanatory place of the latter two has already been dealt with. All these, as well as other institutions less commonly applied to historical explanatory ends, are simply large bodies of knowledge—assemblages of largely related and internally consistent ideas. Institutions and their names provide a convenient means of labeling such bodies of ideas. Such terms are a kind of intellectual shorthand useful for quick and convenient reference to these bodies of knowledge at some particular point in time. These shorthand terms incorporate the vast numbers of related ideas, which have been integrated more or less successfully into such bodies. But most importantly, these institutions enjoy no enduring reality other than the ideations, past and present, which have created and maintained them. They are entirely creatures of the fundamental stuff of culture configured in ways in which these fundamental cognitive ideas and ethical precepts dictate. These fundamental concepts and precepts are plastic and so can be shaped to the formation of useful economic, political, social, etc., institutions. Alternatively, they can shape regressive and repressive and ineffectual institutions.

The state is manifestly one of the principal social institutions created by all of the four great world cultures. The continued historical intrusion of the state into the life of the citizenry has given it a kind of cultural prominence probably well out of proportion to its social value. The bundle of ideas underlying the formation and evolution of the Western state has proved a classic example of the acquisition/creation/falsification/generation of new ideas and hypotheses, and their integration into existing bodies of knowledge during the Renaissance. The recovery of most of Aristotle's works and those of Plato, both of whom dealt extensively with this major cultural question—the city-state being conceived by both as the great and central cultural strength of the Greek society—cast the understanding of the Western state into a wholly new light, even if this understanding was not immediately translated into operational terms.

But it was not simply the ideas related directly to the organization and social place of the state that governed the rapid growth of an operational central state in this period. For example, this growth was greatly facilitated by the seemingly remote but rapidly growing bodies of knowledge with respect to the manufacture of gunpowder, cannonry, small arms, the mathematics of artillery operations, etc. The latter ideational developments in armaments techne were accompanied by the simultaneous growth in knowledge in the architectural and engineering vocations of the designing of city and other fortifications to withstand the increasing effectiveness of the "gunpowder revolution," in short, in the development of the means of aggressive physical control and defensive self-assurance.

More importantly, the fifteenth century was the rapid but subtle change of the organization of political control from that of the hierarchal feudal system to a dynastic kingship. While the ideas associated with and defining the idea of some kind of a nation—and hence a nation-state—were still in the very early formative stages, the older feudal ideas surrounding the kings situated at the pinnacle of the feudal structure and ruling a large body of liegemen were being transmuted into the king as the supreme ruler of all the people within a geographical area. By the end of the fifteenth century, the kingdoms of England, France, Spain, etc., as well as the Holy Roman Empire were identifiable and relatively well-defined, cohesive, and more or less centrally controlled landmasses. Much quarreling over territorial rights acquired by inheritance began to appear in earnest with the Hundred Years' War only to die down out of the exhaustion of human and monetary resources but to be renewed in the fifteenth century with first the fortunate payoffs of the Hapsburg dynastic marriage policy, bringing together the Empire, Spain and Burgundy, followed by the French invasion of Italy based upon French claims to the territory encompassing Naples.

But even in these early stages of the development of ideas of exclusive, dynastic territorial kingdoms and the emerging concepts of a supreme and incontestable kingship, these ideas carried in their wake profound challenges. The presumptions of the aspiring royal families were encouraged and confirmed by the now well-elaborated body of Roman law. This body of law, after all, was originally the creature of one of the most powerful of the late Roman emperors and had its animating principle in the absolute authority of the emperor or king. To bolster their political authority, the fifteenth-century dynastic monarchs retained large numbers of law graduates of the universities offering instruction in Roman law. It was this body of secular lawyers who defended the claims of the state against all other claimants to social authority.

The church advanced the oldest and most fundamental challenge to secular authority. For centuries, the papacy had claimed as the chosen earthly instrument of the Almighty, supreme and final authority in both the religious and secular spheres. The beginning of the end of these claims derived from the writings of Marsilio of Padua (1270–1342), most notably the *Defensor Pacis* of 1324. While written to serve the ends of Louis of Bavaria in the latter's contention with the Vatican, it advanced and immediately became one of the seminal bodies of political ideas in the West. Marsilio held that all political power was derived from the body of the citizenry, that the secular ruler was obliged to respect and reflect the will of the citizenry, that the authority of the church was similarly founded and was subordinate to the secular ruler, and that the sovereign was to be restrained by a number of intermediary institutions. This revolutionary body of ideas was quickly circulated across Europe in manuscript form and then in the early sixteenth century appeared in print. The echoes of Marsilio's ideas have appeared and reappeared in many of the major theoretical reconfigurations of governance—the religious reformers of the sixteenth century, the intellectual wheelhorses of the English Revolution in the seventeenth century, the advocates of the American Revolution in the eighteenth century, etc. By the end of the fifteenth century, the secular supremacy of the papacy was a thing of the past, save in the Papal States, and secular rulers were, if not firmly, largely in control of the church in their domains.

The second great and continuing challenge to the never-ending compulsion, which drives every generation of rulers to seek an omnipotent and exclusive sovereignty, derived from the aristocratic nobility. This body of claimants to shared power was the historical outgrowth of the leading military feudatories that had supported the king in the feudal ruling structure. The fullest playing out of this particular restraint of monarchial power is to be found in England with the development of substantial control of the purse by parliament.

Slowly appearing alongside this mediating class of nobles were other classes exercising powerful constraints—the bourgeoisie, particularly those resident in the free cities and controlling trade; the wealthy bankers and moneylenders, who financed the territorial ambitions of the new model of dynastic kingship; and, of course, other monarchs pursuing their dynastic ambitions by contesting various inheritances with counterclaimants. It must be noted here that virtually all these intermediary classes or contenders reflected the growing body of ideas respecting the political control of a geographically defined social group. It was all about whether or how control of an increasingly complex society was to be exercised and how this control was to be moderated and the remaining residue of power was to be distributed between the various other claimants to it. This growth of the political power of social control was itself the product of other culturally important bodies of knowledge. (The increasing number and complexity of the various bodies of knowledge and their integration was becoming an increasingly difficult cultural undertaking.)

The other major cultural force restraining the power of the state flowed from the classical body of ideas extolling the virtues of political freedom in the Greek city-state and the Roman Republic. Numerous thinkers and writers of the fifteenth century advanced these ideas, citing classical sources in falsifying the dictatorial ideas of the Roman emperors and the analogous efforts of both the tyrants of the Italian cities and the European monarchs.[32] Several of the Florentine writers compared that city's brief interlude of freedom with that of the early Roman Republic.[33]

In short, the cultural inheritance of not simply Greece and Rome but the German tribes remained living and compelling bodies of knowledge, despite the repeated efforts of the political classes to, if not stamp out, at least neutralize the impact of this long and many-sourced body of political ideas.

The consequence of these several and competing bodies of ideas, all being advanced in any number of books—the moribund but still kicking feudal system of political organization; the nascent nation-state; the ongoing, if futile, assertions of secular supremacy by the papacy; the irrepressible claims of liberty and popular sovereignty; and the never-ending and overwhelmingly important contention over the role of the state in the society, as a near-omnipotent master governing a closed society or a limited state providing limited services to an open society—combined in a variety of specific cultural formulations leading to yet another and major locus of confusion, strife, and uncertainty marked the closing of the fifteenth century.

Transitions: An Unexpected and Vastly Enlarged World

Second only to the misery imposed upon unfortunate citizenry by the state and the confusion with respect to the proper role of the state was the crippling of any sustained capacity to deal with larger and more significant long-term concerns. This incapacity is particularly and pointedly reflected in the remarkably ambivalent and feeble responses of the various ruling elites in Europe to the relatively sudden emergence of an entirely New World and the remarkable associated revision of understanding about the extent and configuration of the earth. Save for the pioneering case of the crown of Portugal in the fifteenth-century exploration and opening of the Atlantic, the charting of the sea-routes paralleling the west coast of Africa and so around the Cape of Africa and on to India. No other ruling authority devoted anything like a comparable and sustained amount of time and resources to this stunning geographic opening.

The utterly unknown and unimagined New World of the Americas and the slightly known but essentially closed world of the Orient were largely explored, and their description and characterization of their native peoples added to the bodies of knowledge respecting the extent of the earth and nature of the peoples, plants, and other creatures living therein. This knowledge was largely the work of individual adventurers, driven by motives of personal aggrandizement and by clerics intent upon bringing the "good word" to the largely primitive peoples encountered.[34]

One or another of the European monarchies advanced some limited resources from time to time to one or another exploring venture, and all the maritime states issued various forms of entitlement to their adventurers for the use or possession of their discoveries up to the middle of the sixteenth century. Both were offered with the continuing expectation that sufficient treasure would arrive with the return flotillas to partially bail the monarchs out of their perpetual financial difficulties engendered by dynastic and royal ambition. Given that these expensive and perilous voyages were largely mounted by private groups, the latter manifestly sought maximum financial outcomes for those backing or conducting them. These ventures were almost universally accompanied by clerics seeking a harvest of new souls brought to the true religion.

It is entirely reasonable and culturally defensible that such individuals and joint-stock companies undertook the development of the economic resources and the conduct of the exchanges. They were able to integrate heretofore localized, constrained, usually destitute, and often haphazard microeconomies into a larger, more rational, international framework of manufacture and trading in a way that governments could not. (Think the muddle the Spanish crown made of its empire.) One of the compelling consequences of this integration was a world of cultural exchange and learning. As the now well-proved economic axiom has it that at the end of the day, virtually every participant in the larger economic framework is better off in such an extended, more integrated economy. But the near-universal disregard by the fifteenth-century states of the monumental problems created by the shortsighted practices of the explorers/colonists and the utter failure to advance any understanding of the extraordinary cultural possibilities implicit in the discovery of other lands and cultures remains a clear indicator of the cultural fragility, self-absorption, and uncertainty of the emerging autocratic state.

In any priority listing of the major achievements of the fifteenth century, the discovery of the New World, and the subsequent exploration and elucidation of the earth and its contents must rank as second only to Gutenberg's invention in cultural importance. The advance in the accumulation of knowledge added to those bodies of ideas now identified as geography, cartography, oceanography, navigation, zoology, botany, anthropology, etc., was simply stupendous—and, of course, required decades, and in most cases centuries, first to digest and intrinsically understand and then to falsify many of the reigning hypotheses followed by creating more defensible hypotheses and finally to integrate these new hypotheses into existing bodies of knowledge.

Here there are two observations: First, the possibility that such exploratory voyages might prove of value was derived from some of the flood of books printers/publishers were releasing into the market. Chief among these were, of course, Ptolemy's *Almagest,* known in the West from the late twelfth century, and his *Geography* first translated in 1406. The book that triggered Columbus's vision of a short route to the Indies by traveling West was Cardinal Pierre d'Ailly's (1350–1420) *Imago Mundi*, itself derived from Roger Bacon's hypothesis of a narrow Atlantic.[35] In the meantime, the monks of several German monasteries were trying to come to grips with the mapping of the spherical world on flat paper as promulgated by Ptolemy. This long forgotten mathematization of geography, employing geometric lines of latitude and longitude, was first undertaken by these monks in the early fifteenth century. The mathematics required in support of this effort had proved too difficult for the mathematicians of the medieval period to resurrect. The first surviving copies of some of these maps appeared in 1460 or 1461. Subsequently, the Ptolemy *Geography* was printed in the 1470s and 1480s with the new maps drawn by these monks. It is unclear as to how these new departures in cartography were applied by first the Portuguese and later by Spanish and Italian navigators. But certainly the "haven-finding art" had to be vastly clarified and improved with the widespread availability of printed maps to encourage navigators forward.

Subsequent to his first voyage, Columbus wrote a long letter describing it. This letter went into eighteen editions in Latin and several European vernaculars. Even more famous was the account of the Portuguese voyage, the *Mundus Novus* of 1501 written by Amerigo Vespucci (1454–1512), which, among other things, appeared in at least sixty editions within a couple of decades. In this work, Vespucci also confirmed his nearly exact calculation of the circumference of the earth and established the existence of the Pacific Ocean, which, in turn, established the New World discoveries as continents quite distinct from Asia. In 1507, one of the German monks, Martin Waldseemüller (1470s–1522), drew and printed the map which with accompanying text, *Cosmographiae Introductio,* first incorporated these revolutionary findings. The true shape of the earth was finally starting to fall into place.

Printers/publishers played a major role in putting into place the intellectual foundations underpinning this abrupt initiative of exploration. They also fed the subsequent thirst for further knowledge of voyages, their outcomes, the means of executing them, and on and on. In short, the invention of printing led to the rapid and widespread revelation of a radically different world. But this revelation, in turn, led to yet further uncertainty—not simply about matters of cosmography but more seriously led to the formation of a large cloud questions respecting long accepted ideas about the nature of humankind and its place in the larger universe. In yet another area of knowledge, the invention of printing was launching clouds of uncertainty and confusion at unseemly speeds on increasingly puzzled peoples.

Further, with the invention and mastery of printing line engravings, the printer/publishers were able to print not just maps but all manner of illustrations having to do with the construction of ships; the use of the compass, quadrant, astrolabe, and other navigational gear; the locating of latitudinal position through the use of astronomical navigation; views of the newly discovered lands, plant, animals, and peoples; primitive scientific explanations; geometrical exercises; and so on. To not put too fine a point on it, the printing of illustrations offered all readers, not just the wealth but the opportunity to own and to be instructed by visual means as well as linguistic.

But what to make of all these strange places, plants, creatures, and peoples and their utterly different languages, dress, modes of life, etc?[36] Yet more uncertainty.

What were the immediate cultural consequences that these primitive fifteenth-century explorations brought to the West? It was a mixed bag at best. While a number of relatively successful voyages had been completed, others had failed, and seamen and ships were regularly lost. The arts of navigation were still in their infancy and required significant improvement. The means of keeping vessels and crews in some degree of fitness for extended oceanic voyaging were substantially wanting. Few detailed charts or manuals of transoceanic sailing had yet been prepared or printed, for want of adequate dependable information.

Even greater ignorance and uncertainty accompanied the enormous number of random and often inaccurate reports about how other peoples lived. The confirmation/falsification and reconciliation of these inconsistent reports were to be the stuff preoccupying the natural historians for four centuries prior to the emergence of the discipline of anthropology in the nineteenth century. The early natural historians were responsible for turning these scattered and ad hoc clumps of, often, partial information into the bodies of Western knowledge respecting non-Western ways of forming and shaping religious, linguistic, epistemic, philosophical, political, economic, and social bodies of knowledge. In short, they sought to comprehend and limn out cultural complexes differing in all manner of general and particular beliefs, usages, and practices from those of the West.

But this effort to come to grips with alien cultures was at best a spotty undertaking—the principal thrust of the early explorers and their backers was to impose Western culture in all its particulars upon the natives or to turn them into the engines of Western wealth production. As a consequence, not only were some of these other cultural complexes despoiled, for want of adequate legal protections, a massive failure of the autocratic state, but also useful cultural information forever was lost. Only the occasional scholar, most commonly the rare cleric, concerned with such seemingly lesser matters, conducted the collection of bodies of cultural knowledge in any kind of systematic way.

These same conflicting reports dealing with the geography of these new lands, and the plants and animals inhabiting them, characterized the early days of geography, botany, and zoology. So parallel intellectual endeavors by natural historians were called for to bring some reasonable order to these fields of scientific and cultural understanding. In all cases, it may be observed with some pride by publishers that the community of authentic publishers fastened voraciously upon any such accounts they could learn of. Little of the intellectual results of these sporadic explorations and the organization of this received information into hypotheses by Western natural historians were lost to the Western world for both the reports, and the consequential hypotheses were soon published upon the explorers' return or the conclusion of the falsifiers/synthesizers' work. But like most of the cultural undertakings of the period, reports and their meaning were commonly in conflict. The larger world recently opened was an intellectual jumble as perplexing and awash with uncertainty as the repeatedly debated and fought over cultural and knowledge issues endemic to the West.

The Closing Years of the Fifteenth Century

The early Renaissance was above all a period of extraordinary uncertainty and fundamental confusion. It was for the most part the period when the West was inundated with another flood tide of new bodies of knowledge and new and not easily understood cultural formulations, both classical and the ill-formed reports of explorers. The "new men" of the Renaissance were, in some measure, the product of the "new cultural material" which, in part, they sought out and, in part, had thrust upon them. The latter was the result of the inveterate curiosity, that quintessential mark of the West, which led the more enterprising to open new doors that, in turn, disgorged "new perplexities." But to accept the notion of some of them that the era had turned its back on the Middle Ages when dealing with the new information and new bodies of knowledge, which marked the fifteenth century, is a serious error in historical judgment. The leading Renaissance figures were, in fact, dealing at the base with the traditional bodies of knowledge, which had collectively shaped the Western cultural tradition up to that time. The Renaissance simply added to or falsified some of the ideas contained in various traditional received bodies of knowledge. The same observation may be made with respect to the comprehension and integration of the new information and bodies of knowledge of which the fifteenth was the latest recipient.

In addition to the receipt of new information and new bodies of knowledge, the other novel factor was the wide dissemination across Europe of standard printed texts at radically lower prices than handwritten manuscripts. Almost overnight a vastly increased number of critical and/or creative minds could work simultaneously from common texts on shared problems of comprehension; raise questions and alternative interpretations; falsify received or newly minted hypotheses; generate new, more powerful hypotheses; and propose means of integrating old/new ideas into contemporary bodies of accepted knowledge. A heretofore unimagined mass of mental power or energy was brought to bear on virtually all the intellectual concepts and ethical precepts, which had been promulgated in the West and in Islam. All the problems relative to the institutions of the West—religious, economic, political, social, etc., were, likewise, suddenly and concurrently fair game for the critical masses of thinkers/writers. In short, the printing press had fostered a giant knowledge-generating engine.

Not simply textual material but figurative matter—music scores, maps, charts, geometric examples, procedural layouts and instructions, and plans for building not simply structures but machines, tools, ships, firearms, and on and on—fashioned to support the arguments or ideas being advanced in the accompanying text. The means of accurate, current, and widespread communication had been radically advanced. The consequence was yet a further extending and deepening of the critical mass of minds being brought to bear on virtually every aspect of the culture and culture building.

But this deepening and extending of the mental means of culture building by the agency of printing was not an unmixed blessing. The increasing numbers of titles produced in increasing quantities and their increasingly conflicting intellectual/editorial content contributed enormously to the confusion and uncertainty, which closed the fifteenth century. To compound this confusion were the numbers of titles bearing contents that would in time be proved to be false—simply fabrications addled or intentional—or, more ominously, purely evil—a far more difficult problem to counter than the falsification of a simple mistake. On the other hand, print not only broadened the reach of ideas but also speeded up the search for resolution. No longer was the option of devoting decades to the falsification of an idea and the creation of a broader encompassing alternative hypothesis implicit in culture building. The imperative of resolving falsehoods or conflicting conclusions or countering evil had within a couple of generations assumed an urgency never heretofore known. The premium on individual mental prowess had been vastly increased. The West had become among the world's four great cultures a radically more advanced knowledge-generating engine for the destruction and creation of both single ideas and substantial sections of entire bodies of cognitive and ethical knowledge. While the West was poorly prepared to cope with so unique a cultural outcome, the other three world cultures were—and remained up to recent decades in some cases—utterly unprepared to deal with so fundamental an acceleration and increase in the volume of the falsification/creation/integration of ideas.[37]

But the immediate consequence of the conjoining of this extraordinary constellation of cultural events was to leave the West at the close of the fifteenth century in need for/of the massive restructuring of the masses of new knowledge, both classical and the results of the first opening of the entirety of the earth and all its contents. The next several centuries would necessarily be devoted to the restructuring and resolution of much of this perplexity. The printer/publishers were both complicit in engendering this bewilderment and would be among the principal participants contributing to its resolution. Much of this work was to be accomplished in the sixteenth century to which we must now turn.

Notes

1. Thompson, 1939, 473ff.
2. Ibid., 459ff.
3. Yates, 1964.
4. Manual, 1979, 230.
5. Willison, 1980, 10.
6. Yamey, 1949, 99–114.
7. Braudel, 1984. Braudel does a meticulous job in tracing the evolution of the growing body of ideas dealing with the making and exchange of goods and services from the fifteenth century onwards.
8. De Sota, 2000, 223ff.

9. Kristeller, 1961. Kristeller makes a strong case for impact of this cultural tradition upon the emergence of humanism and its preoccupations.
10. Bolgar, 1976, 8.
11. Ong. "Commonplace Rhapsody: Ravisius Textor, Zwinger and Shakespeare." In Bolgar, 1976, 120ff. Ong offers a quite interesting summary of the high value the Renaissance placed upon imitation in literary work, employing the common turns of phrase, epithets, and events that were the heart and soul of the commonplace books—both those individually maintained and those created by the likes of Erasmus and Textor and printed for broad, general use. He summarizes the strong case T. H. Baldwin makes in his William Shakespeare's Small Latine and Lesse Greek that large swathes of Shakespeare's poetry and dramatic writing depended heavily upon Textor's Epitheta, an often reprinted and widely employed commonplace book.
12. Allen, 1995, ix.
13. Kekevich, 2000, 154.
14. Bolgar, 1976, 19ff.
15. Steele, 1903–7.
16. Hirsch, 1967.
17. Grendler, 1995, II, 59. Grendler points out that "[The Arthurian romances were] … probably the largest corpus of secular vernacular literature to be found in the Renaissance. They rivaled saints' lives in popularity, insofar as such things can be determined."
18. Sarton, 1938. Sarton carries on at some length condemning the printers and publishers of the fifteenth century for their lack of intellectual vigor and understanding as reflected in the absence of "good" classical and contemporary science books from their lists and the abundance of "bad" apocryphal writings therein. Publishers are no more fortune-tellers than are scientists. On the contrary, the printers and publishers were publishing the subject matter that was approved, sought after, and being used by those making some claim to be studying natural history. The fault, if any fault may be properly assigned, rests as clearly with the fifteenth-century scientists. But in truth, no fault maybe assigned for the Renaissance was enveloped in boundless confusion. As pointed out elsewhere in this book, the fifteenth century was deluged with all manners of texts coming from the Middle East—mostly Greek but Hebrew, Arabic, etc. This deluge spilled in over all the rediscovered Latin texts that had fallen into desuetude, most of which were suddenly widely available, thanks to Gutenberg's invention. Scattered randomly throughout this plethora of writings were wildly fantastical mental machinations or fanciful illusions produced by wildly uninformed imaginings. It would take the best part of three centuries to sort all this embarrassment of out-of-control mental exuberance out and consign it to the cultural debris with which historians must work in an effort to create a relatively honest and accurate account of the past. Needless to say, the other great epistemic undertakings of falsification, creation of replacing hypotheses, and the integration or reintegration of these more powerful explanatory hypotheses into existing bodies of knowledge. This ground has been gone over often enough in this book that the reader would lief not be conducted over it again—so, the author will not go over well-trodden ground. As was noted earlier, his patron Cosimo de' Medici required Ficino to set aside the translation of Plato, a work in progress, in favor of translating the esoteric writings of Hermes Trismegistus. Sarton would have these two leading humanists deciding in favor of a writing that Sarton could only identify as wildly unscientific rather than attending to some other work as for example some of the Aristotelian corpus, thereby consigning them to his company of derelict printers and publishers among the scientifically unwashed. The plain

fact of the matter is that no one in the fifteenth-century Florence, or elsewhere in Christendom of the time, possessed the knowledge and understanding to make the kind of judgments of scientific worth, which Sarton could make with five centuries of numerous falsifications, formulations of new hypotheses, and much larger bodies of integrated knowledge. To say that Cosimo and Ficino were misled is to fail to understand the rolling mists of confusion that blanketed Europe for centuries.

19. Rose, 1973.
20. Lang, 1941.
21. Kelley, 2002, 210.
22. Haskins, 1960, 151.
23. Sarton, 1938, 104.
24. Kuhn, 1957, 86.
25. Sarton, 1955, 50.
26. Sarton, 1938, 84.
27. Hundert, 2004, 461–2. See account of Francis Bacon's idea of the place of technology in the search for truth.
28. DeVries, 2002, XIV, 394.
29. Scammel, 1995, IV, 369.
30. Ashtor, 1992, iii, 265. Ashtor also makes the important observation that a part of the continuing decline of the textile manufactures in the Levant was the mounting corruption of the Ottoman manufacturers. "When there was no more free competition [as the Turkish state controlled the licensing of textile plants, among other enterprise, so the operators bribed Ottoman officials in order to maintain their licenses] there was indeed no to improve production methods," iii, 245. A clear case of the positive results of the relating two powerful bodies of knowledge—technological and economic.
31. Momigliano, 1950, 313.
32. Cantor, 1973, 552. Cantor writes "… the political life of the Italian city-states was as sordid as any in Europe.".
33. Baron, 1996, 54–5.
34. Kamen, 2003, 95. Kamen repeatedly makes this point with reference not just to Spain but England, Holland, etc.
35. Randles, 2000, I, 9.
36. Clark, 1966, 2. Clark notes that "The man who lived at a distance of two days journey was a foreigner …"
37. In making this assessment of the present worldwide hegemony of the West, it must be particularly highlighted that all three of the other great cultures actively eschewed the introduction of printing. This was not simply a case of the well-understood lag of implementation of innovation, which is common across all human societies. Rather the elites of these other three cultures actively discouraged the importation and resisted the adoption of this technological and cultural multiplier.

3

The Spread of Printing and Its Consequences in the Sixteenth Century

> *Merely describing the past in its own terms does not constitute the historian's function.... We are not antiquarians. We are called to help the present understand itself by understanding how it came to be. We strive to find meaningful order in the multifarious events of the past and thus, explicitly or implicitly, we pass judgments on the relative importance of events.*
> —Richard S. Westfall, "The Scientific Revolution Reasserted," in *Rethinking the Scientific Revolution*

While it is always convenient for the historian to organize a narrative by century, as has been done here, every relatively informed reader of history has long since recognized that such chronologically convenient divisions often distort multicentury trends. So were it not for the discovery of the New World by Columbus and the French invasion of Italy near the end of the fifteenth century and the Reformation of the early part of the sixteenth century, a more apposite dating might follow the observation of Bolgar: "That in the field [of the collection, publication, and often translation of classical texts] the date 1500 is almost totally devoid of significance. If an era is needed, it should be 1550. By that time most classical texts were in print and it was becoming possible to assess the critical problems [editorial and contextual]."[1]

This history of the cultural consequences of Gutenberg's invention of printing departs from the wise observation of Bolgar, for he was concerned more with the impact of the revival of classical learning in the West. The concern of this history is to trace the enormous impact of Gutenberg's invention of printing upon the cultural evolution of the West in terms of its critical role in the solution of the epistemological problem. So without apology the traditional division by century is retained herein.

This account left the fifteenth century on the note of the painfully grave uncertainty and profound confusion that marked the intellectual and cultural lives of Western Europe. This outcome was attributable, thanks, in very substantial measure, to the catalytic role of the printed book, to the remarkable intellectual and financial risks undertaken, and to the exceptional exertions exercised by the printers/publishers, who had proliferated across Western Europe in the half century since Gutenberg's invention. Perhaps the most telling emblematic motif of the compelling and enduring presence of this confusion and uncertainty is to be located in the politics and pursuits of the papacy at the end of the fifteenth century and the first decades of the sixteenth century—particularly the reigns of Julius II (Giuliano della Rovere, 1443–1513) and his successor Leo X (1513–21, born Giovanni de' Medici of the Florentine de Medicis, 1475–1521). The first was the warrior Pope, still driven by the idea of the secular supremacy of the church and the papacy over the lives and affairs of Christendom. He was bent on recapturing the papal states from the French to consolidate the papal central state while simultaneously inaugurating the lavish and costly reconstruction of Rome. His successor, Leo X, continued, for the same reasons, the consolidation of the papal central state and Julius's extravagant and ostentatious reconstruction and grand decoration of Rome. But he, impelled by a belief in the propaganda value of costly spectacles, staged a continuous series of such costly spectacles. These dramas and festivals were meant to entertain the hothouse coterie of Curial sycophants and simoniacal humanists attracted to papal preferment. As important was his further belief that such spectacles awed those of the mass of the flock who had made pilgrimage to Rome, thereby augmenting their homage and veneration of the church.[2] All of these undertakings were carried forward at vast expense to believers and a pretentious and a palpably manifest indifference to the long-sought twin ideals of the reform of the worldly church and a return to the devotion and practices of the primitive church. It bears noting that one of the witnesses of this vast and costly rebuilding of an imperial papal city was a young German Augustinian monk, Martin Luther, who in 1510–11 spent some months in the order's convent adjacent to the new Vatican.[3] In retrospect, it is difficult to ascribe any coherent or comprehensible view of the spiritual place of the church or Erasmian religious humanism to such radical worldly initiatives. This remarkable instance of cultural cognitive dissonance is, in a very genuine sense, the direct consequence of the widespread distribution of a mounting deluge of printed books supporting and advocating a wide variety of often conflicting worldviews, analyses of human nature and its earthly setting, and doctrines of intellectual and ethical understandings and conduct.

Continuous reference has been made to the great eras of translation, the twelfth- and thirteenth-century burst from the Arabic, following the reconquest of the Iberian Peninsula, and the burst of the late fourteenth and early fifteenth centuries in Italy and Germany, incident to the influx of manuscripts and scholars from Constantinople, translated by the early humanists following in the footsteps of Petrarch and Boccaccio. Although both of these bursts led to genuine renascences, that is, renewals of the intellectual and ethical contents and perspectives of the culture of the West, they were largely confined to a tiny handful of religious or secular scholars who enjoyed a rare good fortune, enabling them to escape the lot of the peasants or that of a largely benighted nobility. Neither of these two revivals nor the earlier Carolingian Renascence effectuated a substantial or widespread improvement in the lot of the generality of the populace. This is not to hold that no lasting or meaningful intellectual or ethical structures were put into place in any of these three cases, as it is hoped this narrative confirms. Each of these renascences manifestly not only built serially upon the cultural structures of the previous eras but also provided an augmented array of intellectual springboards from which inherited hypotheses might be falsified or successive more powerful hypotheses could be put into place. And in every case the circle of beneficiaries of these ideational exertions was progressively widened.

The sense here intended is that the mechanisms devised for the initial comprehension, falsification, creation, and integration of new knowledge structures remained exceedingly primitive, dependent as they were on the transmission of cultural goods by word of mouth—conversations, lectures, sermons, etc.—or a handful of laboriously hand-copied writings, often more or less garbled. Both of these avenues were essentially open only to a limited number of those fortunate enough to be able to follow such not visibly productive careers. This long-standing, constricted access to and pursuit of cultural goods was radically altered in the mid-fifteenth century by Johannes Gutenberg, who provided the critical element necessary to the development of a new methodological/technological structure for the comprehension, falsification, creation, integration, and dissemination of cultural knowledge. With Gutenberg's revolution the fundamental cultural epistemological problem facing every culture was vastly improved.

The happy concurrence of the coming together of the profound intellectual methodological revolution and powerful knowledge-generation engine brought into being by Gutenberg and the receipt and subsequent printing of the flood of most of the Greek texts and a few long-stranded Latin manuscripts not previously known led not simply to a geometric increase in the introduction of knowledge concepts and precepts but to a continually increasing pace of translations and their rapid publication in multiple copies in the sixteenth century. The glacial flow of limited quantities of printed books in the early decades following the introduction of the art of printing rapidly sped up to become a growing torrent of infusions of sometimes half-understood, sometimes novel, and sometimes utterly unsupportable intellectual and ethical ideas. Again the "new men" of the Renaissance boasted of the superiority of their translating skills relative to those of their medieval predecessors—a boast that present-day historians tend to endorse. But as Haskins pointed out more than seventy-five years ago, the Renaissance translators depended in substantial measure upon the deprecated work of those medieval translations.[4] This observation is made only to reinforce one of the continuing themes of the previous chapter—that of the iron law of cultural continuity—an analog of the geological axiom of uniformitarianism.

The element, which was most notably new in the Renaissance period, was not some form of cultural superiority to the cultural achievements of the medieval era but the geometric increase in the number and variety of more broadly available ideas to comprehend, to debate, and to work with. This widening of knowledge sources engendered and supported orders of magnitude greater numbers of minds which could be brought to bear simultaneously upon the critical cultural matters of the comprehension, falsification, creation, and integration of knowledge concepts and precepts embodied in identical texts. This culturally volatile association of the wide dissemination of identical texts, coupled with an explosive swelling in the numbers of acute, intellectually driven minds, bred and nourished the Renaissance. The concocted notion of some kind of special "creativity" which mysteriously appeared in the fifteenth and sixteenth centuries had nothing to do with a "New Humankind." Rather the broadening and deepening of the sheer numbers of widespread identical texts, similar to a mounting number of readers and thinkers, dealing with such cultural matters provided the impetus for the explosion of knowledge in the Renaissance. This explosion was manifestly augmented by the mounting flood of translations from the Greek of the classical texts. But this was not the engendering spark.

A substantial start had been made on these related developments in the last decades of the fifteenth century, as described earlier, but the pace of translation and publication was considerably increased in the first half of the sixteenth century. It can be said that most of the Greek canon available to twenty-first-century readers had been published in multiple copies printed in Greek or Latin by the middle of the sixteenth century. In substantial measure, this massive endeavor was the outcome of direct initiatives taken either by printer/publishers like Aldus Manutius of Venice in the first decades of the sixteenth century or by less notable printers in various printing centers now well established in all the major towns and many of the smaller towns across Europe. This vast corpus of widely disseminated books containing new knowledge or concepts printed in the first decades of the sixteenth century was so suddenly made that it injected another substantially difficult-to-digest bolus of sometimes useful and sometimes deceptive material into the already confusing stew inherited from the fifteenth century.

Consequences of the Book: Religious Reform

In an emerging and growing contrast to concerns with traditional religious or classical writings, some printer/publishers were engaged in commissioning or soliciting or selecting new writings of then-living writers. These initiatives pointed to or elucidated positive agendas aimed at articulating or advancing additional positive and definite ways of comprehension, thought, and judgment. These writings and the books containing them began to introduce some sense of certainty and constructive thought into the sea of uncertainty and confusion then widely abroad. The iconic figures of these new departures were, in the first rank, the reformers Martin Luther (1483–1546) and John Calvin (1509–64), together with their several less-notable but like-minded reformers.

Some historians have held that Luther and his reformation were made by the printing press. This is hardly a sustainable conclusion, but it does point vividly to the central role that books and printing played in this history-changing religious cultural creation.

These imposing historic reformers must be placed in the first rank of cultural formation, for they advanced coherent bodies of integrated intellectual and ethical religious doctrines which were to prove enduring and powerful in shaping the culture and society in succeeding generations—precisely as religious paradigms have always done. The reformations of the sixteenth century were that century's most notable long-term contribution to the shaping of the modern world and, hence, to its rise to hegemony.

Joining the Protestant reformers, even if gingerly, was Pope Paul III (1534–49), who first called the Council of Trent (meeting in three separate conclaves—1545–47, 1551–52, 1562–63), to enact measures aimed at reforming the Roman Catholic Church. This initiative was the response to the break away of the Protestant church organizations—the Counter-Reformation. The second session of the council was conducted by Julius III (1550–55), while Pius IV (1559–65) presided over the third and final group of sessions. The subsequent temper of the Roman Catholic Church was simultaneously partially defined by the founding of the Jesuit Order (1534) by Ignatius Loyola (1491–1556) as "The Military Company of Jesus" and the establishment in 1542 of the Congregation of the Inquisition by Paul III. These massive, combined initiatives can undeniably be said to constitute a reformation, one of the several marking the sixteenth century.

The chastened Roman Catholic Church clearly intended to vigorously fight back against its critics and regain its lost adherents and its universal reach. And its leaders and their lieutenants sought to fight not simply these new voices of alternate spiritual doctrines but a host of other more secondary cultural developments that had been viewed as inimical to the teachings of Roman Catholicism as developed over a millennium and a half. Perhaps chief among these secondary targets was the publishing/printing trade. The book trade had given widespread voice to the growing body of critiques and complaints about the ways in which the church had drifted from long-held Christian teachings and into the worldliness of power politics, the continual grasping for wealth, ostentatious display, clerical luxury, an often untrained, indifferent clergy, and numerous other failings. Further, Luther had made skillful use of the power of printing to recruit a wide and devoted following. He possessed a remarkable gift for language and oratory, which was powerfully employed in the writing and issuing of the numerous pamphlets attacking the Roman Catholic Church, encouraging conversion to the reformed Lutheran Church, and presenting in readily comprehensible form the fundamental doctrines that defined the "catechism" or teachings of the new church.

The Roman Catholic Church proceeded simultaneously on two fronts with respect to the intellectual methodology centered upon printing and the widespread dissemination of printed books. First, the papacy of Leo X (1513–21) actively encouraged and supported three presses designated as "booksellers to the Roman academy" and a fourth serving the doctrinal and political "outreach" of the Curia.[5] The printing press had come to be recognized in Rome as a powerful instrument for the propagation of accepted doctrine, public persuasion, and the shaping of intellectual and cultural relations.

The second front on which the papacy moved assertively was the inauguration of the *Index librorum prohitorium*—the official listing of books of heretical or otherwise disapproved content, the reading of which was forbidden to the generality of Roman Catholic adherents. The first edition of the *Index* was published in 1564. So the printing press was enlisted by the centralized Vatican to positively carry forward the "war of pamphlets" first employed by the reformer Luther, all the while mounting a vigorous campaign to muzzle all the latter's as well as other publications. Here began the still-continuing campaign of both church and state to simultaneously positively foster and negatively constrain the press to doctrinally pure or politically correct content.

From the point of view of confirmed believers of any of the general persuasions, Roman Catholic or the several Protestant sects, this new current of publications bearing messages confirming and promoting their closely held doctrines and beliefs provided gratifying relief from the conflicting and confusing miscellany of often conflicting ideas and propositions that had been the currency of the previous three generations. For many, the officially sanctioned publications, books, pamphlets, and newssheets offered even more, namely, safe anchorages in an uncertain and confused universe of beliefs, doctrines, and principles, all articulated in firm and uncompromising terms.

As Grindler makes clear, "in the 16C books became really cheap."[6] This fact in part consequent upon yet coupled with the compelling needs of growing church and state bureaucracies for literate, trained bureaucrats. The parallel need of trade and commerce for literate, trained staff augmented this demand for trained clericals. All conjoined to generate an enormous growth in the numbers and enrollments of schools and the simultaneous increase in members of the educated middle classes. The need for literate and trained clerics, as well as the literary and liturgical upgrading of a previously casually recruited pastorate, added to this pressure for the establishment or augmentation of both schools and universities. In addition, Luther had early on and repeatedly in subsequent years urged the education of the young and the establishment of school and municipal libraries. He "argued at length for public schools and libraries ... . It was God's command to educate the young."[7] So one of the major arenas of religious contention occurred with respect to the opening and control of schools to assure the recruitment, retention, and doctrinal orthodoxy of the oncoming generations.[8] Such a burst of newly admitted students at every level, in turn, forced the rapid development and widespread distribution of the textbooks aligned to the differing educational objectives of these new schools.

So the commissioning and publication of textbooks became a growing driver of the central place of the book in the transmission of the cultural goods of the West.

Consequences of the Book: The Rise of the Autocratic Monarchical State

Dynastic ambitions were clearly the principal driver in the struggle to establish large monarchial states. Here too the printed book was co-opted as one of the significant tools in this centuries-long struggle for power. All the contending factions engaged in this scrum employed the book to advance their particular interest and belittle that of opposing groups.

Beyond the vicious and continuing churchly sectarian contentions fought over doctrinal and ecclesiastical matters as well as over the recruitment and enduring allegiance of followers, the early sixteenth century was beset and confused by the place of the increasingly powerful dynastic state. Perhaps the most compelling element in this controversy was the altered nature of the long history of contention for primacy of the Roman Catholic Church. Now the church was constrained to jockeying for place and position with a transmuted, dynamic, and growing leviathan. This more powerful, emergent, autocratic, monarchial state was driven by a newly energized version of the traditional garb of dynastic and divine right cloaking sixteenth-century sovereigns' lust for power.

As the Protestant churches—the Lutheran first, followed by the Reformed Church of John Calvin—matured and gained progressively more adherents across wider reaches of Europe, both increasingly found themselves entangled in complex webs of church–state relationships. The several sectarian contingents in these church–state imbroglios soon sought to co-opt the state's monopoly of force both within and external to its borders to force religious orthodoxy upon the inhabitants thereof. For their part, the increasingly autocratic dynastic states sought to promote their authority and enhance their revenues by seeking control of the church(s) in their domains. The iconic example of the sectarian drive for state protection is probably that of Luther's recruitment of the numerous German princes to his Reformed Church. This relationship was advanced under the doctrine that the religious beliefs of the prince were to control those of his subjects. This principle, while actively employed by Luther in his lifetime, was not cast into a permanent form until 1648 in the Treaty of Westphalia ending the disastrous Thirty Years' War, which, although ostensibly fought over religious principles, was one of the more egregious examples of the compulsive drive of the European autocratic monarchs for territory and domination.

The classic example of the seizure of the church by the state (1531) is likely that of Henry VIII of England (reigned, 1509–47). In this revolutionary venture he depended upon his theories of his divine right to ultimate control of the English church formulated in part by those within his political and religious circles. Associated and consistent with that doctrine was the consequent right of possession of the vast land holdings and wealth of the English churches. His confiscation was thus simply the exercise of his divine right as the head of the church within his territories. (NB: The Tudors were exemplars of the drive for monarchial power and so forever short of money.)

The ultimate outcome of these contests in church–state dominance in this cultural battle of ideas proved to redound largely to the augmentation of the power of the state. Large bodies of religious adherents felt more comfortable and secure within the borders of an emerging state identified and shaped in part by the domination of a single sect. However, the poison in that comfort was that the centralizing or centralized state was always contingent upon the life as well as the unpredictable notional and dynastic views of the sovereign. A new king or a reigning king successfully wooed by a contending sect could withdraw and replace these monopolies of belief and liturgical practice. This typically horrendous and disconcerting outcome frequently resulted in a substantial loss of life and invariably the loss of virtually all the accumulated wealth of those who insisted upon continuing to adhere to the suddenly outlawed old faith. Almost without fail this confiscated wealth flowed to the benefit of the state. This unhappy outcome was widespread not only in Germany and the Low Countries but in the case of the French Huguenots and the multiple shifts in religious affiliations of the crown in England as well.

Indeed, given the increasingly passionate religious beliefs resulting from the sixteenth-century sectarian confrontations and differences, these sectarian quarrels served as a major source of not only added monarchial power but the rising tide of national feeling.[9] As such the co-opting of religious exclusiveness augmented the concerted drives of the autocratic states to consolidate their power and wealth. These latter objectives were facilitated in part by fostering religious identifications beyond the traditional local affiliations to an identification with a larger spiritual realm and incidentally leading to an expansive territorial dominium. Clark aptly depicts the sense of the mental space in which humankind lived in the late fifteenth and early sixteenth centuries in the following way: "The man who lived at a distance of two days journey was a foreigner."[10] State-mandated substitution of state-endorsed religious sects helped overcome this sense of the foreign. The notion of the large territorial monarchical state fostered by such switches of sect choices and allegiances contributed to the formation of an entirely new conception of native and foreigner.

To the same end the writing of laudatory national histories was increasingly strongly encouraged and often supported by the crown. As the power of Gutenberg's art in shaping and in focusing the mind-sets of people became increasingly evident in the course of the ideological/cultural wars of religion growing out of the Reformation and Counter-Reformation, the developing secular institutions of the state, covertly and often overtly, underwrote such publications. The court enlisted authors (typically from among those associated with the state apparatus), printers, and publishers (often recruited by the state) in defining and justifying the ideas of a nation and of a state apparatus which controlled that monarchical state. This rediscovered identification with a state territory within which they lived, an identification virtually unknown since the fall of the Roman Empire, proved to be one of the consequences of the new ideational conception of the state advanced by contemporary writers. The publishing of such works markedly augmented the rising feeling of national identity, which, in turn, vastly increased the power of the monarchical state by binding its subjects more closely to itself.[11]

But it was not only the writing of self-serving histories that helped cement the notion of a nation-state in the eyes of the populace. Literature, for example, the English historical plays of Shakespeare, contributed to the same end. Perhaps more effective in generating allegiance to the dynamic of state control was the increasing torrent of pamphlet material aimed at the populace, promoted and subsidized by the state. Here the book played a role akin to dynastic iconic art.

The ambitions of these autocratic monarchical states were greatly and impressively shored up and given expression by the growing body of lawyers graduating from the proliferating universities offering training in the law. As described in a previous chapter, the legal concepts being inculcated in the young men of the Renaissance were those of the Justinian Roman jurisprudence. (NB: The nearly universal usage of Roman law throughout the West, save only for England and a few small and isolated regions, is a remarkable testimony to the central cultural role of the book being advanced herein. In this case a single manuscript dating from the sixth century, containing a huge and cohesive body of Roman legal concepts and precepts formulated out of centuries of progressive falsification and creation, was discovered someplace in Italy in the twelfth century. This lone manuscript was laboriously and repeatedly hand-copied and served as the standard text first in Bologna in the thirteenth century and then in following decades radiated out to most of the universities of the West. In the course of travels this body of legal concepts was progressively falsified and augmented to adjust the code to governing the never-ending stream of problems that inevitably arose in its initial medieval setting and subsequently in its new setting of the centralizing state.) This Justinian corpus of Roman law was oriented around the pivotal notion of a powerful central authority dictating both basic principles and a code dictating practice. Conceptually, it fit snuggly with the sense and aims of the nascent autocratic monarchical sovereignties.

The lawyers trained in and acclimatized to the concepts of this elaborate body of legal knowledge were, for the most part, entirely comfortable with serving the concept and interests of the centralized autocratic state and its controlling monarchy. They were only too well prepared to support and enjoy the prerogatives of power, which they increasingly came to enjoy in this superior vocational option—superior, that is, as an alternative to a career in the church bureaucracy.

This new centralized and increasingly powerful monarchical state offered its populace some modest protection from the predatory ambitions of neighboring monarchs. More important, it supplied an explicit body of law with which to settle differences between fellow citizens rather than depending upon the often-arbitrary decisions of a local baron or other feudatory. Consequentially, the Roman law introduced yet another reassuring institution that provided further relief from the uncertainty and confusion that the advent of the widely available printed book and the flood of ancient Greek learning had loosed upon the West.

So the emerging centralized monarchical state of the sixteenth century was second only to the reformations of the same century in offering a firm base of cultural certitude in what had earlier become a bewildering and precarious cultural universe. Indeed, the argument advanced here might be turned around, as a thought experiment, to assert that the reformations and the new centralized monarchical state were the necessary outcome of this growing and widespread cultural perplexity and bewilderment. The argument being that the generality of people cannot for long comfortably abide high levels of uncertainty with respect to central cultural institutions and beliefs and so would readily fabricate and accept the intellectual and institutional resolution of such uncertainties.

But such an explanation, dependent as it is upon the causal explanatory notion of the working out of conjured primal and mysterious forces of some kind, is quite indefensible. The work of subliminal historical forces has long been the refuge of charlatans and those advancing hidden agendas sustained by arcane historical explanations dependent upon such poltergeists of explanation. Rather, as has been the constant theme of causation employed in this writing, the working out of cultural knowledge and institutions arises out of the progressive falsification of received hypotheses by various thinkers and writers. The latter were consciously seeking to respond to the continuing flow of emergent unforeseen problems. In so doing they necessarily created new, more powerful, more general hypotheses to explain both the matters subsumed by the falsified hypotheses and the resolution of the triggering problem. This continuing and arduous work has led to the increasing body of intellectual concepts and ethical precepts which have marked the evolution of the culture of the West. All of this intellectual work is conducted by living human beings and then transcribed to a written or printed form—not conjured by hypothetical historical phantoms or specters or fabricated/modeled forces.

To return to the historical thread of this writing: In the formation of these new bastions of cultural certainty the widespread distribution of print plainly played a central role. The printed book, pamphlet, and newssheet were the vehicles routinely employed by the contending religious sects and the aggrandizing young monarchical states to articulate their doctrines and principles and to justify their raison d'être to a growing literate populace. Even in the midst of the armed conflicts engendered by the contention of ideas animating these martial outbursts, the printing presses were kept busy by the principal actors in their continuing efforts to convince the uncertain and opponents of the superiority of their political claims or religious codes of belief.

But these cultural wars of ideas, while reassuring and intrinsically confirmatory to the committed monarchical supporters or confirmed believers, offered the contrarian effect of freeing the minds of an increasing fraction of the society by implicitly offering choices. The opportunity to escape both the rigid feudal political/economic and exclusionary religious strictures that had marked the previous centuries as well as the increasing rigidities of an overweening dynastic state was an option being exercised by increasing numbers of the literate. With the growing numbers of intellectual and ethical options being opened by these overt confrontations appearing in print, the numbers and depth of possible conflicts and contradictions increased geometrically.[12] Just so, Gutenberg's "arte" provided the key unlocking the Pandora's chest of intellectual and ethical uncertainty and consequent confusion of the late fifteenth century. The same "arte" in the sixteenth century encouraged the partial resolution of that uncertainty and confusion with the emergence of the reformations and the autocratic states. However, print simultaneously opened the way to pose or offer or transmit a wholly new sense and means of choice and freedom and so to compel, at least a fair number of the literate, to make reasoned choices between the growing numbers of politico-constitutional and religious alternatives proposed.

In Germany continuing religious strife and peasant revolts marked much of the sixteenth century. The best remembered of the peasant revolts is that of Thomas Münzer (1489–1525) and associates in 1524, which was put down in 1525, shortly after which Münzer was executed. Their notions of social organization in terms of the common ownership of property, the radical social egalitarianism of the citizenry, and the equal sharing of wealth, coupled with a messianic cult of "true believers," have held a continuing place in Western utopian thought right up to the present and were considered by Marx and adepts as the first model and harbinger of their communist vision. (Subsequent history attests to the numerous and repeated subsequent failures of ventures based on these premises.) Further, these peasant uprisings in Germany, which many historians attribute to the influence of the freedom of belief implicit in Martin Luther's ideas that every believer had to come to the true faith of his or her own volition, served as the inspiration and models of similar failed revolts elsewhere in Europe. However, all these militant, utopian outbursts simultaneously added cultural confusion among some, while confirming alternative cultural conceptions among the majority.

To the east the Ottoman Turk menace continued on victoriously despite spasmodic, halfhearted Western efforts to halt its advances. Before the sixteenth century was out, the Mediterranean was virtually a Turkish lake; the Venetian and Genoese Middle East trading cities were in Turkish hands; the Balkans, including Hungary, were occupied by Ottoman armies; and the Islamic armies of jihad were pressing Austria. Looked at from the perspective of the Middle East, Islam had returned to the *jihad* and was likely to become the hegemonic power from the steppes of Inner Asia to the Atlantic. Many in the West were acutely aware of this looming threat to the culture of the West, but the European sovereigns of any import commanding large armies of mercenary, battle-hardened soldiers were so caught up in their dynastic ambitions, territorial avarice, and competition for wealth that they were unwilling to undertake any sustained common action against the Ottomans. At the end of the day, the armed resistance of the West had a minimum to do with its escape from a final and, probably, complete and total replacement of its cultural heritage by that of Islam.

So, what might be the explanation for this fortuitous escape? In brief it had to do with the internal cultural nexus of these two great cultures. The cultural complex, which in all likelihood saved the West in this third Muslim *jihad*, was the faltering and decaying inner core of Islamic culture itself. This cultural malaise was fostered by a rigid, closed, and inward-looking religious/political *weltanschauung* that had seemingly concluded two or three centuries earlier that Islam possessed all necessary truth and had nothing more to learn either on its own initiative or from others. The contrast with the West in this new episode of cultural confrontation is matter for exposition later in this chapter.

Two further general and complicating factors emerged in sixteenth-century Europe, which must be noted in passing. The first was a rapid resurgence of the population following the widespread decimation of populations in the two previous centuries due to the coming and repeated outbreaks of famine resulting from global cooling and of the black death and other newly experienced diseases.[13] By every measure of population growth, which has been reconstructed from the scant, and often confusing, data still available, every decade from the late fifteenth century on experienced a substantial population boom. This enormous increase in the number of hands to do the culture's work and the number of mouths that had to be fed manifestly led to severe, shifting local economic and political difficulties from time to time. These rapid distortions in population resulted in often excess numbers of marginally employable people. It was from among these groups of floating often under- or unemployed males that the buildup of large mercenary monarchical state armies, which had become the standard fighting forces employed by the dynastic monarchies, was essentially recruited. It was also from among this group of often genuinely impoverished agricultural laborers now fled to become minimally employed city dwellers that the rioters and millennial movements, which marked the century, drew many of their participants or adherents. Further, the same causes and sources provided many of the "foot soldiers" of colonial conquest and settlement in the last half of the sixteenth century and in the next several succeeding centuries.

The other important general factor that more or less affected all the regions of Europe was a rapidly expanding economy accompanied by substantial economic inflationary pressures.[14] By the sixteenth century the productive bourgeoisie had reached the sheer mass needed to sustain a rapidly growing financial, manufacturing, and trading complex capable not only of sustaining the economic engine of the West but to fund the ever-unsatisfied appetite for economic power and showy wealth, which was driving the monarchs to extraordinary lengths. To this internally generated economic improvement and the ever-widening circles of inhabitants lifted from the margins of poverty to some semblance of sustainable livelihood was added the massive influx of mineral wealth, particularly gold and silver, from the New World.[15] The latter led to often out-of-control inflation, in the classic manner of too much wealth pursuing relatively limited supplies of goods. This inflation added to the economic burden of the populace of the West but simultaneously provided the means of employing some of the burgeoning population.

When endeavoring to assess the consequences and likely outcomes of these multifarious religious, economic, and political upheavals and confrontations resulting from the bitter religious reformations and the raw, rude wrestling for power and wealth of the new monarchical states exacerbated by the exercise of common desires for pleasure and increased consumption, the historian is quickly put in mind of the foundations and grounds of the dreadful fourteenth century. In a genuine sense the underlying ideational conflicts and discontinuities of the late fifteenth/early sixteenth century were even more acute than those that had precipitated the near-catastrophic cultural decline of the fourteenth century. The severity of the problems implicit in the aspects of the cultural inheritance had reached the point of widespread acknowledgment and distress. Many of the received bodies of knowledge were now more or less openly recognized to be burdened with accumulated contradictions and mined with long-repressed perceptions of the multitudinous departures from accepted, venerated, and widely professed cultural norms and objectives as well as social needs. In the responses of several generations of fifteenth- and sixteenth-century thinkers and writers, an avalanche of alternative hypotheses had been advanced, some tested locally in the increasing hurly-burly of affairs but many yet only incorporated into books. However, in a matter of decades all of these accumulated problems and the various alternative hypotheses aimed at their resolution were on the table. Often they arrived at the table as the "bloodiest of raw meat," as in the case of the emergence of the dynastic monarchical state or some of the religious conflicts.

These sixteenth-century Western ideational paroxysms and the almost unending rounds of raw exercises in the display of and quest for power and booty by military means seemed to promise another extended descent into a period of reduced cultural stasis. It seemed poised upon another episode of exhausting self-induced and self-inflicted period of the massive letting of the blood and treasure of its social body. The state of the West exhibited signs analogous to the calamities that marked the ninth/tenth century and the fourteenth century, following the renascences that had flourished in the preceding centuries.

However, the sixteenth-century West failed to fall into a parallel kind of cultural exhaustion and spiritual hopelessness. The cultural capital accumulated in prior centuries successfully withstood a repeat of the tenth- and fourteenth-century debacles. Even at the last minute, the amounting ambitions of a renewed and reinvigorated Ottoman Muslim expansionary impulse was successfully routed.

This quite remarkable sixteenth-century demonstration of a new cultural resilience in the West opened a continuing chain of culturally remarkable achievements. The source of this remarkable cultural power was the product of the more or less successful integration into some substantial measure of sustainable coherence and tolerable synthesis of the multiple cultural inheritances of the West by the mid-sixteenth century. A kind of muscular self-assurance replacing the uncertainty marking much of the fifteenth century was widely evident. The West had again established a new and substantially firmer footing in contrast to the insecurity of the previous century. It is likely that this newfound confidence was partially bred by the evidence of the manifest integrity and vitality of the accumulated cultural heritage in the face of the numerous fronts opened in the religious cultural wars and the predatory search for power and wealth by the civil authorities.

Consequences of the Book: The Renaissance Preserved

This remarkable cultural outcome in another potentially quite desperate passage in the West's history can, in large measure, be attributed to the rapid and relatively successful bringing together of the several intellectual streams that had engendered the West, each comprising numerous large bodies of accumulated and increasingly defensible and usable knowledge. The more or less adequate integration of the distinct cultural streams bearing the enormous and bulky cargos of the Greek, Jewish, Roman, Christian, and Islamic ideational stocks had been substantially completed sometime in the mid-sixteenth century.

This gigantic intellectual feat was the work of increasing cadres of thinkers and writers conducted over a period of several centuries. This enormous enterprise demanded several qualities that were rapidly becoming distinguishing characteristics of the West: an intense curiosity about all the things about them in the world, including other peoples and their cultures, and particularly their ideas; a "pack rat's" instinct to collect all manner of these fascinating cultural "objects"; an omnivorous appetite for comprehending, at least in a roughly satisfying way, the substance of these collections of cultural goods; an almost playful interest and joy in manipulating, turning, and trying these ideas in a variety of configurations; and a compulsion to fit all this brew of ideas and observations within the cultural stocks they already possessed. But these cultural characteristics were of considerable fragility, liable to interruption or submergence in a chaotic setting. There were, in the early centuries of this enterprise, no assured means by which all but the most commonly used bodies of knowledge, the record of which was therefore copied many times over, could be retained and made a continuing force in the conduct of intellectual and ethical undertakings. The evidence provided by the repeated discoveries of Latin manuscripts stowed away in what were thought to be safe places, which subsequently proved in many cases to be a variety of out-of-the-way places, offers overwhelming proof of, and fully supports, the fragility of the cultural memory recorded in handwritten manuscripts. It was the coming of the printed book that corrected this previously persistent cultural shortcoming. Books printed in multiple copies of an identical text suddenly assured the preservation of knowledge.

Further, it was, in substantial measure, the large and widespread numbers of thinkers and writers able to focus intensively on identical texts and present their falsifications and alternative hypotheses through the medium of the book that rapidly advanced the remarkable fusion of these widely dispersed cultural streams. In short, it was the book, intrinsically and instrumentally, that provided the safe passage around the reefs that had engendered the cultural submersions of the eighth- and twelfth-century renascences and, on the contrary, led the West to the Renaissance, which was to prove the time and place in which the foundations of the West's hegemonic role were finally set.

To attribute the historical fact of the success of the survival of the fifteenth-century renascence in avoiding the decline incident, when compared with that of other earlier renascences, to an "awakening from a long sleep" or some such metaphor in explaining the Renaissance, as has been a common stock-in-trade ever since a few late-fifteenth-century- and many of the sixteenth-century thinkers and writers declared it so, is hardly convincing. The turn of the historical events precipitated by the Reformation; the destruction of lives and wealth by the autocratic dynastic states in their never-ending warfare; their energetic mercantilist abuses of the growing economy; the increasingly oppressive fear induced by the sporadic and seemingly capricious outbreaks of the black death; the radical changes in the long-term weather patterns, leading to repeated episodes of starvation and famine across Europe; the renewal of Islamic *jihad*; and other unfavorable historic factors, described earlier, could have as readily led to the same cultural malaise that stifled the earlier renascences in the sixteenth century. What was different in the sixteenth century that ameliorated the deleterious cultural impact of these substantial historical negatives and gave the color of truth to the assertions of the fifteenth/sixteenth bluster and braggadocio of intellectual superiority?

There are substantial grounds for construing this seemingly egregious claim by Renaissance figures to preeminence relative to their medieval predecessors as largely contrived. As noted earlier, the Renaissance writers were, in fact, in substantial measure dependent on the religious, philosophical, linguistic, political, legal, and economic bases for their ideas upon accumulated medieval foundations. So these repeated Renaissance assertions can profitably be seen as an effort to establish some alternative grounds of and for future historical judgment of their accomplishments. Such a remarkable claim was able to gain widespread currency exemplary of and thanks to the new means of broadly distributing and preserving ideas in the form of the book, pamphlet, and newsletter. This largely successful Renaissance effort in claiming to be "up to date" and to be the fountain of a rebirth of Western civilization can well be viewed as the second great ideological campaign, or "book war" waged with and around the printing press. The first of these book wars was the one associated with the Archbishop's War in Mainz in which Gutenberg seems to have been a participant[16]. The third example of book wars is the religious struggle launched by Luther and soon emulated by the Vatican in the battles for adherents virtually contemporaneous with that of the boosters of the apologists for the Renaissance. Although not as overtly partisan as these religious campaigns, the Renaissance writers were as insistent and bent on casting their nets as widely as possible to assert their claims. The leading figures of the humanist Renaissance were almost universal in the inclusion of such claims in virtually every one of their numerous publications and in their correspondence. The promotional power of the printing press was perhaps more broadly proved by its successful employment in this Renaissance campaign than Gutenberg and later Luther were in theirs—hardly surprising given the passion and dedication with which the Renaissance humanists pursued the theory and practice of rhetoric.

Consequences of the Book: Exploration and Discovery

A quite striking example of the sixteenth-century synthesizing of the various cultural streams in the West is to be found first in the common explanation of another of the great cultural initiatives of that century—the discovery, exploration, and colonizing of the New World. Brief mention has already been made of the pioneering voyages of the Portuguese; the associated and primitive cartographic recordings thereof; the progressive refinement of the lodestone into a functional and usable surveying and navigation instrument; the development of ship hulls and their rigging, making them capable of withstanding the rigors of open-ocean sailing; the successive translations of Ptolemy's geography; the geographic and map-making work of the German monks; and the resolution of the conceptual conflicts engendered by the Aristotelian explanation of the structure of the earth and oceans. It was from this ferment of knowledge concepts that Columbus derived his plan for discovering the Indies by sailing west and it was this that guided him in his explorations aimed at proving the truth value of his deductions.

All of these bodies of knowledge—geographic, physical, and technological, and the ideational conclusions Columbus drew from them—were prelude to the larger meanings drawn from his successful navigations. The first group of meanings resided in the confirmation of the validity of the hypotheses employed by him. Yes, he had not landed in the Indies as he opined, but very quickly he and subsequent explorers had provided the grounds for Amerigo Vespucci to assign the name *Mundus Novus* (New World) to his discovered lands. This remarkable confirmation of the bodies of knowledge employed in Columbus's predictions positively proved that the West was on the right track insofar as these specific knowledge bodies were concerned and could be confidently employed in making other uses of them in other contexts.

The Columbian venture was yet another spectacular confidence-building fact—the centuries of intellectual effort in falsifying hypotheses, creating new hypotheses, and reconciling conflicting ideas derived from the various intellectual streams noted above were producing usable new knowledge and adding certainty in an uncertain world. These confirmations of the work of numerous thinkers were adding additional islands of dry, intellectually viable land in what had seemed an endless sea of confusion and uncertainty. All of this knowledge, received and newly conceived, was being duly written up; published as books, maps, and other forms of printed material; and widely distributed throughout the West. Growing cadres of newly recruited thinkers and writers were critically studying these hypotheses and conclusions and adding in increasing volumes of new and more powerful ideas to the inherited stock thereof.

The second and more important body of meanings was the demonstration that the West had manifestly created over a period of eight centuries—in twenty-four generations—a powerful, book-based, knowledge-generating engine for the exponential increase and preservation of knowledge bodies that possessed ever-closer approximations to the truth and ever-sounder approaches to the good. The primitive knowledge-generating engines prior to the printed book were only powerful enough to lift the veil of unknowing over periods of time marked by generations. With Gutenberg's invention, a wholly new engine was put into place powerful enough, within a couple of generations of adoption that knowledge could be generated and disseminated in but a fraction of that time. This engine was, and remains today, the most spectacular culture-generating engine humankind has ever conceived and successfully constructed—more powerful than steam, internal combustion, electric, or computer—all of which are simply the products of cadres of "out-of-the-box" thinkers employing this knowledge-generating engine.

Just as clearly, the central controller or regulator of this remarkable knowledge-generating engine was/is the printed book. Several of its late-fifteenth- and sixteenth-century products—the Reformation, the Counter-Reformation, and the monarchical state—have been noted earlier. Others are to follow. All of these products of the increasingly productive knowledge-generating engine contributed to the surge of certitude and confidence so much in evidence in the sixteenth century despite the perennial malign exertions of the autocrats, religious and secular.

The third massive body of meanings flowing from Columbus's discoveries was a wholly new and previously unknown series of intellectual vistas opening to the entire world. The first of these vistas, a vastly augmented human understanding of the extent and contents of the earth, is perfectly evident. No other culture heretofore had any comprehension of more than some limited region and its immediate surrounds in which untold generations of the incurious had lived and continued to live. The success and excitement in this geographic enterprise, slowly generated following Columbus's voyages, inaugurated the great age of Western exploration and discovery. This massive and enduring epic of discovery, undertaken exclusively by the West, filled in within two centuries—six generations—most of the complex geographic outlines and topographies of the earth.

The second vista might well be identified as the first glimmerings of a formal anthropology as an infant body of knowledge. Yes, every one of the four great cultures, as well as probably their primitive outliers, possessed a miscellaneous store of haphazard, more or less distorted travelers' or speculative accounts of other peoples, their beliefs, customs, and practices. But none was suddenly deluged with numerous first-hand and increasingly informative reports of previously unknown peoples and their folkways as was the West. None of the other three great cultures possessed anything comparable to the incredible knowledge-generating engine to record and formulate increasingly integrated and coherent senses of these reports.

The third major vista might well be styled the botanic analog to the budding anthropology. All manner of plants were as suddenly being discovered, recorded, and organized in a systematic way by botanists, employing the Western knowledge-generating engine, as were compendiums documenting other peoples. Equally importantly, these newly discovered assemblages of plants contained several plants of immense economic and environmental importance—as food, as medicinals, as raw materials, as a source of a host of useful chemical substances, and as fine ornamental species (of which there is a plethora). The exploration of, and collections from, the New World launched a giant, worldwide plant exchange, which over the next several centuries enormously profited the various peoples across the world then and since. Perhaps the iconic example of the worldwide gains deriving from the creation of this global plant exchange network is the New World potato, now a near-universal food.

The fourth major vista opened by, first, Prince Henry the Navigator of Portugal, later Columbus, and subsequent Western explorers was to emplace the economic foundations for the eventual formation of a far more extensive pattern of world trade, economic development, and the consequent growth of economic wealth and well-being. European manufacturing and mercantile enterprises had grown vigorously in the sixteenth century. Note was earlier made of the reversal of the cloth trade with the Middle East markets as the manufacturing capabilities of spinners, weavers, and dyers in the West continuously improved thanks to the growing Western knowledge and printed recording of the processes involved and those related to the harnessing of sources of power to its production, thereby making European cloth both better and cheaper than that produced in the Levant. A parallel story could be traced with respect to firearms, cannon, etc., the fearsome Turkish army, for example, depending progressively more on Western knowledge, products, and personnel.

Within Europe itself manufacture and trade grew rapidly as did the numbers and influence of the bourgeoisie, the guild tradesmen, and the financiers involved in or underwriting these pursuits. This enormous economic growth was, like every other human undertaking, both dependent upon previously created and tested knowledge as well as upon the continued creation of more profound and powerful business and economic knowledge. This body of capitalistic knowledge while fine-tuned to the needs of internal trade within the West was readily generalizable to the demands of the growing international trade. This expansion of trade was not simply confined to the new European trade entrepôts and colonies established in the train of Western exploration and discovery but also led to the invention and manufacture of trade goods suited to overseas demands.

The pioneering Portuguese explorations around Africa to the lands of spices in Asia had as one of their most fundamental motives the wresting of control of the lucrative East–West trade in spices and other Oriental goods from the Islamic world. A similar body of economic ideas and objectives drove the subsequent Spanish ventures to the New World—but this undertaking resulted instead in the discovery of a different raison d'être. The search for precious metals, a far richer immediate prize, quickly displaced the previously primary ideas of trade in spices and Orientalia. As Weber noted, "Spaniards had come to the frontiers of North America hoping to change little in their own lives except to enhance their wealth and status"[17]—commonly by acquiring precious metals, then returning to Spain richer and better able to become estimable landholders.

Thus were world economics rapidly changed, changes that were to continue and radically alter the economic system governing the world trade and national economies. As for the Spanish crown, the newly founded empire was to furnish the wealth required to continue its sixteenth/seventeenth-century dynastic wars, which radically altered the shape and history of Europe.

Another major vista opened by the age of exploration and discovery deserving of mention here is the profound impact the voyages of

Columbus and successors had upon the internal cultural formulations of the West. This is not to say that the vistas described above had no impact upon or were of minimal import with respect to the cultural understandings of the West. In plain fact, these cultural transformations and understandings were first evident in and unique to the West—yet they have by the twenty-first century not been entirely understood by many around the globe and, more surprisingly, even among elements in the West.

Perhaps the most important of these transformations in cultural understanding were the mental horizons, both intellectual and ethical, which were subtly imposed upon the entire body of Western cultural understandings. A number of elements in that body of intellectual concepts and ethical precepts which had been created in a single, somewhat remote, western corner of the Eurasian continent simply fell short of coming to grips with that wider world being opened by the venturers of the West. The odor of provincialism emanated from various subsets of the Western mind-set, which was remarkable by the sixteenth century. A wider horizon of more or less coherent cultural traditions and a more extensive inventory of peoples, cultural practices, and intercultural relationships had to be accommodated. Where people could for a millennium think in regional, narrowly provincial terms they were now compelled to reformulate their cultural constructs into broader and more universal terms suitable to the wider universe of people and ideas newly encountered and made real.

The construction Columbus himself made of the meaning and import of his discoveries in the course of his successive voyages and subsequent reflections thereupon is highly suggestive of the changing sixteenth-century frame of mind and the dawning of a wider and more inclusive sense of the need for coming to grips with this larger, more complex world. He saw himself as the millennial messenger of a new and better world. He wrote, "God made me the messenger of the new heaven and the new earth, of which He spoke in the Apocalypse of St. John ... and He showed me the spot where to find it." He further saw his discoveries as fulfilling the millennial prophecies of that enigmatic Cistercian monk, Abbot Joachim of Fiore (1132–1202).

Amerigo Vespucci turned to Dante's vision of a new world for the apposite precedent a few years later.[18] Both explorers had seen and visited what they conceived as the locus of paradise. At long last that longed-for precinct of perfection had been revealed—and the route and gates thereto had been revealed. So Columbus and his fellow early argonauts, while all the time standing and acting and drawing upon the accumulated bodies of knowledge noted above and derived out of two-and-a-half millennia of arduous Western labor of thought and occasional judicious intellectual acquisition from elsewhere, were caught up in the thrall of the prospect of a better world. In short, they and the growing number of their succeeding enthusiasts looked both back to their medieval and humanist heritage and forward to a new and better world encompassing the entire earth. Not that they turned away from the Judeo-Christian vision of the afterlife but rather that they envisioned a marked improvement in the lives of mortals. A wholly new confident march into a far more rewarding future for the living on earth seemed to have been embarked upon.

Although implicit in Columbus's sense of the outcome of his voyage and Vespucci's harkening back to the images of Dante in his reprise of his journeys to the New World, the importance of the content thereof deserves highlighting. Both conceived of their travels in terms of the soon to be ushered in long-promised and long-yearned-for millennium. And both referenced by way of illustration earlier utopian writings by admired medieval figures. Utopian visions had periodically captured the minds of men for two millennia or more both in the classical world and in the earlier Christian era. These occasional assays into the mental fabrication of better or more nearly perfect societies for humankind included Plato's *Republic* and St. Augustine's *City of God*. Dante's *Divine Comedy* can also be construed as such a fabricated utopian vision. The last two Western Christian utopias found much of their meaning and substance in the characterization of Eden and of heaven, the paradises long explicit in Judeo-Christian teaching. These same Judeo-Christian ideational motifs were to form the ground of the subsequent formulations in the West of such utopian places and societies.[19]

But it is in the sixteenth century, with the opening of the vistas of the explorers and the seeming promise of a better life deriving therefrom, that this genre became a more appealing and common form for writers critical of the present shape of cultural matters.[20] These new castings of utopias often incorporated bits and pieces of reported or perceived features of the other cultural complexes being opened by Western venturers, but most were recastings, in more universal terms, of the received Western cultural tradition. The first of the notable writers in this new genre was Sir Thomas More (1478–1535). More, for a period Henry VIII's lord chancellor, wrote his *Utopia* ("no place") while serving on Henry's privy council and published it in 1516. The title of More's book gave the name "utopia" to this literary form, which employed the rhetorical devices of fiction but was freighted with eminently serious content. More's casting of this better life was followed by Rabelais's *Gargantua,* containing the section describing the utopian depiction of the Abbey of Thélème, published in 1532. The genre was repeatedly employed in the following centuries to depict a more perfect society. And virtually all shared the characteristic of greater or lesser dissatisfaction with major aspects of the current state of Western culture. All grew out of the newly found confidence emerging in the sixteenth-century West that provided the cultural latitude and cultural resilience to withstand and occasionally profit from the often-sharp-edged criticism implicit in the form. All sought to formulate a somehow better set of conditions suitable for all the peoples of the world.

But while moved by perceptions of current shortcomings, often stemming from traditional and conventional cultural formulations, coupled with explicit or implicit proposed correctives, it is important to keep in mind that virtually all utopian writings share the Janus-faced character of that of Columbus—they look both backward to earlier cultural exemplars and forward to a presumably better organization of cultural matters. In the centuries before 1500 the Western mind was almost entirely focused upon the received cultural formulations and the means of and prospects for salvation. There was little thought or speculation devoted to the shape of the secular future or all humankind's worldly prospects in the centuries leading up to that time. This was hardly a surprising outcome given the complexity of the intellectual demands of understanding and mastering the enormous collective bodies of knowledge that had come in a tiny handful of manuscripts in an often-incomplete or error-ridden form to a still-only-partially-civilized populace hemmed in by an actively hostile culture to the East and across the Mediterranean, and by the still-largely-impassable Atlantic and the rigors of the North. Beyond this enormous task was, as has repeatedly been pointed out, the daunting undertaking of falsifying received, and creating and integrating alternative, hypotheses.

This exercise in cultural formation in the early centuries of the West had to be repeated often thanks to the fragility of the means of recording and disseminating both the original inheritances and the subsequent knowledge-building and integration efforts. The means of recording and disseminating knowledge sufficiently widely and securely for its preservation and broad employment in the affairs of humankind were simply not up to the demands of the repeated strains thrust upon the Western cultural corpus from two distinct directions, imposed internally by the commonly taken but as commonly ill-advised and unwise ventures of secular and clerical elites or externally by shocks of unexpected invasions by peoples from the East and North, new disease organisms, or massive climatic changes.

The sixteenth century, by way of contrast, was by early in the century well schooled and practiced in the arts and procedures of more or less imperishably recording knowledge, both received and newly created. The intellectual requirements required for building arguments falsifying received hypotheses by critiquing previously composed texts; for formulating new hypotheses together with the evidence in support thereof as well as arguing in support of such newly minted hypotheses; and for integrating newly created hypotheses into received bodies of knowledge, thereby organizing into relatively coherent wholes ever-enlarging bodies of relatively consistent principles and precepts of knowledge. All these culture-building exercises required the widely disseminated, identical text of books of considerable amplitude. At the primary hub of all the sorting-out and switching of these complex relationships of falsification, knowledge creation, and dissemination were book printers/publishers. Further, they were as practiced and industrious in disseminating the concepts and precepts contained in their books widely across Europe as they were in seeking out, prompting, and editing into publishable shape these multifarious intellectual ventures. The Europe-spanning distribution network—which they developed to peddle their progressively more diverse knowledge wares—together with the burgeoning number of extensive libraries, both private and public, proved to be the sovereign antidotes to the loss of knowledge and its debasement by individual scribes characteristic of earlier centuries in other cultures.

The sixteenth century had every reason to view itself as standing at the threshold of an entirely new world with such a firm foundation of evermore dependable bodies of knowledge to support their willingness to engage in heightened risk-taking and previously foreclosed ventures. These new ventures ranged across the entire spectrum of human undertakings: from preparing by means of wider offerings of education to the growing number of people for all manner of manual vocations to the far reaches of investigation and scholarship; to the launching of trading entrepôts across oceans; to ever-extended geographic explorations and alchemical experimentation; to embryonic studies of the other great cultures; and to the progressive recasting of Western cultural traditions into more inclusive, expansive, and universal terms better suited to dealing intellectually and practically with a wider more diverse world than had heretofore been assumed.

The Janus-faced posture of the writers of utopias deserves further emphasis. In almost every case the writers displayed a strong strain of millennial thinking/belief employed in the form dictating the liniments of the ideal outcome. This outcome was to materialize at some point in the not too distant future—perhaps in some more remote place. This millennial content was adopted from, and has remained in, almost all such subsequent writings, more or less directly and fully from the Judeo-Christian descriptions of the paradise to come.[21] As much as some later utopian writers have sought to dissociate themselves from this received religious utopian tradition and content, their commonly pallid and narrow depictions of "the better life for humankind" betrays both the poverty of their preoccupations and their reliance upon the far more expansive Judeo-Christian conception. A profound religious impulse impels and infuses almost all utopian writing—both authors and readers thereof. But this millennial sensibility came to encompass far more than utopian writings. As shall be recounted in the following chapter, millennial roots and expectations informed much of the cultural preoccupations and thrust of the seventeenth century.

The tracing of the new era of discovery and exploration in the sixteenth century was necessarily momentarily set aside by the necessity to sketch out one of the most pregnant cultural forces engendered in the West in that century by the discoveries of the Portuguese explorers and more particularly by Columbus's discovery of the New World and its subsequent exploration. But as is patently evident, this cultural force was far from the sole cultural consequence of these discoveries and subsequent more detailed explorations. An equally important and far-reaching cultural thrust was the revival of an intense Christian missionizing initiative. Throughout most of the sixteenth century, this missionary effort was mounted by the Roman Catholic Church. The focus here is on the missionizing activities undertaken in newly discovered lands not the even more intense effort mounted within Europe itself in the search for converts or the restoration of fallen-away parishioners by both the Roman Catholic Church and the Reformed churches. Rather the point of consideration here is the overseas missionizing idea.

This idea was soon incorporated into the instructions given by the crowns of Spain to the explorers and traders dispatched to both the New World and Asia. These high-minded instructions with respect to the saving of the souls of the peoples the explorers were routinely encountering by conversion to the Christian faith were given concrete embodiment by further instruction that priests were to be made a part of the personnel of every ship, whether engaged in trade or exploration. The priests willing to be recruited for such uncertain ventures and problematic outcomes were largely drawn from the ranks of friars of the older orders of Dominicans and Franciscans as well as the more recent Counter-Reformation order of Jesuits, formed in 1540.

The satirization and deprecation of these religious ideas and ideals as well as the Roman Catholic priests and Protestant clergy charged with their implementation has been the common butt of contempt since the age of the eighteenth-century Enlightenment. This cheap parlor game has been, and continues to be, played by contrasting the many and manifest failures in the realization of the high-minded intentions contained in the state-mandated instructions and the declared aims of the clerics. There is no question that the a substantial number of explorers and colonial settlers were little short of beastly in their treatment of many of the native populations they discovered and conquered and in their rapid adoption of an economy built upon impressed or slave labor. It is equally clear that the clerics were often rigid and high-handed in their treatment of native religious practices as well as in their frequently brusque and crude efforts at conversion of uncomprehending or reluctant natives. But the consequential fact remains that many of the bestial native religious beliefs and practices were eliminated; at least, equally barbarous political despotism was simply replaced and occasionally improved, while the cruelties of impressed or slave labor more or less remained roughly comparable to what had apparently long been the native practice. Moreover, and of paramount importance, the ameliorating cultural formulations then being framed in Europe were soon transplanted into the New World. Thus, in the course of a century or two both the lot of the natives surviving the introduction of previously unknown diseases and that of the colonists, largely recruited from the excess populations of Europe, were substantially improved. In short, while the West has but little reason to boast of the first century or two of the settlement and development of the New World, in the longer reach of history such a judgment must now be reversed in substantial measure.

Consequences of the Book: New Departures I

To return now to the narrower locus of Europe, the formation and propagation of another major stream of knowledge deriving from several tributaries must be attended to. Desiderius Erasmus (1466–1536) was another of the iconic figures of the sixteenth-century Renaissance. His learning was so extensive as to lead some to opine that the last Westerner able to master the entirety of the then body of Western culture and knowledge was Erasmus. His book of *Adagio* (*Adages*) (1500 and later successive augmentations) became a near universally used collection of pithy and useful quotations—the very model of the medieval florilegium updated with addition of the flood of apposite adages from the Greek. The *Adages* became the standard form and basis of the commonplace book for the next several centuries.

More important, for this account, were his enormous contributions to the settling of the standard forms of many of the defining Christian texts—the numerous Latin editions of the church fathers he edited and saw into print and above all his revised edition of the New Testament. He had written several books (many published by Johannes Froben of Basel), criticizing the worldliness of the church and advocating a simple devotion, coupled with a life based upon reason. Of these his *Enchiridion Militis Christiani* (*Manual of the Christian Knight*; 1503, printed 11 times before 1520 and translated into most of the European vernaculars) and his *Moriae Encomium, Laus Stultitiae* (*In Praise of Folly*; 1509, and again reprinted 19 times before 1520 and translated into most of the vernaculars) were probably the most influential. His sharp critique of the Roman Catholic Church and some of its doctrines led Luther to believe he had a major intellectual ally in Erasmus. These hopes were severely disappointed when Erasmus sided with the Vatican.

While trained in his early years in the schools of the Brethren of the Common Life, Erasmus's mature writings were much more in the tradition of an active but simple piety reminiscent of Nicholas of Cusa, coupled with the far-reaching skepticism as to the human capacity to ever arrive at final certainty with respect to the true and the good. This skepticism extended to dogmas of every kind and was to become a continuing intellectual constituent of Western thought henceforward. The most notable of Erasmus's previous exponents of this approach to the fundamental limitations of the human mind with respect to First and Last Things were Ockham and Cusa. Both had, in their writings, breathed new life into an arcane and little-noted body of thought, turning on the question of comprehending God—of understanding His nature, qualities, powers, and plans and purposes in creating the universe and life. Both had concluded that the acquisition of such knowledge was beyond the reach of the human mind. The sources of this common proposition were derived from quite different bodies of thought: Ockham's was via the rigorous employment of scholastic rationalism and tradition, whatever the outcome of such an unalloyed line of reasoning. Cusa's, on the other hand, was from a mystical insight derived from reading Proclus while on his return voyage from Byzantium, seeking to mend the schism between the Western and Eastern churches. While in the mode of identifying ancestral sources of this powerful and culturally fertile conclusion, three of the other most noteworthy were Ficino, informed by the Neoplatonist writings and *Corpus Hermeticum* of Hermes Trismegistus he translated; and Plotinus and Proclus, who, building upon Plato's *Timaeus* and other writings of the later Platonic Academy, concluded that First and Last Things were unfathomable. This view had been articulated by Islamic proponents of astrology, alchemy, and natural magic, who also depended heavily upon the Neoplatonist writings. These Islamic writings entered the West with the twelfth- and, more notably, the fifteenth-century receptions of Islamic learning.

Now what is to be made of this remarkable mélange of comingling antecedents, which look on the face of things such an unlikely combination of bodies of thought and knowledge? All manner of notable consequences were to flow from this fundamental axiom or proposition concerning the human understanding of the nature of God. These consequences, in their Renaissance setting, can be sorted out along the following lines. In discussing Ockham earlier in this writing, a note was made that his new approach to acquiring knowledge now designated as "science" is founded on the metaphysical proposition that given the human incomprehensibility of the nature, qualities, powers, and guiding principles of God in the formation of the universe and life, mankind was reduced to a close examination of the universe and the life which had been created to begin to understand God. This assemblage of propositions neither was made in one fell swoop nor was the means of implementing them pronounced ex cathedra. On the contrary, a disparate company of thinkers subsequently built up a body of thought and propositions of the scientific approach over several centuries. But the fact remains that the basic metaphysical proposition which opened the door to both the building of these later intellectual principles governing the scientific discovery of the information about the natural world and the formulation of that information into scientific hypotheses and knowledge as well as those principles guiding the actual conduct of such intellectual activities derived from Ockham and the Franciscan school of thought. It should be evident to the reader that one of the more general ideational consequences flowing from this crucial intellectual departure was some degree of skepticism with respect to the received ways of thinking about all manner of matters and many of the received knowledge propositions.

Cusa's was quite a different intellectual trajectory. Cusa had concluded in his "moment of illumination," incident to reading Proclus, that God was of such power and majesty that humankind possessed no means to comprehend, understand, or describe Him. The only means open to some form of a relationship with the Godhead was a mystical appreciation growing out of a cultivated "learned ignorance," first articulated in his *De docta ignorata* (1440) and followed by related writings. He too urged, among other remarkable dicta, that religious dogma was to be viewed skeptically as all dogmatic tenets were human constructs and thus susceptible not only to error (falsification, as used in this writing) but to possible revision in light of new revelations or insights (creation of new more powerful hypotheses, as used in this writing). Incidentally, he also advanced the then outrageous dicta that the church council was superior to the papacy; delegates to the council should be elected by church members following Marsilio of Padua and Ockham; the planetary system is heliocentric; *The Donation of Constantine* was a forged document; it is not by works but faith that salvation is gained[22]; together with notable advances in mathematics.

As has been noted, the profound sense of skepticism with respect to the formulations of humankind advanced by Erasmus closely paralleled that of Cusa and seems to have been informed not only by Cusa but by Erasmus's close familiarity with the thought of Plato and the Neoplatonists and the Scholastics such as Duns Scotus and Ockham. This new and different turn in reform was manifestly supported by Erasmus's acute observations of the world around him. He was a widely traveled, freelance intellectual, having spent much time in not only the Rhineland but England (he was a close friend of More); France, where he had a major influence on Jacques Lefèvre d'Étaples (1450–1536, a librarian, leading French intellectual, translator of the Bible into French, and commentator on the Epistles of St. Paul and Nicholas of Cusa) and Guillaume Budé (1467–1540, founder of the Collège de France and creator of the massive library at Fontainbleau, which formed the nucleus of the Bibliothèque Nationale); and Italy. This wide-ranging exposure to the customary beliefs and practices throughout much of Europe confirmed this skepticism underlying his thought, as reflected, for example, in his *In Praise of Folly* or in his ultimate refusal to endorse Luther's program of religious reform. More important from the perspective being advanced here, this skeptical attitude informed an entire line of succeeding thought in the West. Indeed, van Gelder sees this tradition of skepticism as a third sixteenth-century reformation quite distinguishable from the Reformation of Luther, Calvin, and Zwingli and the Counter-Reformation of the Roman Catholic Council of Trent. He points to a quite notable line of thinkers and writers in succeeding generations all employing skepticism as a basic principle of philosophical inquiry and explanation and as one of the foundations of knowledge. Among this line of thinkers and writers were the leading scholar-publisher Etienne Dolet (1509–46) and the writers Christopher Marlowe (1564–93), Michel de Montaigne (1533–92), and Jean Bodin (1530–96).[23]

It must be stressed that none of those identified here as initiators/followers in a third wave of reform sought to deny the central place of religious faith in the culture or to reject the body of ideas identifying God as the creator of the universe and humankind and Jesus Christ as the vehicle of salvation. Rather those exemplars of this third catenation of reform produced a continuing, alternative tradition of thinking about and understanding the world and humankind's place in it. They became increasingly critical of any human dogmatic formulation convinced that so doing only deferred or distorted the pursuit of genuine, if limited, knowledge. To radically and overly simplify, these skeptical thinkers and writers were unwilling to utterly and irremediably entrust knowledge or belief to any humanly constructed dictum or dogmatic assertion. Rather they sought to test all such pronouncements and assertions by close examination and analysis of their historical and contemporary relevance or approximation to the true and the good, as best these awesome standards could be and were understood at any particular historical time. Only those statements and beliefs that had endured and withstood the tests of time and present understandings were to be accounted an asset in the cultural treasure of the present. The informal fellowship advancing this third stream of reform found the received religious beliefs to fulfill the criteria of the true and the good. So they neither wished nor sought to set these beliefs aside but rather to endorse them and use any available, valid means to further prove their soundness.

Although this skeptical approach was first developed and deployed in the context of religious dogma, it quickly became a habit of mind and a habitual way of thinking which could be readily adapted to thinking about all manner of cultural goods. The founders and partisans of this tradition of thought even sought to call into question the economic and political ideas then extant and put into practice by the civil authorities. In the next century this mode of thinking and method of inquiry would manifest itself in the quite remarkable efflorescence of the seventeenth century in multiple bodies of knowledge. But this is matter for the next chapter.

This volatile and fecund intellectual ferment was in the most substantial measure the direct consequence of the now readily accessible presence of identical printed texts across Europe. These new directions in thought and culture are perhaps the most forceful affirmation of the book as the engine of knowledge creation and knowledge testing.

Consequences of the Book: New Departures II—The Gnostic Hermeneutic and Magic Arts

Little notice has yet been taken with respect to the other great, historic stream that contributed to the rise of skepticism but also alternative modes of intellectual hypothesis-making and modes of thought: astrology, alchemy, and magic. These bodies of ideas, introduced into the West in any substantial measure in the sixteenth century, became a powerful intellectual force for the reason that they seemed to offer an ancient and alternative means, other than Scholastic reason, for understanding and explaining the material, human, and spiritual worlds. It will be recalled that Ficino was instructed by his employer, Cosimo de' Medici, to interrupt the former's translation of Plato's works and turn to the translation of a Greek manuscript of the *Corpus Hermeticum* received from a Macedonian monk about 1460. De' Medici's reason was that this body of writings was conceived to contain much Gnostic wisdom of vastly greater intellectual value than that of the Athenian philosopher. While this body of esoteric writings and doctrine was known to many of the church fathers, including St. Augustine, it did not enjoy wide currency during the first fifteen centuries of the Christian church. It was Ficino's translation of the bulk of the works of Hermes Trismegistus, buttressed by other sources of natural magic (the Orphic texts, The Orphic hymns, the sibylline prophecies, etc.), and repeated references from Greek via Arabic to the Gnostic traditions of not only astrology but alchemy and the magic needed to access higher spiritual powers of various kinds, that kindled the fifteenth-century enthusiasm. This enthusiasm in turn led to the explosive concern with and influence of these doctrines in the sixteenth/seventeenth century. While belief in these bodies of ideas is now entirely falsified, save among evanescent and fluctuating groups of marginal sectarians, they were widely studied and cultivated beginning from the late fifteenth century and for several centuries thereafter.

Anything like an inventory of the diverse adepts of these bodies of ideas and the varying nature of their relationships and the varied configurations of their thought is beyond the intent and limits of this writing. But it may be pointed out that they provided the intellectual substance for the widespread endorsement and intellectual and ethical employment of the twin and parallel concepts of *prisca theologia* and *prisca sapienta*, ancient and primitive theology, and ancient and primitive knowledge.

Medieval commentators had repeatedly noted the classical parallels or anticipations of many of the doctrines of the Christian church (*prisca theologia*). This parallelism is hardly surprising given the extensive Neoplatonic training and background of the church fathers who had framed these doctrines in the early centuries of the church and the continuing influence of the Latin translation of the only widely extant book of Plato, *Timaeus*. But the Hermetic writings and the newly formed hypotheses of many Renaissance thinkers went well beyond the patristic and medieval notions of classical premonitions of Christianity.

The *prisca theologia* was conceived as having been derived by the ancient Greeks from Old Testament figures, commonly Moses, as well as related Egyptian and Chaldean/Phoenician sources. As such it represented the true origins of the Christian faith, requiring, in principle, only the advent of Christ and His Resurrection to validate or complete the Christian faith. This belief was strongly reinforced by the Hebrew Gnostic writings found in the Kabbalah.[24] One theory of advanced by a scattering of rabbis was that the *prisca* was derived from this collection of wisdom literature, was passed along by some rabbis as immediate intermediaries between the ancient sources of *prisca theologia* and their classical Greek recipients.

By parallel lines of reasoning the ancients were perceived to have fully understood the structure and functioning of the universe and the life therein and to have recorded this knowledge in arcane writings to protect it from desecration and misconstrual by the great mass of the untutored. This Gnostic knowledge dealt with not simply the cosmos, its functioning, and its influence upon humankind (astrology); and the nature of the substances that form it and their influence upon humankind, including the treatment of disease (alchemy); but above all, the spiritual ordering of the universe, the nature and powers of each order, and the abstruse and recondite means humankind had discovered for contacting and influencing these powers (magic). These bodies of thought were all considered to be not simply primary examples of *prisca sapienta* but the intellectual substance thereof.

The publication of the underlying translations of these works and the flood of secondary writings derived therefrom became a veritable torrent over the course of a century.

Two of the leading sixteenth-century figures must be introduced here to illustrate both the power and the broad sway of these *prisca* pursuits in that century and to furnish the foundations for the enormous impact these ideas were to have in many domains of knowledge in the seventeenth century, most notably the formulation of the sciences. The two iconic figures, best representing the import and impact of this tradition are Philipus Paracelsus (1493–1541) and Giordano Bruno (1548–1600).

Paracelsus was trained as a physician in the traditional Galenic school of medicine. Early on he became interested in alchemy, the study and practice of which became a lifelong preoccupation. He soon became a harsh critic of the practice of Galenic medicine, the books used to teach this body of received knowledge, and the practice of Galenic medicine, with its narrow and unswerving reliance upon rigid humanistic parsing of the Galenic texts, and commonly without any specific reference to the actual condition of a patient, the course of the disorder, and the context of the infirmity. Paracelsus concluded that alchemy, and its associated experimentation, was the ancient key to unlocking the physical secrets of the nature and functioning of all living organisms, including the sick or infirm human.

The surviving writings of Galen (AD 160–200), first translated in substantial measure in the sixteenth century, were among the most notable Western inheritances from the Greek. Galen, a Greek, was the greatest synthesizer of classical medicine and represented an immense intellectual improvement in Western medicine over the shamans and primitive folk remedies of the Germanic tribes and the folk medicine based upon the miscellany resulting from the repeated augmentations/ substitutions of Dioscorides' *Materia medica*, still largely dominating Western medicine. But the Galenic corpus and tradition had been captured by the humanist doctors, who simply ignored the Galenic admonitions to continually study the actual condition and symptoms of patients in order to improve or devise cures. By Paracelsus's time, "The medical Renaissance was essentially philological (not clinical or physiological); it was humanistic with a vengeance. Its humanism discouraged the discovery of new methods, and it was largely restricted to Greek and Latin literature."[25]

It was the repeated and heated critiques of these humanistic practices that greatly contributed to the decline of these practices and the introduction of the experimental method in medicine, which probably represented the principal contribution of Paracelsus.[26] He did, however, introduce several chemical drugs into the medical armamentarium—arsenic, iron, laudanum, mercury, sulfur, etc. The tradition of experimentation with the combination and separation of substances and the methods devised for so doing forcefully advanced by Paracelsus in his lectures throughout Europe and, more important, in his writings can be said to have helped put into place the foundations of experimental chemistry.

It was the profound skepticism advanced by Paracelsus, stimulated by the quite different body of alchemical explanation, that underlay his attacks on Galenic medicine. These critiques contributed significantly to the erosion of confidence in the practices of Scholastic reason and the humanistic preoccupation with parsing classical texts. Paracelsus was one of the forerunners in the introduction of experimentation as a basic element in what is now called scientific thought and practice.

Bruno was of an entirely different intellectual lineage and one whose thinking was devoted to objectives entirely unlike those of Paracelsus.[27] The Nolan, Bruno's birthplace and as he was commonly referred to, was trained as a philosopher, theologian, and Dominican monk of the Scholastic school. Accused of heresy for dabbling in Neoplatonic speculations in his early years, he fled Italy to a life of wandering from one university to another throughout Europe.

He became committed to the idea of a heliocentric solar system, of the infinity of space, and of an infinity of heavenly bodies, and the relativity of space, all in contradiction to the Aristotelian and Ptolemaic systems. These ideas were derived, in part, from those of Cusa[28]; in part, from the Copernican astronomical formulation; and in part, from the elaborate ontological constructions of the universe to be found not just in the metaphysical writings of the Neoplatonic inheritance but, more important, in the formulations to be found in the Hermetic writings. These latter bodies of ideas posited an elaborate hierarchy of states of being and the description of the occupants of each of the steps on this ladder of increasing sanctity and power. Each ascending level of the hierarchy of beings possessed a greater power to intervene, for good or ill, in the affairs of those beings arrayed beneath them. God, the creator and the omniscient sustainer of the universe and all the beings therein, including the hierarchy of saints, angels, archangels, powers, dominions, etc., was the omnipotent pinnacle of this hierarchy. Bruno related these levels of states and beings to the cosmology he had derived from the Copernican hypotheses. These relations were to be described by monads that connected all aspects and manifestations of the universe and the beings therein and by the mathematical relationships that he, as one of the foremost mathematicians of the sixteenth century, believed he had discovered.

In addition, Bruno, informed by the Hermetic body of ideas, advanced the view that humankind could make contact with many of these beings and discover a deeper spiritual illumination as well as a more profound understanding of the structure and function of the material world. The means of so doing were to be discovered by the cognoscenti buried in Gnostic prescriptions disguised in not only the Hermetic texts but also the Egyptian hieroglyphics, or alternatively from astrological phenomena, or from the "philosophers' stone" of the alchemists, or by means of various occult linguistic incantations and rituals of "magic" known only to the discerning initiate.

In his travels about Europe and in his extensive writings he popularized this broad and heady mix of speculations among such notable figures as John Dee (1527–1608), Queen Elizabeth's advisor and one of the leading mathematicians and geologists of England; Philip Melanchthon (1497–1560), Luther's right-hand man and the principal creator of the German school system; and even the English playwright Christopher Marlowe (1564–93), who, it has been suggested, used Bruno as the model for his play *Doctor Faustus* (1588.)[29]

Again, the quite different means and mechanisms of creating alternative hypotheses employed by Bruno, in the context of the rapidly expanding world of sixteenth-century ideas and bodies of knowledge, seeking both to falsify older formulations and create new and more powerful hypotheses to explain the universe and its function and meaning, could lead only to an increasingly skeptical assessment of currently accepted dogmatic assertions. Further, Bruno's wide-ranging hypotheses exerted a powerful influence on subsequent thinkers and writers for at least another century, following his burning at the stake for heresy in 1600. Traces of his doctrines and influence appear in virtually all cultural undertakings for years after him.

With respect to his execution by the Roman Inquisition, some have seen Bruno as the first victim of the Counter-Reformation opposition to the Copernican–Galilean cosmology. Yates, however, attributes his execution to true heresy.[30] And in itself, this execution intrinsically further encouraged the gathering skepticism of the century as to the intellectual and ethical legitimacy of the Roman Catholic Church.

Both Paracelsus and Bruno were profound believers in the power of ideas to mold ways of religious, social, and cosmological thinking, alter common social practice, and shape the future. Both were convinced that they were restoring older bodies of ideas that more closely approximated the true and the good or ways of thinking that were culturally more profitable than the Scholastic reason or humanistic rhetorical parsing that were commonly used at the time. Both thought they were falsifying recent ways of thinking as well as the received maxims and principles of traditional views. Both thought they were creating or, better, restoring "old"/*prisca*, alternative ways of thinking and creating/"restoring" more defensible hypotheses with respect to the spiritual and material orders of the universe. And both were convinced of the centrality of books to the explication and promotion of these new/"old" bodies of ideas. They both authored numerous books aimed at falsifying received hypotheses and explicating the new/"old" hypotheses that they held better comprehended and explained a number of major cultural formulations. They found adventurous and often like-minded publishers, prepared to risk printing and distributing books that bore a stronger or fainter odor of sulfur and brimstone, as both had vaguely been identified as adepts of Satan, or at least heresy.

Note has been made that the views of both Paracelsus and Bruno involved what in retrospect may be identified as bearing upon matters that is now called science: Paracelsus with medicine, pharmaceuticals, and chemistry; Bruno with astronomy. They can, therefore, be roughly cast among the early and motley assemblage of sixteenth-century thinkers and experimenters who may be styled scientists. Arguably, the most important achievement of this ill-assorted group of those interested in or concerned with understanding the material world was the translating of and mastering the scientific and mathematical thought of the classical world. The manuals have identified both as leading forerunners of that phalanx of outstanding seventeenth-century thinkers and writers advancing a body of ideas mixing Gnosticism with the nascent sciences, which they have styled the pansophists[31] The widespread dissemination of the writings of Paracelsus and Bruno with their radical messages of attacks on narrow humanism and their advocacy of radically alternative ways of thinking about and explaining the nature and meaning of the universe and humankind led to a flood of books refuting, sustaining, or advancing yet other alternative means of analysis and explanation—all of which the fraternity of the book was intimately involved in.

Consequences of the Book: The Growth of the Sciences and Technology

The first of the sciences to begin to assume a modern shape was botany, the study of which was closely related to the formulation of the then only available pharmaceuticals mostly derived from plants and used in the practice of both learned and folk medicine. Building upon the classical compilation of Dioscorides' *Materia medica* and the writings of Theophrastus and Pliny the Elder, the medical schools of, first, Padua (1545) and Pisa (1545) established herbaria for, first medicinal plants, but in time others that might possess medicinal properties derived from the worldwide exploration for plants noted earlier. By the end of the sixteenth century more than twenty herbaria had been established.[32] By the same date the German fathers of botany had formulated the first systems aimed at describing and classifying the burgeoning collections of plants from around the world in cultivation in Western herbaria and gardens.

A roughly parallel, if temporally later, undertaking with respect to zoology had been inaugurated as well. The monumental handbook *Historia Animalium* (1551–87), in five volumes, compiled by Conrad Gesner (1516–65), performed an analogous role with respect to bringing substantial order to not only most of the animals of Europe but many from elsewhere collected and brought back to Europe court zoos and menageries by the captains of the by then numerous worldwide expeditions of discovery and trade.[33]

It can be confidently said that by the end of the sixteenth century the West had put into place the foundations and much of the preliminary scaffolding upon which the modern biological sciences were to be built. Coupled with the placing of these preliminary but necessary intellectual structures relating to biology, parallel precursory structures were being put into place with respect to others of the sciences and mathematics.

The impetus for the renewed pursuit of interest in the biological world was largely derived from the renewed developments in the understanding and practice of medicine. Paracelsus, as already noted, was a particularly forceful exponent of a patient- and disease-based medicine rather than convoluted conclusions deduced from received texts. Certainly, one of the decisive turning points in the intellectual evolution of Western medicine came with the publication in 1543 of the fact- and evidence-based anatomy of the Flemish Andreas Vesalius's (1514–64) *De humani corporis fabrica*—an early example of the experimental approach forcibly advanced by Vesalius's contemporary, Paracelsus. This book not only falsified much of the Galenic anatomy but, in its numerous vernacular translations, rapidly altered the approach to medicine in the West.[34]

The body of geographic knowledge dealing with the shape, extent, and character of the earth was earlier detailed in connection with its decisive impact upon the launching, first, of voyages of exploration, largely from the Iberian Peninsula, and the subsequent reduction of the resulting discoveries to two-dimensional and printed form as maps and accompanying explanatory books. So note must be taken here of it only in the immediate context of the rapidly forming bodies of related scientific knowledge.

Intimately associated with the rapid development of the navigational art of the sixteenth century was the study of astronomy. The story of the development of the science of astronomy is sufficiently widely known to require little explication here other than to note that the Polish astronomer and canon of the Frauenburg Cathedral in East Prussia Nicholas Copernicus (1473–1543) was the first to publish his findings supporting a theory of the sun as the central focus of the planetary system based upon the science and mathematics of his observations. The resulting book, *De Revolutionibus Orbium Coelestium*, was not brought into print until he was on his deathbed in 1543. The next significant succeeding astronomer was the German Johannes Kepler (1571–1630), who, basing his calculations and conclusions on the remarkable observations of the Dane Tycho Brahe (1546–1601) and the recent advances in mathematics, provided through his three mathematically based laws not only an accurate picture of the planetary system but the relation of astronomy to mechanical physics. His *Commentaries on the Motions of Mars* (1609) contained the first two laws and *Harmonice Mundi* (1626) contained the third. With Kepler's work the foundations of astronomy as an observational and mathematically tractable science had been firmly laid.

The study of physics remained, in the sixteenth century, largely an exercise in understanding and coming to terms with Aristotelian physics. Only a few new physical concepts, and those of minor importance, were advanced during the century. The most important of these were spin-offs from the great burst of astronomical hypothesis-making, which marked one aspect of the century in science. As noted earlier, in connection with the monumental intellectual breakout of navigation and discovery, a handful of the Aristotelian maxims were falsified. But with these few exceptions, the innovative work in physics remained for the extraordinary minds of the seventeenth century.

The sciences, most notably the so-called hard sciences, have been associated, since the work of the sixteenth-century thinkers and writers, with mathematics and the mathematization of scientific inquiry and explanation in that century. Perhaps the most decisive contribution of the sixteenth-century mathematicians was to translate and get into comprehensible form the writings of the Greek and Arabic mathematicians. By the end of the century virtually all the significant work of these predecessors had been brought into print and widely distributed.[35] One of the seminal figures in the application of mathematics to scientific matters was Copernicus. He not only employed trigonometry and geometry to explain and support the heliocentric planetary system, which he advanced, but as a mathematician did a good deal of work to develop the mathematical concepts in the fields of both geometry and spherical trigonometry. By virtue of priority, the name of Regiomontanus, which was introduced as an important early Nuremberg scientific publisher in the previous chapter, deserves mention, for some of his work in spherical trigonometry, unpublished until the sixteenth century, was employed by Copernicus in his mathematical work.

The other leading astronomical figure of the century, Kepler, must also come into this brief account of the high points in the evolution of the mathematical knowledge, for he had to make important contributions to mathematics to state and define his three laws of planetary motion in a mathematically rigorous form. It is not inappropriate here to observe that, as with most mathematicians, Kepler was intellectually compelled not simply by the beauty of the solutions that he had developed but by the positive identity between mathematical statements and physical reality, which he attributed to God's plan for shaping the universe according to mathematical laws. Thus came the source of the title of his last major work, "the harmony of the spheres." This same profound sense of the order, beauty, and reasonableness of the universe in both material and mathematical terms had informed a number of thinkers of earlier periods and would animate many in subsequent centuries.[36]

Note must be made of the work of the French mathematician Francois Viète (1540–1603) and the Flemish Simon Stevin (1548–1620) in the enormous developments in both arithmetic and algebra in the sixteenth century. These two men brought both fields of calculation up to new levels of usability for those in the seventeenth and subsequent centuries.[37] The latter was also the first to develop decimal fractions and instructions as to how to use them.

The long-neglected interest in and investigation of the material world in the sixteenth century in itself marked a disquieting turn in Western cultural concerns and the cultural trove of substance and meaning. Culturally, more decisive was to be the resort to close and extended observation, detailed classification, experimentation, and the recruitment of mathematics into the framing of questions respecting the nature and functioning of the physical world and as the subsequent means of explanation. The new and unexpected outcomes of the raising of such unfamiliar questions and their resulting explanations posed another profound problem. How were these yet paltry bodies of knowledge to be integrated into the currently quite extensive Western universe of bodies of knowledge? Such strange and unfamiliar reflections and concepts possessed no obvious place in a cultural universe substantially organized around theological, philosophical, and linguistic concepts and precepts. One answer, of course, was to deny or endeavor to extirpate such "foreign" inquiries and concepts. But thoughtful members of the society sensed this was a blind alley. Whatever was to be made of this nascent method of inquiry and explanation, it generated one more nexus of skepticism.

This enormously intensified pursuit of new knowledge in the sciences was virtually entirely dependent upon the publication of books advancing new and testable hypotheses. Thus, the substantially reanimated study of the material world and omnipresent life forms was largely energized and made possible by the knowledge-generating engine of the printed book.

The intimate relationship of technology and science, which is largely simply assumed in the twenty-first century, was not true of the centuries before the nineteenth. On the contrary, in the historic period with which this writing is concerned, the development of technology was entirely self-contained. Technological evolution grew out of technical solutions created by users in response to clearly identified problems, shortcomings associated with predecessor technologies, and new existential problems.

The sixteenth century differed in no appreciable way from this pattern, save that the overall speed of technological innovation and achievement seemed to increase. This increase in speed of innovation is perhaps most marked in the realm of sailing and navigation. The development of ship architecture suitable to open-ocean voyaging and naval warfare (the capacity to carry many heavy cannon and projectiles as well as the ability to withstand the repeated shocks of broadside battle) made possible, as noted earlier, the opening of all manner of new existential opportunities. These extraordinary nautical ventures, for they were extraordinary given the maritime practices of that time, necessarily required the development of the mathematics, instrumentation, and knowledge of ship management necessary to exploit the characteristics of the new ships.

Not far behind were improvements in agriculture in the Low Countries and England involving new techniques of draining waterlogged ground, the better rotation of crops, and the inclusion of new crops in the rotation. The consequence was the improved nutrition of the populace of these two regions relative to that of the inhabitants of neighboring regions.[38] Associated with these agricultural improvements and improved productivity was an upsurge of books dealing with all manner of crop-growing and animal husbandry, manuals dealing with drainage and fertilization, the introduction of new crop species, etc. A new class of farmers was beginning to emerge—literate, in search of improved understanding, prepared to innovate, and capable of departing from tradition and of adopting new ways. This led to a class of farmers better able to support the growing populations of parts of the West and would, in time, provide a wholly new and beneficent abundance of food, grown in a more hostile environment—an enormous achievement in a world heretofore largely accustomed to something between subsistence nutrition and a mean and famished existence.

The technological advances of the sixteenth century in general markedly increased the need for serviceable metals. The successful casting of bells and cannon, for example, demanded ever more improved and more efficient extraction and fabrication methods. Further, the opening of the rich precious metal mines in the New World geometrically intensified the interest in mining and the need for better understanding of mining and metal extraction. As a consequence of these demands, substantial intellectual effort was spent on improving traditional practices or developing new practices and the requisite auxiliary technologies for lifting ore, dewatering and ventilating deeper mines, smelting ore in metal fabrication, etc. Several notable books appeared in the sixteenth century dealing with the mining and preparation of metals. They include Vannocio Biringuccio's (1480–1539) *De la Pirotechnia* (1540) and Georgius Agricola's (1494–1566) *De Re Metallica* (1556), together with several other foundational texts.[39]

The appearance of these numerous texts, a new departure in learning and the dissemination of knowledge in an ancient industry, can be viewed as a quite sensitive and accurate "barometer" of the growth and evolution of knowledge in the general field of mining. In parallel other fields of trade and industry employing other bodies of long-practiced undertakings, analogous problems, seemingly intractable obtained and perfected from the increasing number of books new and better practices. In the majority of these fields the broad distribution of printed manuals of new practices led to the rapid and widespread dispersal of more productive and efficient trade practices.

Consequences of the Book: The Political Imperative of Freedom

One other major intellectual cultural current, which came to prominence in the sixteenth century, is necessary to limn out the tentative but emerging cultural configuration of this and subsequent centuries. That was the beginnings of a radical departure in political thinking from the long-accepted doctrines of feudal/manorial noblemen and autocratic monarchies in complete charge of political/economic propositions, institutions, and practices and the Roman Catholic and Protestant hierarchical clerisy in complete charge of religious beliefs, institutions, and practices. That current is the revival of the concept of freedom.

This widening appreciation of the cultural alternative and opportunities of freedom was formed out of two long percolating streams of thought. The first was intrinsic, if still largely veiled, to the late medieval period. The most powerful articulation of this stream was made by Marsilio of Padua in his *Defensor Pacis* written in 1324 and by Dante in his *De Monarchia* of the same century.[40] As noted earlier, the *Defensor Pacis* of Marsilio, basing the rule of both the monarchies and the church on the will of the people, had been written in 1324 but, although widely circulated in manuscript form over the succeeding centuries, was brought into print only in the early sixteenth century and so finally put into a form available to a wider and larger receptive audience dismayed by the rapid growth of the centralized state. In addition, the dismal history of the conversion of the Roman Republic to the Roman Empire was still a vague exemplar in medieval minds, even if only in broad outline.

In support of this medieval stream of thought was Christianity, which had from its beginnings promulgated the idea that the fundament of salvation was dependent upon the freewill choices made in daily life by every person as an individual. While the idea of individual free will was a continuing matter of debate through the centuries, some of the church fathers advanced the contrary idea of salvation as the consequence of divine grace. Yet the free exercise of choice remained a major and continuing thesis of Christendom. Indeed, free choice became the ground of Luther's reform. (Calvin retained the old Augustinian doctrine of salvation by grace cast as predestination.)

This still subtle medieval tradition of the freedom of the individual was notably augmented by the reception of the Greek philosophers and historians, widely published in book form. This second stream of thought extolled the intrinsic value of freedom and the free citizen of the city-state as well as the enormous cultural benefits derived therefrom. Perhaps the two most powerful exponents of this classical tradition derived from the recently recovered body of Greek thinking were Nicholus of Cusa and Pico Della Mirandola, both of the fifteenth century.[41]

The medieval stream of ideas was to a degree augmented by royal or feudal/manorial charters, grants, and proclamations. But these charters and related writings remained of distinctly secondary moment whenever the secular or religious powers chose to exercise their presumed greater prerogatives. So, for example, the feudal lords of England were only occasionally able to invoke the Magna Carta in their defense against the Crown. All other classes were helpless in the face of the exercise of abusive English kingly or feudal power. The free towns invariably paid dearly for their charters often only to see them seriously abridged if not abrogated by a king or nobleman needing money or seeking retribution for some perceived fault or slight. The most evident repeated exactions and departures from professed practices of the church have been detailed elsewhere herein. But again the laity had no effective means to secure themselves from such exactions or oppressions.

The arguments for freedom and the first, if feeble and futile, efforts to realize the actuality of the free individual began in the late Renaissance. Adding to the sixteenth-century flow of ideas of freedom were Niccolò Machiavelli's (1469–1527) *Il Principe* (*The Prince,* 1532), *Istorie Fiorentine* (*History of Florence,* 1532), and *Discorsi sulla Prima Deca di Titus Livy* (*The Discourses,* 1531)—all appearing in print after his death. The first, of course, received instant attention for its quite amoral advice on dictatorial governance from which the neologism "machiavellian" was soon coined and which remains to the present a cautionary tale with respect to the thinking and practices all too often employed by political authorities. So its cultural role may be construed as of a piece with the Marsilio as well as Machiavelli's clear support for republican principles evident in both *The Discourses* and the *History of Florence.*

Bruno's name once again must be cited in this account of the growing body of sixteenth-century writings advocating political reform. Bruno's account in his *Spaccio de la Bestia Trionfante* (*The Expulsion of the*

Triumphant Beast, 1584), published while he was in England, advocated a great purification and regeneration beginning in the heavenly reaches of the elaborate cosmological ladder he had formulated from Neoplatonic and Hermitic sources and then descending downward to the earth and humankind. Both flawed religious structures and tyrannical political structures would be cleansed and returned to a free state of primitive worthiness.[42] While urging/predicting religious and political reform, the initiative for this reform stems from heavenly sources rather than from earthly sources in Bruno's judgment, not by earthly agents as conceived by the other advocates of religious and political reform.

Other writers, perhaps of lesser impact, contributed to this growing stream of opposition to the traditional forms of authoritarian governance—"... John Knox's *First Blast of the Trumpet* and the *Bekenntnis* of Magdeburg which proclaimed a divine right of resistance; in George Buchanan's *De jure regni* and Christopher Goodman's work on *Superior Powers* ... in Francois Hotman's *Franco-Gallia* and the *Vundicae contra tyrannos*, in which rebellion against tyrants becomes both a right and a duty."[43]

The cultural foundations of freedom and liberty, first tentatively laid in the medieval period, were substantially augmented in the sixteenth century, as noted. One of the inevitable consequences of the advocacy of such radical notions in a traditionally constrained culture was a significant skepticism in some circles with respect to prevailing institutions and their obligatory and foundational ideational structures. The sole, immediate sixteenth century, substantive responses to this questioning and skepticism were a rash of peasant and journeyman revolts in a handful of towns—none of which came to other than a quick and bitter end.

The Consequences of the Book: The Knowledge-Generating Engine and the Close of the Sixteenth Century

The very considerable cultural achievements adverted to here, in a number of diverse domains, including the invention of the new mode of inquiry and explanation—science—were the outcome of not simply the revival and eager acceptance of the classical tradition or the widespread distribution of the classical writings with the advent of the printed book. More important, they speak to the vastly enlarged cultural involvement, which the same widespread distribution of the printed book made possible. Within two generations, the printed book had, in effect, made of growing sectors of the West a vast intellectual "symposium." All of a sudden, relative to the vast time frame of the presence of *Homo sapiens* on the earth, a previously unthinkable immense host of minds was able to focus and reflect virtually simultaneously upon not simply common texts but the common bodies of knowledge packaged therein and further to then write out the products of their own reflections and deliberations to be distributed to the other members of this culturewide symposium for their critiques and further knowledge-generating use. A radical restructuring of the "system" of generating and qualifying (creating and falsifying knowledge concepts and precepts) had resulted from Gutenberg's "arte." A heretofore unknown, powerful knowledge-generating engine had been constructed and put into operation.

The nascent sciences, for example, represented the first body of knowledge that can, with some conviction, be called a new departure in the ways in which humankind could seek out, think about, and formulate hypotheses about the world they lived in and themselves. The sciences, as presently understood, can be considered in one light as one of the most promising children of the powerful knowledge-generating engine of thought resulting from the advent of the printed book and the symposium of minds it brought into being.

While some contemporaries in the fifteenth and sixteenth centuries rightfully extolled the virtues of the printed book, few comprehended the far more overwhelming and astonishing fact that an entirely novel and powerful knowledge-generating engine had been devised, which had, in turn, brought into being a new and previously unforeseen intellectual and ethical world. Few, then or since, genuinely understood the cultural and world-shaking impact of the printed book, and the knowledge-generating engine it fostered, as an unintended consequence.

This remarkable Western knowledge-generating engine reflects another almost equally remarkable Western characteristic, which is a marked increase in the exercise of the long-standing, extraordinary Western cultural curiosity. This quality led to not only a search for the full consequences of traditional knowledge but also an openness to the reception of knowledge accumulated elsewhere. Beyond this the West possessed a ready willingness to incorporate these principles of foreign knowledge found sustainable in the Western context. Obviously, a measure of this increased curiosity was the inevitable outgrowth of the newly created mastery of the open ocean by the West. But some significant measure of this augmented curiosity about and acceptance of selected, tested non-Western thought derived from the rapid opening of the intellectual and ethical horizons of the West was the product of enormously increased appetite for knowledge fostered by the newly created knowledge-generating engine. This strain of curiosity about and openness to foreign knowledge was unique to the West and offered, by the end of the sixteenth century, premonitions of the cultural hegemony of the West. And all this massive accumulation of foreign knowledge was carefully and extensively bundled up in the readily distributed package of the printed book to be made widely available to any who sought such cultural accumulations for further use.

It is of fundamental import to note that the close study of the culture of the other great cultures became a widespread Western undertaking in the seventeenth century. Matters that seemed of no importance in their homelands became the stuff of both amateur investigators and the foundation of newly established fields of scholarly enterprise in the West.

More easily and commonly overlooked is the central role in the initial building and continuing operation of this astonishing knowledge-generating engine that the many knowledgeable publishers/editors played over the roughly six generations following the invention of the "arte." The enterprising few in every publishing/editing cohort who were able to recognize the cultural enormity and import of the engine with which they were involved took deadly seriously the central cultural role they played in the sound maintenance and operation of this new engine.[44] They invented and carried forward the practices that have become the touchstones all subsequent serious publishers/editors have employed—the "gate-keeping" role of earnestly attempting to assess the cultural worth of every writing they publish; seeking out and encouraging of competent writers; critically sorting out of genuine falsification of hypotheses and the advancing of new, more powerful hypotheses from the far more usual, casual, and trite carping and the ordinary, common proposals arising out of the formulation of shallow intellectual and ethical complaints and the positing of ad hoc trivial intellectual Band-Aids; assisting writers in getting ideas into the comprehensible forms necessary to the readiest comprehension of readers; assuming the often serious risks inherent in injecting into the public square genuine cultural building hypotheses; and actively campaigning to get the printed book out into the hands of the widest possible readership.

Despite the widespread warfare, the advance of another Islamic *jihad,* the recurrent local outbreaks of the plagues and other infectious disease, episodes of fairly widespread agricultural failures, the continuing economic burdens of nascent mercantilism, dynastic war, the overweening search for honor and glory by the dynastic houses of Europe and other dislocations, the renascence of the late fifteenth and the sixteenth centuries did not sink into the cultural torpor and intellectual stasis which had marked earlier parallel periods of Western renewal followed by cultural decay. Why? This chapter has sought to locate the answer to this profound historical conundrum not singularly in the invention of printing but rather in the development of the powerful knowledge-generating engine created by Gutenberg's invention. The argument in support of this is not so simple or straightforward as to suggest that the advent of print alone led to this marvelous departure from past cultural crises. Rather the argument is much more complex, pointing to the dependency upon the collaborative efforts of several generations of a wide variety of translators, writers, thinkers, and book people scattered across Europe. Mention has been made of a number of the foremost figures all of whom worked in concert with several generations of printers/editors and associated book people to the difficult and uncertain end of seeking progressively clearer understandings of the true and the good. This knowledge-generating machine became the locus for pursuing all the numerous and related religious and philosophical questions and concerns that have dogged humankind since time out of mind. And it was upon the enormous accruals of knowledge that had been repeatedly tested and tried and found sound that the hegemony of the West began to emerge in the sixteenth century.

And to the good fortune of the culture of the West yet another highly productive century-and-a-half lay ahead. The momentum of advance of cultural generation had become so great as to produce a continuing flood of new intellectual concepts and moral principles. These were both the product of Gutenberg's knowledge-generating engine and its place as a continuing partner in the epistemological facility of the West, leading to further fertile cultivation of further concepts and principles.

So massive were these seventeenth- and early-eighteenth-century advances that only the leading cultural currents of the seventeenth century, and further only those advanced in the single fecund isle of Britain, can be detailed within the necessary space limitations of this book.

So this narrative now turns to England as it sets much of the cultural direction of the West.

Notes

1. Bolgar, 1971, 127.
2. Rowland (1999) presents a well-founded and well-rounded survey of this telling exemplar of the "high Renaissance" and the astonishing disconnect between the Curia and the supreme Pontiff and their flock.

3. Ibid., 245.
4. Haskins, 1924, 152.
5. Rowland, 1999, 217.
6. Grindler, 1995, III, 22.
7. Jenkins, 1968, 35.
8. Ibid., V, 779.
9. Kamen (2003) notes that about the mid-16c. the Spanish people began to refer to their peninsula as the "Spanish nation," 333.
10. Clark, 1966, 2.
11. Kamen, 2003, 333.
12. Bouwsma (2000) structures the thesis of his history of the waning of the Renaissance around the deep and multiple contradictions he finds among the leading figures of the period.
13. Garraty and Gray, 1972, 488.
14. Ibid., 488.
15. Ibid., 488.
16. See Ch. 4 for a brief account of this episode.
17. Weber, 1992, 313.
18. Lasky, 2004, 20.
19. Manuel and Manuel, 1979, 33ff.
20. Ibid., 33.
21. See the works of Manuel and Manuel (1979, Ch. 1) and Lasky (2004, p57ff) tracing this Christian lineage.
22. Watanabe, 2001, 223.
23. van Gelder, 1964.
24. As one of the aspects of the mounting critique of the Church and its massive apparatus of dogma, a return to the simpler practices and teachings of the primitive church was widely urged. In part, and further as the result of the continuing recovery of ancient manuscript material, the Hebrew *Kabbalah* was brought into print and introduced to wider European readers. The study of the Hebrew language, as the language of the Old Testament, was also widely encouraged, particularly in Lutheran circles. So there was widespread familiarity with Hebrew learning—and with Hebrew Gnostic writings that contributed markedly to the ideas of *prisca theologia* and, to a lesser degree, of *prisca sapienta*.
25. Sarton, 1955, 50.
26. Hall, 1966, 132.
27. The seminal, modern study of Bruno is that of Frances Yates, 1964.
28. Kuhn, 1957, 235.
29. Gatti, 1989, 77ff.
30. Yates, 1964, 355–6.
31. Manuel and Manuel, 1979.
32. Sarton, 1945, 66–7.
33. Ibid., 132.
34. Ibid., 116.
35. Kline, M., 1972, 240.
36. Ibid., 246.
37. Sarton, 1945, 159.
38. Derry and Williams, 1961, 69–74.
39. Ibid., 140ff.
40. Ibid, see Ch. 3.
41. Cassirer, 1942, 323.

42. Lasky, 2004, 196.
43. Ibid., 182.
44. There have always been several publishers of books of fictions and other popular entertainments largely seeking personal affluence and momentary recognition, littering the publishing/editing scene. But the iconic publishers in every generation have been those taking seriously their cultural responsibilities.

4

The Cultural Triumph of the Seventeenth Century and the Role of Print Therein

> ... the images of men's wits and knowledges remain in books, exempted from the wrong of time, and capable of perpetual renovation. Neither are they fitly to be called images, because they generate still, and cast their seeds in the minds of others, provoking and causing infinite actions and opinions in succeeding ages: so that if the invention of a ship was thought so noble ... how much more are letters to magnified, which, as ships, pass through the vast seas of time, and make ages so distant to participate in wisdom, illuminations, and inventions, the one of the other.
> —Francis Bacon

The Cultural Inheritance of the Seventeenth Century

This history, as have other recent histories of the period, left the sixteenth century with a surfeit of cultural goods. The cultural table was inundated with intellectual and ethical ideas: some portion of them, long familiar; another portion of old, vaguely familiar, little used but now revitalized ideas; a substantial portion, the veritable flood of sometimes partially recognizable ideas deposited by the rush of translations from the Greek; a great portion, the consequence of the stunning upheaval occasioned by the unpredicted serial appearance of three Reformed churches (Luther's, Calvin's, and Zwingli's) and one rehabilitated church (the post-Tridentine Roman Catholic); a portion, the emergence of a continuing stratum of skepticism; a portion, the irresistible advance of ideas promoting the autocratic, monarchial state; and as a counterpoint to the latter, the swift emergence of advanced concepts of liberty; a portion, the growing economic dislocations and previously unimagined and continuing increases in wealth consequent upon the rapid growth ideas of capitalism leading to an explosive increase in manufacture and trade, as well as the influx of precious metals from the New World; a portion, the awe, wonder, and uncertainty flowing from the voyages of discovery and subsequent colonization; all compounded by another outbreak of dynastic wars, the continuing *jihad* of the Turks, and the sporadic resurgence of the plague and other epidemics. To further compound this superfluity, whole bodies of quasi-knowledge in the form of various more or less believable versions of Hermetic doctrine, Gnosticism, astrology, alchemy, magic, Kabbalistic writings, and divination were imported or reimported into the West as some of the baggage received with the Greek and Arabic sources.

This already sagging table of intellectual and ethical fare was further freighted with the blending of some of these rich intellectual and ethical comestibles by the continuing discarding of a few of the dishes on offer and their replacement by new, more nourishing combinations. Of substantial but curious interest in this progressive cultural process of falsification of received hypotheses and creation/integration of new hypotheses is the role that the subsequently falsified tenets, such as Hermeticism, alchemy, astrology, etc., were used by the likes of Paracelsus, Bruno, and so on, to falsify other received hypotheses. This sometimes-unfathomable process has been a constant force at work in the intense fermentation of received and traditional ideas in the West—a process that makes a mockery of the neat and orderly and systematic march of history, "progress" so beloved by social system makers—not simply historians but social scientists of various breeds, as well.

The publishers and booksellers (for bookselling had partially broken away from publishing in the sixteenth century to become a separate and distinct profession), who had set this table and kept adding to its riches, did not confine their efforts to a handful of places—Florence, Paris, Oxford, Wittenberg, Utrecht, Vienna, etc. Rather they set up nearly identical tables across the length and breadth of Europe. No corner of Western Europe was entirely denied this bountiful offering. Every succeeding generation saw not only new faces but added recruits who shared in this inexhaustible intellectual and ethical fare and who would, in their years, identify, define, and frame new problems requiring falsification of received, and creation and integration of new cultural hypotheses. The process of culture building and formulating ever-closer approximations to the true and the good in any vital culture is a never-ending cultural task.

New intellectual and ethical problems seem to be one of the genuine constants of not just each individual life but of the life of the culture. If these problems are not constantly and vigorously dealt with, they simply become festering sores sapping the vitality of the individual or culture. It was, and remains, the essential function of the job of publishers and booksellers to encourage and advance this cultural problem resolution or cookery (to maintain the culinary metaphor being employed), with all the substantial risks of so doing involved.

In light of what was likely a geometrically increasing body of knowledge and its equally rapidly proliferation of complexity, how was even the most astute and gifted mind to encompass this vast range of understandings and the nuances of their evolution and bring such a mind to bear in a meaningful way in the lived life of the culture? How was this immense task to be realized in the face of the widely agreed but notably underappreciated and under-recognized traps and snares of innate intellectual limitations, those that were incorrect, the illogical, the contradictory, the cognitively dissonant, the evil, the immoral, the decadent, the half-baked, and all the other intellectual and ethical infirmities with which humankind is burdened? How were the intellectually unsustainable and ethically compromised/corrupt ideas or bodies of ideas to be progressively identified and extirpated from the cultural accumulation so the latter did not turn toxic and plunge the culture into a descending trajectory as had happened not just to the Greek and Roman cultural structures but to those of several other major cultures? And assuming that these massive and sound but hard-to-win formulations could be put into place, how is that cultural body of knowledge and understandings to be relatively accurately and faithfully passed on to oncoming generations?

Clearly, a massive collective, social effort had to be progressively organized and maintained in a vigorous state of health. The West had successively endeavored to solve the same problems on a simpler and less extensive scale, first with monasteries and then with universities, but by the sixteenth century, something more was required. To a considerable degree, answers had been found in the formation of the new Reformed churches and the Tridentine Catholic church, a growing national identity formed around despotic dynastic houses as well as a reinvigorated monastic impulse and university mission. But the knowledge-generating engine centered on the printed book was engendering new ideas and falsifying traditional ideas faster than the West could comfortably deal with them. The epistemological problem had, within a couple of generations, mutated from that of inadequate cultural resources to a problem of superfluity.

The recent but yet only marginally tested initiative to assist in keeping the burgeoning inventory of more complex cultural goods under control was the entrance into the cultural maintenance and formation role of individuals from the gentry and the growing body of bourgeoisie. So we see those like Machiavelli, a relatively low-level civil functionary; Marsilio Ficino, the son of a doctor, only entering religious ranks after many of his major translations and writings had been completed; Pico della Mirandola, the son of a minor count, who spent his life wandering from city to city in Italy but never took religious orders; Nicholas Copernicus, the son of a wealthy Polish trader, a physician who joined the church bureaucracy but never became a cleric, but laid much of the foundation of heliocentric astronomy; Tycho Brahe, the son of Danish gentry, who laid the foundational observational data used by later astronomers; Calvin, the son of a Catholic church bureaucrat, who in turn studied for the clergy but turned to found a Reformed church; and the multitudinous other laymen of the seventeenth century, possessed of either patrons or personal wealth permitting them to follow cultural pursuits. In short, the knowledge-generating engine catalyzed by Gutenberg's invention was soon able to attract an entirely new cadre of knowledge workers from a recently emergent segment of society. Increasingly, this cadre of adepts of the knowledge-generating engine was to augment, shape, and husband the explosive Western culture.

The other initiative to firm up control of this burgeoning feast of cultural goods embodied in books was the founding and growing support of libraries of all kinds. The augmentation of existing libraries and the formation of new libraries were quite obvious next steps in the effort to gain better control of the growing bodies of knowledge flowing from the knowledge-generating engine. Foundational models for this initiative were long extant in the monastery and church libraries as well as the notable handful of private, court libraries of late medieval and early Renaissance times. The universities had, late in medieval times, begun to form libraries, largely through the generosity of a few high church officials and a handful of the nobility who gave significant personal collections of manuscripts and printed books. The great De Medici Library in Florence provided an early example of this new initiative. It was to be soon followed by imitators in intellectual centers across Europe, as, for example, the Ambrosian Library in Milan and the Bodleian in Oxford founded early in the seventeenth century. Further incentive for the founding and development of libraries, especially school and municipal libraries, was offered by the sixteenth-century reformers, particularly Luther, as adjuncts to the encouragement of literacy and public education. The profession of the librarian had a long history, but that profession took on a new meaning in a culture of increasing literacy, increasing knowledge, and increasing numbers of "violls of the purest efficacie and extraction of that living intellect that bred them." The librarian was enlisted into the Western community of the book of publishers, printers, and booksellers essentially formed by the sixteenth century. The professional community of the book had, together with writers and readers, become not just the engineers operating the knowledge-generating engine of the printed book but the vanguard sector of and the access gate to Western culture as well.

But the larger environment in which this cultural explosion was going forward in the seventeenth century looked no more propitious to the distribution and ordering of this torrent of cultural goods than had part of the sixteenth century. The by-now well-defined dynastic "royal" families in pursuit of the ideas of familial honor, glory, wealth, and power not only continued the mayhem inaugurated late in the sixteenth century but also raised it to new heights of expenditures of life and treasure. The Bourbons and the Hapsburgs were the foremost houses fomenting this nightmare. Adding to this warfare in search of prestige, place, and wealth were the royal houses of Denmark, Sweden, Poland, and Hungary together with an assortment of German kings and princes. By the time of the Treaty of Westphalia in 1648, which incidentally established the long-standing diplomatic axiom that the internal affairs of a state were exempt from interference by other states, Germany was, in substantial measure, a wasteland, the outcome of the Thirty Years' War, from which it was to take the best part of another century to recoup. But Germany was only the most aggravated and pathetic example of the noxious consequences of the seventeenth century pursuit of national grandeur by the divine right monarchs of the now established national, autocratic, dynastic states.

Less obvious was the increasingly vexatious burden of taxation and intervention into the lives and affairs of their citizenry imposed by these self-important monarchs and their "clerks" (now bureaucrats). Versailles, and imitations thereof across the capitols of Europe, and the associated fawning courts staffed by sycophantic courtiers, themselves seeking wealth and advancement, were all built and supported on the backs of the productive citizenry. All of these irredeemable exactions were to ultimately lead to other ill consequences, but that is matter for other studies and books.

The consequence of these malign governmental initiatives and actions had several marked deleterious consequences for the population of Europe. "When the Roman Empire came to an end ... a serious national reverse, perhaps her decline was even greater than in the European crises of the fourteenth and seventeenth centuries."[1] Further, it led to the exhaustion of huge numbers of lives and the waste of huge financial resources. Spain, at the beginning of the seventeenth century, was the West's wealthiest and most extensive empire yet was exhausted and lost its primary role in European affairs by the end of the century. It had had to forfeit the United Provinces, the latter now a sovereign state. But more importantly, Spain acceded to the Dutch dominance of the trade between Seville and America, the Dutch reaping the rich economic rewards thereof.[2] The Spanish Navy had been destroyed in its two Armada attempts to eliminate the pesky English privateers preying upon both its Atlantic and Pacific gold fleets in the late sixteenth century. The Danes and Swedes retreated from the larger European scene to their northern haunts. Poland had become the plaything of neighboring states. The devastation of Germany has already been adverted to. Only the immediate dynastic objectives of the Austrian line of the Hapsburgs and the Bourbons, in France and Spain, had been served by over two centuries of virtually constant warfare and the savaging of most of Europe.

Seventeenth-Century England: Precursors

Whatever the distraught character of the European continent, harbored off to the west was an island which had had, by and large, minimal recent impact on its neighbors—England. It had periodically been drawn into the royal marriage trading game and had been recruited as a sometime ally by one or another of the warring continental states—usually on the side of the underdog in an effort to maintain a balance of power. By the same token, this little island had begun to come into its own in the sixteenth century and was arguably to become the principal paradigm for the modern shape of Western culture in the seventeenth and following centuries. The economic distress of the sixteenth-century Tudors was being rapidly turned around, thanks to the increasingly astute conduct of international trade in wool and cloth and trade with the Orient.

For these paramount reasons, the balance of this history of the book, as the central shaper of modern cultural history, will focus on seventeenth-century England. The argument for English exceptionalism will be the substance and charge of this chapter. It is fully recognized that significant numbers of historians will bridle at this judgment, quickly citing the work of such important seventeenth-century cultural continentals as Ullise Aldrovandi, Tycho Brahe, René Descartes, Galileo Galilei, Hugo Grotius, Christiaan Huygens, Johann Kepler, Gottfried von Leibniz, Justus Lipsius, Blaise Pascal, Joseph Scaliger, Francisco Suarez, and others as well as the continental publishers and booksellers, who gave the work of these men their status. None of these undoubted cultural luminaries will be noted further, save as they made contributions to the intellectual life of their English colleagues at the time or subsequently.

Further justification for this decision is to be found in the English exceptionalism so forcefully and convincingly argued by Gertrude Himmelfarb in her seminal analysis and portrayal of the Enlightenment.[3] The contention here is simply that the foundations of this exceptionalism argued by Himmelfarb are to be discovered in the English history of the seventeenth century and prior English traditions.

Several of the leading cultural factors forming the distinct quality of English history in previous centuries have already been mentioned; the seventeenth was to see the augmentation of these cultural factors together with the strengthening of the internal structure and coherence in their formulation and additionally with the introduction of new and commanding cultural ideas. It can be said, with no likelihood of serious contradiction, that not only did the seventeenth-century cultural formulations of the English massively influence the future cultural history of Europe but also that the English modus operandi for successfully founding permanent, viable colonies across the world firmly established the subsequent dominance of English ideas, institutions, and practices in much of the developed world around the globe. No other nation so successfully established and extended its influence with comparable long-term beneficence.

The historian seeking to explicate the lineaments of the English cultural archetype capable of launching such a widespread and lasting influence is faced with puzzling out the convoluted and tumultuous currents and crosscurrents of the seventeenth-century England—and most particularly that period of twenty years, from 1640 to 1660—in which the subsequent framework was set. Perhaps the most promising place to start to unravel this history is in tracing out the tortuous and embattled playing out of the final settlement of the religious issue and the place of religion in the culture of England. This entry point seems most propitious for several reasons. First, because the body of religious thought and belief plays such a central and perpetually defining role in the formation and ongoing trajectory of all four of the world's great cultures. But more particularly, religion lay at the heart of the English revolution (1640–1660), the Glorious Revolution (1688–1689), and the founding of the Puritan colonies in North America.

The initial cataclysmic religious dissociation associated with the founding of the Reformed churches has been noted previously. Just so, the establishment of the independent English Church by Henry VIII and his assumption of the role as supreme head in the early 1530s can be seen as the beginnings of another of the Reformed churches, although it did not fully assume this role until later.

Second, because one of the outcomes of the sixteenth-century turmoil leading to the religious settlement of this new sect was its massive contribution to the final formation of the English language. Perhaps the greatest culture-organizing principle following religion is the symbol system of language. Just as Luther's translation of the Bible into vernacular German gave the various German regional variants the framework to shape a national language and John Calvin's Bible the French standard language[4], just so the various versions of the English Bible based essentially on William Tyndale's (1494–1536—burned at the stake in Flanders) translations and culminating in the King James Version (1611) set the framework for the English language.[5] So the present-day form of English used worldwide today was one of the progeny of the tortuous working out of the English reformation.

The last foundational effect of the English religious settlement, to be dealt with at this point, was its impact upon the political settlements of "The Restoration" of 1660 and then the "Glorious Revolution" of 1688. By the mid-seventeenth century, the general reformation postulate of freedom of conscience and associated freedom of speech had matured to the point that English Christendom was well on the way to the acceptance of the idea of religious toleration and a more generalized sense of liberty. As this body of ideas was augmented as well as conformed and reconciled with other bodies of knowledge, its consequences were adapted and synthesized with and into bodies of political knowledge. These new formulations (hypotheses) of political thought in turn led to the powerful reinforcement of ideas of political freedom then widely abroad in the whirlwinds of English political debate and resolution. So this sense of religious freedom also substantially contributed to the enormous bodies of constitutional, legal, and political knowledge of a limited government and liberty of the person forged in the furnace of seventeenth-century England.[6]

But this is getting ahead of the story, so to more fully trace the evolution of the English body of knowledge supporting these religious cultural outcomes, a return to the reign of Elizabeth I is necessary. At Elizabeth's coronation, she was the supreme head of the Church in England. The church had become a nearly exclusively state church, controlled by the crown. The reverse side of this coin was that covert Protestants (several groupings of which were soon to styled "Independents" or "Puritans") saw these government measures as an opportunity to introduce the reformed religion, first of Luther and then that of Calvin. The latter followed the lead of John Knox and the reformers in Scotland in the early sixteenth century and the establishment of the Church of Scotland in 1560. Opposition to this disestablishment of their church was not only widespread among English Roman Catholics but also strongly disfavored by foreign powers, most notably Spain. Almost needless to say, these now more or less openly contending religious factions led to years of internal unrest and uncertainty. Elizabeth sought to stifle this unrest by proclaiming a body of measures, including the compilation of a revised Book of Common Prayer, which was aimed to compromise the religious differences of the major groups and so establish a state church more or less satisfactory to the liturgical and doctrinal demands of the various contenders—the so-called Elizabethan settlement.

Elizabeth had inherited not only the crown and the state church but also a remarkable state institutional apparatus. Her Tudor predecessors had established a quite encompassing theory and practice of monarchial divine right. This theory spliced together with disparate elements of the Common Law; the traditional county offices of sheriff, justice of the peace, and coroner; the newly created office of lord lieutenant responsible for the training and maintaining of a military force to defend the shire and provide troops to the king's army; and augmenting the duties of the traditional parish churchwardens and vestrymen to include a number of local civil responsibilities, such as care of the poor, maintaining roads, overseeing local taxes. While the result was, until the early seventeenth century, a cheap (the Tudors always needed money) means of centralizing the government, for all these local institutions were staffed by leading men of the county, parish, shire, or hundred at little or no cost to the central court. Yet this cobbled-together system was an effective means of imposing the dictates of crown and Privy Council across the land.

This noteworthy body of institutional ideas defining the English national state under the rule of a dynastic monarch differed markedly from the body of ideas animating the institutions of the Continental monarchs, most notably the models formed by the autocratic French and Spanish states. The latter employed agents answerable solely to the crown to administer the edicts of the crown, collect taxes, and man and command the military. By way of contrast, it was from among the English country gentry, all of whom in the course of their lifetimes held several of these local offices that members of the House of Commons were elected thereby exercising some control of state policy. In the course of the over hundred years of Tudor supremacy, the number of commons seats increased to about 450. As will shortly be seen, this unusual body of ideas guiding the formation and operation of the English administrative institutions was to prove a major source of strength in the seventeenth-century making of the classic parliamentary state.

Elizabeth had inherited this distinctive administrative system, thus making her edicts and those of her councils readily enforceable. Thus despite opposition from both the traditional Roman Catholic believers, on one hand, and the radical Protestant reformers, on the other, the Tudor state church was temporarily accepted. The queen's establishment of a single state church employing a common body of doctrine, a common prayer book, and a common liturgy was successfully emplaced. But all the while, local officials, including the state church priests, the church-wardens, vestrymen, and assorted county and other local volunteer officials, talked and considered and debated across the kingdom. In part, they talked about the implementation of the edicts bearing upon matters of religious practice and belief, but more often about more general matters of administration and taxes. It is utterly impossible for any law or regulation or administrative procedure to be articulated in such a way as to be universally applicable in every relevant situation. So the talk turned in part not only upon how to apply the new and standing bodies of laws but also, inevitably, upon the meaning, utility, soundness, and more importantly the policy implications thereof. This local talk and consequent conclusions were salted with ideas brought back by members of the House to London, informing future parliamentary sessions.

Meanwhile, several quiet, subtle religious reform impulses advanced, gathering numbers, doctrinal definition, and strength among identifiable bodies of like-minded believers. To get a bit ahead of the story chronologically, these various religious groups can be grouped as follows: an increasingly assertive body of Roman Catholics; a larger body favoring the state church; several quite rapidly growing bodies of more or less strict Calvinists, usually gathered under the general heading of Puritans; reform-minded activists or Congregationalists; and finally the genuinely radical reform fringe groups such as the Levelers, Diggers, Fifth Monarchy Men, Anabaptists, Quakers, and other assorted utopians[7]. In the more or less accommodating environment fostered by the Elizabethan court and the widespread affection enjoyed by the queen, these various groups largely held their peace and refrained from pressing their beliefs in the expectation that, in a subsequent reign, they might come to enjoy and assert their doctrinal views. This manner of compromise and expectation of change over time, to which Himmelfarb[8] attributes many of the qualities of the English Enlightenment, was to prove one of the central or controlling characteristics of the emerging, modern English character.

England: 1600–1641

But this relatively accommodative religious posture hardened even as James I, Elizabeth's successor, was en route from Scotland to London to take the English, and hence soon British, crown. A petition drawn up by about one thousand English clergy (the Millenary Petition) sought modifications of Elizabeth's dictates with respect to liturgy to make it more acceptable to both Anglicans and Puritans and called as well for a new translation of the Bible. At the end of the day, James turned away any amendment favoring the Puritans and hardened the rules of clerical nonconformity. The only sop offered to the believers was the superb newly revised Tyndale translation of the Bible, the King James Version.

This edict grew out of the body of ideas constituting the divine right of kings on which James had spent much of his time, while king of Scotland elaborating in great detail and which he was to pass on to his lineal descendents to their great misfortune. He, therefore, viewed a state church as an inseparable and necessary adjunct to the absolute state he intended to rule.

A nearly analogous drama was played out in James's first parliament. On this occasion, the issue turned on the rights and privileges of representation of the citizenry in the Commons, which the king saw as a direct assault upon his royal authority. So opinion was hardening on both sides, this hardening confined not simply to matters political but matters of religion as well.

And in this period of growing controversy are to be found the beginnings of a gathering storm of the printing wars, which were to open every facet of life in England to critical examination and debate for the best part of two generations. This cultural war for the minds and hearts of Englishmen—or at least those possessed of any significant concern for the future shape of the way they and their countrymen were to live—touched religious, political, legal, social, economic, and other aspects of the common culture. This cultural war, conducted in the public square with respect to the country's future, involved many of the people of the world of books not simply as printers, publishers, and booksellers—as straight away brokers for the ideas of others, a job which they, of course, undertook—but as writers of many of the tracts produced and distributed or as active members of one or another of the large number of groups advancing enormously differing bodies of ideas on various cultural concerns. However, the bulk of these tracts dealt with religious and political matters, which were increasingly dealt with in common. These print wars exceeded in magnitude and intensity even those accompanying the Reformation and Counter-Reformation cultural wars. Virtually, every belief, every major body of knowledge, and every idea was a matter of contention and up for grabs. And despite the sudden raising of the crown's control of the press, this newly combative press was flooding not simply London but all of England with increasingly radical reform publications—books, pamphlets, broadsides, newsletters, etc. This mounting deluge of print soon recruited numerous adherents to the cause of radical sectarian and parliamentary reform, leading to a growing body of citizen adherents throughout the land.

England: 1641–1660

As the century advanced, the quarrels between the crown and the parliament intensified, accrued an ever-greater number of incidents fostering suspicion and division, and drew religious, political, legal, and financial (taxation) concerns more tightly together in both the popular mind and that of parliament. James I died in 1625 to be succeeded by his son, Charles I, who was as convinced of monarchial divine right to rule without reference to parliament as was his father. Forced in 1640 by financial stringencies, the crown summoned parliament. In the meantime, the country gentry, local officials, parliamentarians, and London professionals and tradesmen had been talking and arguing policy—always aided and abetted by the stationers (the guild of printers, publishers, and booksellers). A few had even formulated a moderate plan of religious and governmental reform—one matter of concern dealt with the imprisonment, torture, and notching of the ears of some of the Puritan pamphleteers—reform of which was introduced early in the session.

This, the Long Parliament, was, however, soon overtaken (by 1641/1642) by the minority of the radical reform groups. Differences between parliament and the crown soon hardened to the point that, in the summer of 1642, the king fled London and gathered an army of supporters around him. War was now inevitable—while the radical and utopian elements in both the general populace and the commons gathered the reins of power into their hands. Soon, a countervailing parliamentary military force was formed. The men in the parliamentary forces were also talking and reading some of the floods of books, pamphlets, and newsletters, forming diverse bodies of religious and political ideas—all civilians drawn to the cause of reform and soon to be revolutionaries—and they formed a multitude of debating societies. Out of these religious, political, social, and economic debates, some members of the army joined civilian groups bent upon radical reform of both government and religion.

Shortly after the capture of Charles I by the parliamentary forces, then led by Oliver Cromwell (1599–1658), this independence of mind soon led to the effective governmental control of the army, with Cromwell as the dictator.

Then another previously unimaginable event occurred—Charles I was found guilty of treason and beheaded by some of his subjects. The centuries-old Western idea of the sacerdotal kingship had been falsified!

The next decade was to see both a continuing revolutionary impulse and a struggle for power between Cromwell, the lord protector resulting in and a succession of experiments aimed at establishing some form of parliamentary constitution. Needless to say, Cromwell also set the pattern for all subsequent revolutionaries endeavoring to establish an absolutist state in rigorously controlling the press. The publishers/printers responsible for the pamphleteering, which had been one of the principal avenues of Cromwell's ascent to power, were then seen as clearly definable adversaries and were severely constrained.

A period of instability and uncertainty followed Cromwell's death. Nearly all the contending parties were now exhausted in company with the utopian dreams, which had animated the previous twenty years. So too were the vast proportion of the citizenry who had not shared in this fantasy of the radical uprooting of the culture and its replacement by all manner of idealistic programs and who supported the idea that the island must seek a stable government. But the die had been cast favoring freedom of conscience and a return to the liberties of the citizen thought to be embodied in English law and practice.

The figure around which this stability was to crystallize was widely agreed to be the son of Charles I, Charles II (1630–1685). The monarchy of the Stuarts was restored in May 1660. A new parliament consisting of a House of Lords composed of the old members and the House of Commons of members largely dedicated to the restoration of the Stuarts came into existence at the same time.

After only a few months, a substantial proportion of the religiously, politically, and economically active began to develop increasingly well-founded concerns that the new king was not abiding by the extensive inventory of articles of agreement negotiated prior to his restoration. And even more alarmingly, he, in concert with his council, seemed increasingly to direct state policy in the directions that had led to the execution of his father. Compounding these growing concerns was a major recurrence of the black death in 1665, followed by serious Dutch and French threats to England's dominance of the seas and foreign trade, won in substantial measure by the superb organization and captainship of Cromwell's military. This evidence of military decay under Charles II then deepened the despair provoked by the Fire of London in 1666, which demolished most of London, all aggravated by the magnificent court and extensive company of courtesans, which Charles II maintained in imitation of Louis XIV of France. An informal council of Charles's cavaliers had successfully replaced the Long Parliament of Roundheads. The stage was set for yet another vicious confrontation between the claims of a monarchial government bent upon complete religious and political control and those of a citizenry seeking limited government.

The discovery, in 1677, of the king's repeated negotiations with Louis XIV, aimed in part at the restoration of Roman Catholicism in England, and the allegations of a Popish plot possessed of the same objective, led to the calling of new parliament, which proved to be heavily weighted with strongly pro-Protestant members. Thereupon, Charles II resorted to the repeated dissolution of this and successive meetings of the parliament, the members of which had divided into the classic Tory and Whig parties that marked English politics for the next century and a quarter. A stalemate, controlled by the crown, marked the remaining years until Charles's death in 1685, leading to the succession of his brother, James II.

The early years of James II's reign left little doubt that he was a firm adherent of his ancestors' divine right doctrines and as firm an adherent of the Roman Catholic Church. In short, once again a Stuart king was bent upon imposing his views on not just simply a reluctant citizenry but one of largely a quite different set of mind as well.

England: The Glorious Revolution and Its Aftermath—1660–1700

Late in Charles II's reign, the issue of succession had arisen because he had no male children. The king in parliament settled the succession on James, Charles's brother, then Mary, James's daughter. The latter married the rising Dutch leader, William of Orange. As the distance between James II and the opinion and allegiance of not just the parliament and the two infant political parties—Whig and Tory—but the citizenry increasingly diverged, it became apparent to several of the leading

The Cultural Triumph of the Seventeenth Century

English political figures that this succession could not await the death of James II. They, therefore, undertook secret negotiations with William and Mary to assist in ending the reign of James II.

In the short reign of James II, another major pamphlet war developed, the antimonarchial objective of which was to consolidate literate opinion against James II—again validating the central cultural role of print and that of publishers and booksellers, who not only printed the pamphlets, etc., but also authored some.

The precipitating event in the bloodless replacement of James II by William of Orange was the birth of a son to James II in 1688, thereby implicitly a continuation of the Stuart monarchy. William of Orange, now William III, invaded England with a force of Dutch soldiers augmented by a large contingent of English volunteers. This force met virtually no resistance from James II, who quickly and surreptitiously fled to the court of Louis XIV.

This series of events soon dubbed that the Glorious Revolution was a markedly impressive victory for the parliamentary party and that substantial body of English commonwealthmen, who sought freedom of conscience and limited government. Within a short period following William's and Mary's accession, a foundational body of parliamentary acts effectively sealed the future of not simply English constitutional instutions and arrangements but set the pattern for first the limited governments initiated in the English colonies and then, in time, many of those of the continent. Those statutes included the following:

1. The Coronation Oath of Office (1689) in which William and Mary promised to govern by the statutes of parliament and the laws and customs of the realm.
2. The Bill of Rights (1689), an act reminiscent of Magna Carta to which it has often been compared, which forbade the suspending of the law, levying taxes saved by acts of parliament, maintaining a standing army in times of peace, condemned the various courts establish by previous monarchs, requiring excessive bail, influencing jurors, establishing free elections to the Commons, freedom of parliamentary speech, and the broad "… claim, demand, and insist [ence] upon all and singular the premises as their [Englishmen's] undoubted rights and liberties."
3. The Toleration Act (1689), an act extending toleration and underwriting the independence of the religious sects and their ministers. In this case, the general construal of this act also tolerated the worship of Roman Catholics, Unitarians, and similar previously forbidden religious bodies.

4. Discontinuing the Licensing Act (1695), which essentially assured freedom of the press.
5. The Triennial Act (1694), requiring a new parliament every three years.
6. The Act of Settlement (1701), defining the requirements and prohibitions governing the succession to the crown, denying the crown's right to dismiss judges thus assuring that their terms would run for the full term of their commission, statutory control of foreign policy, and substantial limitations on the authority and competences of the Privy Council.

William III died in 1702 to be succeeded by Anne, James II's youngest daughter. With this succession, it may be said that religious and political pattern of England until well into the twentieth century was now in place. The reader may well ask why this conventional tracing of the history of English religious and political history so familiar to many in contrast to the method of tracing the history of key cultural ideas used in previous chapters. This is because the English Civil War and the Glorious Revolution were first and last a war of ideas—a cultural war. It was in the continuing and frequently dangerous intellectual thrust and parry of ideas that eventually led to armed warfare in which this cultural formation was conducted. It was the hard, dangerous, often uncertain, and brilliant work of an astounding assortment of thinkers, writers, and publishers/booksellers, most of whom stood at one time or another on the battlements of armed conflict but always in the public square of civic debate that brought these momentous and enduring events to their successful conclusion.

This enormous and remarkable cultural work was accomplished roughly in a century. Seventeenth-century England was a hot, dangerous workshop in which the cultural ideas and practices that have become models of freedom not just in the West but also around the world were forged. This century in England has proven to be one of the crucial episodes in the cultural formation of the West. It proved, in that remarkably brief time, one of those few luxuriantly bountiful smithies of cultural formation guiding subsequent Western cultural practice and development marking every cultural florescence. It required the falsification of a broad array of previously accepted ideas in the cultural bodies of knowledge, defining and epitomizing religious, social, and political thought in the West. And accompanying this vast enterprise of falsification was the immense, parallel risk-driven endeavor required to create new and more powerful hypotheses to substitute for those ideas falsified followed by the integration of these new, alternative hypotheses into the relevant bodies of knowledge.

Not only was this remarkable work fabricating the fundamental shape of England from the seventeenth century through much of the first half of twentieth century but it was to provide the model for large numbers of the countries making up the rest of the world. In many cases, however, the value of the English model was not to be realized for up to another four centuries and even then not in all places. By the time of this writing, some benighted and autocratic, oligarchic religious and/or political regimes persist. Further, new generations of oligarchs continually appear, possessing remarkable capacities to reestablish such command-and-control structures—commonly by invoking an assortment of usually shopworn, utopian, and populist slogans and political cant to realize their raw search for power and wealth.

Seventeenth-Century England: Religion, Constitutionalism, Philosophy, and Law

What were these seventeenth-century English contributions to the stock of ideas making up the bodies of knowledge with respect to religion, politics, and related matters? The most important from a religious point of view was the laying of the foundations of toleration of beliefs and forms of worship other than those of an approved state church. This major cultural achievement was, of course, a significant modification of the Treaty of Westphalia concluded only a half a century earlier, and so religious toleration was only slowly and reluctantly adopted in other Western countries—and hardly at all in those of other cultures. The immediate consequence of the idea of religious toleration was to put an end to the routinely disfiguring and disquieting cultural spectacle of continued religious conflict.

One of the necessary accessories of religious toleration was freedom of speech. The cultural importance of this basic right was amply confirmed by the several attempts to repress the work of the printers/publishers in the great pamphlet wars, which marked much of the seventeenth century—first by the crown, then by Cromwell, and subsequently by the restored Stuarts. One of the leading voices in the pamphlet wars opposing the Stuarts was the writer of *Paradise Lost* and other pillars of English literature, John Milton. His *Areopagitica* remains the outstanding statement of the right of free speech. This right of free speech inhering in the individual citizen has proved over the subsequent centuries one of the principal bulwarks against the never-ending press of those in political positions to infinitely extend their power, control, and wealth.

The contributions of England to the Western body of constitutional and political knowledge were at least equally impressive—both at the theoretical level and at the level of institutions and practices: at the theoretical level, the formulations of John Locke (1632–1704) in natural law, constitutional organization, political theory, and above all the clear and firm articulation that the desire for individual freedom. The latter has been a paramount and continuing aspiration of humankind and remains a living tradition.

Hardly as well-known but of equal importance in providing the modern basis of English constitutional law and that of the Common Law employed throughout much of the English-speaking world was the work of Sir Edward Coke (1552–1634). Both participated in setting the principal constitutional and legal ideas foundational for a limited government subservient to the law in which the freedom of the citizenry was the paramount political objective. This freedom directly involved the possession by every citizen of the natural rights to the ownership of his/her person and life, property as the crucial means of exercising personal and public freedom, and freedom of individual choice as against any claims of the state.

They were both architects at the institutional level by advancing the ideas of the free election of representatives to a free parliament called on a regular basis the members of which were immune to prosecution for statements made in framing legislation. These reforms were perhaps the foremost achievement in formulating the structural arrangements governing the nation. Parallel to these structural changes were others aimed at providing against arbitrary administration of the law by according immunity to judges and juries in court deliberations. Another institutional reform of roughly equivalent importance stipulated that the body of the Common Law could not be contravened by interventions at the hands of the crown when administering the law.

But these remarkable new bodies of constitutional, legal, and political ideas and knowledge did not develop in the course of English history in some rational and orderly fashion. Their evolution and institutionalization were marred by several decades in which their recently proposed and antecedent hypotheses leading to these cultural outcomes took on a strange new life as ideologies. Only after the revolutionary passions of the ideologues had been exhausted in futile massacres and pointless authoritarian repressions fueled by beautiful and compelling but unrealizable utopian expectations was the final settlement made by the plain, unromantic, moderate men seeking achievable solutions to cultural problems of genuine merit realized. So the last of the inventory of contributions to the Western cultural inheritance deriving from the English Revolution was the cultural truism of the strange psychological inversions to which the epistemological exercise could be turned when driven by the ideology of activist "true believers." Morally defensible and eminently sensible solutions to genuine problems recast in the overwrought minds of a cadre of radicals could be turned into the apparatus of evil and into avenues of ideological correct despotism and carnage.

The years from about the second year of the Long Parliament (around 1642) to the restoration of Charles II (1660) were the first of, and became the model for, a continuing succession of major cultural upheavals or revolutions in the West. Yes, there had been all manner of peasant and urban revolts and uprisings in previous centuries, and kings had been killed but always in warring against other kings. But no comparable total, bloody cultural upheaval of a kingdom had ever previously been mounted. This period of the Civil War and Protectorate was to provide the pattern, thereafter, for every such cycle resulting from the conjuring up of utopian systems and expectations aimed at solving some substantial group of perceived, usually randomly pieced together, cultural/social problems in one sudden episode of cultural/social change. This misbegotten strategic objective has always been followed by the seizure of power by a tiny activist minority. This illicit seizure of near-absolute power inescapably establishes an authoritarian and increasingly repressive regime. The concluding episode in this woeful historic sequence is a reversion to a semblance of the known and long-established practices.[9] Lasky appositely notes, "... the ideological forms of the first great revolutionary experience and its aftermath had molded the modern political mind were never to be broken or discarded or even significantly reshaped."[10]

In the case of this first Western revolution, the sheer license of the civil war and protectorate began to exhaust support for the utopian reformers. It was made clear in this first spasm of the exercise of revolutionary ardor that the impelling vision was essentially religious in nature. By way of clarity of example of this dislocation, the French Revolution was a classic example of the replacement of heresy from the realm of religious belief to state-imposed politically acceptable beliefs. It was only when significant and moderate sectors of the community tired of these doctrinal excesses that a return might be made to ordered liberty and the responsible exercise of freedom. "The things with which we were primarily and mainly concerned are inward passions and not outward arrangements, ..." wrote the English poet William Wordsworth

(1770–1850) in endeavoring to explain the infatuation he and his fellows had for the French Revolution in the European "arts community" and to express his regrets for so doing in his *The Convention of Cintra* (1809).[11] Such a return to moderate and informed debate restored the interrupted cultural process of accountable falsification, creation, and integration of the latter hypotheses. Only this return to rational dialog could provide the grounds for further realization of the final achievements of seventeenth-century English experiment.[12] But one of the enduring images left in the mind of the historian is the narrow margin in human thought processes between genuine falsification/creation of ideas and the messianic vision of the "true believer."

Seventeenth-Century England: Commerce and Dominion

In the course of the seventeenth century, the English, together with the Dutch, enormously advanced the theory and practice of foreign trade. This development depended upon the rapidly evolving bodies of knowledge with respect to banking and large-scale company finance. As importantly, it depended upon the identification of products, markets, and sources necessary to successful trading. It further depended on the physical development of the means to conduct such trade. The latter depended upon both the building of ships of such strength and capacity to engage in voyages of several years and the rapidly growing knowledge of successful long voyage, open-sea navigation. And to draw these several quite disparate bodies of knowledge into a useful and efficient symbiosis called for and impelled the rapid evolution of high-level investment and management skills.

The following observation should be noted here. That is the fact that two small nations with comparatively small populations located on the periphery of the continent of Europe, England and the Dutch Netherlands, played such an enormous role in the shaping of the world trade. Both were essentially Protestant. Both proved better at organizing and building substantial naval and merchant fleets (often at this time these two classes of ship were interchangeable). They fought several drawn naval battles for control of both the near seas and those of the East and West Indies in the seventeenth century. Both became equally adept at mounting and managing profitable overseas trade and colonies. They both increasingly excelled in the conduct of these major classes of affairs, which were emerging as paramount bodies of knowledge consequent upon the opening of the world's seas by the West. Both fostered the rapid development of the Western economy, the latter substantially dependent upon the swiftly evolving bodies of economic and business knowledge. These two heretofore minor players in European affairs proved better able to organize and manage their limited resources of men and money than were the mainline continental powers. Early in the sixteenth century, Spain (including Portugal, which had been annexed by Spain for much of the period here dealt with) had taken the lead in overseas trade. Contemporary and latter observers of the confrontations of naval prowess and economic initiative in the seventeenth century routinely attributed the success of the English and Dutch forces to a combination of better organization/management and determination.

These two, then second-string powers, were able to not only repeatedly fend off the military and naval forces of the larger, more populous, and wealthier states of the continent but also come into effective control of the foreign trade of Europe with the larger world. This codominance of foreign trade, of course, led to repeated military and naval confrontations. But the important point here is that the body of ideas making up the Protestant mind-set seemed, as Max Weber[13] (1864–1920) concluded in one of his seminal studies, almost inescapably to lead to a more profound exercise of reason, order, and application in all aspects of life. This body of cultural tradition incorporated into the larger body of Protestant ideas and knowledge, repeatedly reinforced by their successful application in the wide area of worldly undertakings, continued to have major implications up to the present.[14]

The English reach of foreign trade in the early seventeenth century shared many of the characteristics of the preceding Spanish and Portuguese traders. Initially, the captains of English vessels were also authorized to trade directly for the account of the shareholders for that single voyage. But early in century, the English, together with the Dutch, had developed the legal concept of the joint-stock company. Such companies were commonly formed by a group of traders together with investors from other professions (shareholders) for the initial investment in trade goods and the rental of a ship. The ship's captain was deputized to trade for desired import commodities and goods. Often the shareholders also acquired an insurance policy for the safe return of the ship—the origins of this body of knowledge devoted to the assessment of and mitigation of risk had been developed in earlier centuries but was vastly elaborated in the seventeenth century in parallel with the expansion of overseas trade.

It soon became clear that there was much to be gained by forming longer lived corporate organizations the objective of which was to establish a permanent overseas presence to carry on continuous trade—The East

India Company, the Virginia Company, etc. Locales particularly rich in one kind of valuable trade commodity or another useful to the mother country or for intra-European trade were identified; fortified trading posts possessing ready access to shipping were then set up; and using staff sent out for limited periods of time, proceeded to acquire economic quantities of the commodities sought by trading European as well as goods of others' manufacture desired by the local peoples or gold/silver. The founding of permanent colonies as a substitute for limited-term staff soon became the practice—most notably by the Dutch and English. Overseas colonies served other purposes as well—strategic, religious, and naval.

The quite sophisticated and complex bodies of knowledge—maritime, navigational, religious, legal, economic, managerial, and financial—which remarkably quickly undergirded this rapid advance of foreign trade are in their many details difficult to trace and beyond the intent of this writing. But they create a monument to the creativity of the Western culture, the Western mind-set, and the knowledge-generating engine developed in the fifteenth century. What is, also, perfectly clear is that this rapid increase in knowledge and understanding of a highly significant cultural undertaking was documented and dispersed in books. This widespread availability of knowledge relevant to all aspects of global trade fostered by books greatly accelerated the widespread improvement in the welfare of immense numbers of people worldwide.

The colony established by the Pilgrims in North America is perhaps the best recollected of all those planted in North America, thanks to two factors. First, because its founding became a symbol of the quest for religious freedom and independence from state churches. Second, because it was the first to proceed from a well-conceived plan aimed at making it economically and politically stable within a couple of years of founding. Some historians decry the singular historical focus on the colonization of North America as being an English affair. They argue for according a greater role to the Spanish and French, the former of longer involvement in the settlement of the Americas. But the fact remains that it was the English colonies, first of Virginia and New England and subsequently of most of the Atlantic east coast of North America that made manifest the rapid development of a number bodies of knowledge necessary to the successful establishment of overseas colonies, the founding of a remote empire, and a viable colonial empire.

Perhaps even more compelling was a strongly informed religious sense of the return to the primitive church made possible by living and worshipping in a new land. The latter motive, a working out of the long-advocated and widely promoted in tracts and books, offered a way back to a closer relationship with God and a simpler form of worship. America "... must consider that we shall be a city upon a hill. The eyes of all people are upon us, so that if we shall deal falsely with our God in this work ... and so cause Him to withdraw His present help from us, we shall be made a story and a byword through the world." Those words of the Pilgrim Father, John Winthrop (1588–1649), are perhaps the clearest expression of the realization of this centuries-old current in Western religious history.

It has been previously noted that the Iberian colonizers of both South America and the southern reaches of North America had little intention of settling. Rather, most sought to make a financial stake of sufficient size to return to the homeland, acquire some desirable property and live a life of at least some local, if not nationwide distinction. Additionally, the Spanish crown and church were concerned with the spread of Christendom—a trivial matter in the eyes of most of the venturers. In this divergence of ideas regarding overseas ventures and motivations, the quite dissimilar subsequent histories of the respective territories settled were put into place.

It is a matter of some considerable difficulty to unravel the development of the rapidly evolving bodies of ideas with respect to those bodies of knowledge now titled macro- and microeconomics from that of international economics. Both were greatly and simultaneously informed by the parallel growth of worldwide trading networks and the swift recasting of the traditional means of structuring, procuring, producing, and marketing of economic and trade goods. Enough here to make the point that within about a century—the latter decades of the fifteenth century and the better half of the sixteenth century—the English nation had together with its doppelganger, the Netherlands, put into place the enduring outlines and characteristics of a capitalist economy based upon individual initiative, risk-taking, the spreading of economic risk via insurance, forming capital markets of sufficient depth to fund the extraordinary expansion of economic activity, and the requisite legal structures. The finalization of the economic structures and the budding of the theoretical foundations of economics crowned this evolution in the seventeenth century.

Seventeenth-Century England: The Cultural Integration

The quite striking evolution of almost the entire spectrum of bodies of sixteenth-century knowledge in both extent and complexity, as well as the opening or developing new bodies of thought, made in the course of seventeenth-century English history—religious, linguistic, political, economic, social, technological, and scientific—led some commentators, late in the seventeenth century, to point to this historic trajectory as forming an entirely new direction in the history of the West. This new character they styled "progress." The concept seems to have begun as a generalized sense of moral improvement, the significant amelioration of the lot of the lower orders of society due to the Poor Laws and emigration, the markedly increased political and economic freedom enjoyed by the citizenry, and the quantum increases in the various bodies of knowledge. In prior centuries, there had been various classical and Christian notions of both progress toward a millennial beneficent time or a regression from a more beneficent age. But the budding body of ideas in England looked only in passing at all these earlier bodies of ideas dwelling rather on the human initiative and role in the realization of these achievements. This sense of progress was an entirely earthbound concept and the product solely of the human mind. This concept was to massively influence the thinking of Western culture for at least three centuries and was another of the English contributions to what was to become a worldwide cultural worldview.

And here to close the circle initiated by the revolutionary English practice of foreign trade riveted in place by colonization and/or empire, it must be pointed out that not only were the remarkable knowledge bodies—religious, linguistic (the Tyndale/King James Bibles), and political theory and practice—hammered out in the smithy of the seventeenth century on that island but also these bodies of knowledge were planted in all the English colonies and political/economic outposts. So vigorous and vital were these seeds that they defined the world of the seventeenth century onward. Only slowly have other nations in Europe been able to make halting and troubled gestures in the direction of the liberty—religious, political, and economic—for which England provided the theoretical and working model. Elsewhere, other nations have also sought to replicate the English model, but again with only hit-or-miss outcomes. The patterning bodies of knowledge and ideational *weltanschauung* of England and its progeny have proved the driving forces of the world of the seventeenth and succeeding centuries.

While these bodies of knowledge were in limited measures carried in the minds of the English populace and those of the colonists the heavy lifting of these ideas across the globe to be used in the shaping of the culture for succeeding and dispersed generations was the work of the book people of the motherland and the colonies. This important work of culture transmission and culture-building in unfamiliar settings was often conducted under quite adverse circumstances. The continuing intellectual struggle being waged in Europe between the forces of authoritarianism—cultural, religious, political, economic, social, etc.—and the new patterns of freedom in many aspects of life and limited government were almost immediately reflected in the overseas settlements. Then there were the inevitable mechanical difficulties resulting from the great and difficult distances from the concentrated centers of technology for repair and replenishment.

Most of the colonists were greatly and charitably disposed out of Christian duty to assist the natives and to help them participate in the introduced culture. That sense of mission led, in turn, to the enormous undertakings of reducing diverse native oral languages to alphabetic form and then teaching the natives how to read their own languages. However, such an undertaking may be viewed by some today, that effort called for substantial moral, human, and financial resources, thus placing a further burden upon the settlements and their printers and/or the importers of such books from the mother country.

For centuries, the continuing shortage of manpower typical of all the settlements presented yet another difficulty for the colonial book trades.

Seventeenth-Century England: The Advance of Science

There remains one more seminal English cultural achievement that must be dealt with to present a well-rounded portrait of that pathbreaking nation in the seventeenth century and the cultural heritage it set in motion in the West. That is the final cultural seating and acceptance of science, much as it is known today, into the Western cultural nexus. It must be acknowledged that some knowledge in mechanics, astronomy, geography, some aspects of biology, mathematics, and the application of the mathematics to all these budding fields of science had been accumulating in the West from the thirteenth century on, but was still largely confined to the fitful revival of the classical inheritance. Roger Bacon in the late thirteenth century had urged the close study of the natural world, based upon Aristotle and employing close observation. William of Ockham in the early fourteenth century had, as noted earlier, set the metaphysical course for the study of the natural world. But all of these departures from the classical were little more than tentative initiatives.

The reader is again reminded that in focusing so narrowly on the English experience and contribution, significant continental figures—Aldrovandi, Brahe, Descartes, Galileo, Kepler, Leibniz, Pascal, and so on—who contributed hugely to Western science are ignored.

One of the most remarkable and illuminating episodes in the history of ideas had been progressing in the creation of the Western body of medical and scientific knowledge for a period from at least the times of Paracelsus until after the death of Newton. It will be recalled that Paracelsus is generally credited with the initial attacks upon and falsification of the Galenic theory of the humoral nature of disease states. He contended that Galen's hypotheses dealing with the diagnosis and treatment of disease as exercises in humanistic reasoning from the received Greek medical texts without any reference to the symptoms and their progression as manifested in the sick person were useless.[15] It will be further recalled that Paracelsus is also credited with setting the preliminary footings of both pure and medicinal chemistry.[16] Yet the underlying and motivating theories employed by Paracelsus derive almost entirely from the traditions of Gnosticism, Ficino's "magic," the Kabbalah, alchemy, and centrally the doctrines of *prisca theologia* and *prisca sapienta*. In short, Paracelsus was and remains a commanding, if ambiguous, figure in the evolution of Western medicine and chemistry.

More widely and certainly accepted as seminal players in the formation of the bodies of scientific knowledge in the seventeenth century were Francis Bacon,[17] Robert Boyle,[18] Isaac Newton,[19] and numerous "lesser others" of that century's canonical scientific community. Just to confuse matters, however, all of these figures shared Paracelsus's theoretical groundings in alchemy, Hermeticism, related Neoplatonic beliefs, and millenarianism. All were, furthermore, confirmed believers in both *prisca sapienta* and *prisca theologia*. In short, nearly all of those commonly classed by most triumphalist historians of Western science as the founding fathers of the new scientific way of arriving at knowledge were followers in the footsteps of Bruno, Paracelsus, and the remainder of the band of Gnostics of the sixteenth and seventeenth centuries. Further, most were millenarians, including Newton, but all were confirmed Ockhamites still viewing their new way of knowing as fulfilling William of Ockham's search for an unknowable God's plans for not only the universe but those of humankind's purpose as well. As Pagel, focused particularly on medicine and biology, so perspicaciously put the matter, "One of the spiritual tendencies leading to modern [science] was mysticism and one of the motives ... was religion."[20]

It was Francis Bacon (1561–1626), first in his *The Advancement of Learning* (1605) later expanded in Latin to *De Augmentis Scientiarum* (1623) and then the *Novum Organum* (1620), who most persuasively provided the economic (a better understanding of the natural world would yield material benefits to the generality of humankind) and religious (a clearer understanding of the natural world would produce greater reverence for God) motivations for pursuing scientific studies more aggressively.[21] Bacon's writings served to convince the growing body of gentry, urban middle class, and professionals of the intellectual worth of pursuing scientific investigation and supporting a small band of those dedicated to making such investigations. As Lord Chancellor to James I Bacon's ideas bore the weight of monarchial prestige.

Bacon has been commonly characterized as an original thinker breaking a new path in ways of conceiving and thinking about the world. As previously noted, he was, together with contemporaries, a skilled adapter and reviser of ideas that had been floating about in the West for some centuries. These ideas had taken some hold in the minds of those benefiting from an education and so gained increasing acceptance with the continued widening of educational preparation. In the heady atmosphere of the acceptance of all manner of new thinking that marked late sixteenth- and early seventeenth-century England—religious, geographic, political, economic, social, etc.—these ideas gained a kind of impetus that an astute mind, such as Bacon's, could utter and find a receptive audience. Bacon was, like other Renaissance reformers, a great popularizer but in the precincts of philosophic reform.

Bacon's ideas soon found a practical expression in the formation of a loose association of those we would now call scientists, such as Robert Boyle (1627–1691), and those we would now call interested laymen who met sporadically to discuss the most recent scientific findings, usually communicated by letter. Boyle referred to this ad hoc group, usually meeting at Gresham College in London, as an "invisible college." These meetings were interrupted during the 1650s. But in 1661, Abraham Cowley (1618–1667), poet and dramatist, proposed a small society of members limited to physicians, academics in science and mathematics, members of the gentry, and some of the aristocracy to discuss and pursue or encourage others to pursue scientific investigations of one kind or another. This idea almost immediately took visible form in 1661 and by 1662 had attracted the attention of the restored Charles II. At the behest of John Evelyn, one of the members of the society, Charles II, duly bestowed a royal charter, and in time some land by way of a financial endowment, on the new society, after which it took the name of the Royal Society.

The society quickly gained a larger membership of those of the same societal segments interested in the vigorous investigation of all aspects of the natural world. The society formed committees dedicated to the pursuit of specific areas of research—several of which reflected the interests of the membership: the gentry, an agricultural committee; the urban traders and merchants, the histories of trade committee; the physicians, the committee on anatomy—as well as the more theoretical sciences. A committee on correspondence assumed the responsibility for the exchange of findings from researchers outside London, including foreign investigators.

Soon launched by the society was another seminal undertaking—a regularly published journal, *The Philosophical Transactions,* recounting the scientific work done not just by members of the society but elsewhere in the British Isles and on the European Continent. Yes, other scientific journals had been started elsewhere in the years immediately preceding the founding of that of the society, but the *Transactions* was the only one which long survived—up to the present as a matter of fact.

The Royal Society established a new form of organization—a private, nonsectarian membership corporation. Such an idea and such a legal creature, like the limited liability corporation, was another of the remarkable innovations launched in England. This body of ideas, made manifest in the nonprofit, nongovernmental organization (NGO), proved another example of the intellectual innovation that typified seventeenth-century England—a practical answer to an emerging intellectual need. This legal creature served England not only well but also served as a useful model virtually worldwide in subsequent centuries.

Bringing the story back to publishing and the place of print in the West, the founding of the journal, *Transactions*, set the model for a practical means to disseminate the limited and diverse bits of information arising out of research and other investigations. Together with the indexes that make the assorted and varied contents of a backfile of a journal accessible, the journal format is a better means of dissemination and storing varied and miscellaneous bits of information than a multitude of pamphlets or similar short pieces.

But the Royal Society did not confine itself to the dissemination of discrete bits of information—the results of discrete observations and experiments—it also sought to advance the publication of soundly based syntheses of these data/bits of information into scientific bodies

The Cultural Triumph of the Seventeenth Century 155

of knowledge demanding the format of the book for the exposition thereof. So it soon launched a book publication program of which the most notable early title was Isaac Newton's *Philosophiae naturalis principia mathematica* (1687).

This publishing program can well stand as an icon of serious and authentic publishing. It demonstrates all the long-since established principles of publishing—the publisher as intellectual gatekeeper, the publisher as the initiator of books needed to flesh out/advance the dissemination of ideas, the publisher as editor, and the publisher as rewriter. (The most famous case of rewriting at this time was Newton's and Halley's recasting of Flamsteed's astronomical observations published by a committee of the Royal Society, not over the latter's imprint, however). As such, the Royal Society is a classic example of the role of the publisher in the work of culture building.

In order to work out the immense problem of calculating the curved orbits of the planets caused by mutual gravitational forces at work in the solar planetary system, Newton (1642–1727) developed a new mathematics now called the calculus. Newton did not, however, publish this new mathematics or give the sense of using it in his *Principia.* In the meantime, the German polymath, Leibniz (1646–1716), developed an analogous body of mathematics. A continuing quarrel between Newton supporters and Leibniz supporters for priority in the development of the calculus arose—and continues in a low key to this day. Whatever the rights of the matter, the fact remains that the invention of the calculus was a major mathematical achievement—one that might well be styled "a breakthrough," for this body of mathematical knowledge opened the door to all manner of subsequent augmentations of other bodies of both mathematical and scientific knowledge. Incidentally, Newton's achievements provide a remarkable illustration of the epistemological paradigm employed in this writing—falsification of an existing hypothesis, creation of a new hypothesis, and the integration of the new hypothesis into the existing body of scientific and mathematical knowledge.

This remarkable seventeenth-century expedition into the organization of investigation of the natural world and the continent-wide dissemination of the results manifestly required a new or augmented philosophical underpinning to provide the intellectual foundations for this new cultural initiative. Further, such a philosophical groundwork must necessarily broadly set the future directions of the scientific enterprise. The foundational guiding assumptions of the science that had yielded such marvelous fruits as Kepler's and Galileo's planetary system, Newton's physics, and Boyle's chemistry, to name but a few of the foremost scientific hypotheses launched in the Renaissance, were simply not those of the eighteenth century, to say nothing of twenty-first-century science. As noted previously, the hypotheses flowing from the presses of scholarly publishers were rooted, at least in part, in and motivated by the foundational hypotheses of Gnosticism, mysticism, and millenarianism. As Collinson remarks with a parallel sense of disjuncture, "... the brains of the best mathematicians [of the seventeenth century] (including Newton's) were engaged in calculating the most likely date of the millennium. The most powerful mind of all, that of Joseph Scaliger (1540–1609), was almost unhinged by his efforts to reconcile the discrepant chronologies of the Bible with what other the ancient records had to say about age and history of the earth, a matter of much more than academic embarrassment."[22] The alert reader will then question whether the far more intuitively arcane scientific hypotheses of the twenty-first century might be founded upon and guided by assumptions other than those ostensibly employed. A nice riddle.

But turning back to the first seventeenth-century efforts to provide a philosophic foundation and justification of science, the foremost figure we meet is Thomas Hobbes (1588–1679). Now Bacon, like the scientific giants noted above, was careful to set the realm of the new science he was advocating to those matters about which conclusions might be established by reason. This was to distinguish these bodies of knowledge from those bodies of knowledge derived from religious thinking. This was hardly a novel idea having been repeatedly articulated in the literature for several centuries. So the historian must look elsewhere for the beginnings of the needed new philosophical foundations of the new science.

Hobbes by contrast sought to falsify and so dispel all ideas of a supernatural power in seeking to understand the natural world, including that of humankind. Hobbes is best known as a political philosopher; his most important work in this area of knowledge is *Leviathan* (1651) in which he was the writer who introduced the concept of the "social contract" into political theory. Hobbes was, from early in his adult years, profoundly interested in the scientific exploration of the natural world. He soon came to the position of radical materialism. The natural world, including humankind, was nothing more than matter. This matter is worked upon by natural forces, which when fully discovered and codified into a body of scientific laws will provide the full explanation of the universe and of the behavior of humankind. He did not deny the existence of God, but argued that the attributes assigned to God were not provable philosophical truths but rather terms of the highest respect and piety for this unknowable Being.

Hobbes's radical materialism was bound to raise a storm of criticism and the confuting voices of large segments of the society. But despite these critiques, the philosophical principles of materialism were soon adopted, even if silently, by the scientific community and have remained the guiding doctrine of scientific research and explanation to the present.

Seventeenth-Century England: The Roles of the Authentic Book Publisher

To return to the continuing and primary premise of this writing, the printed book was the vehicle that advanced this welter of conflicting falsifications and newly created hypotheses in the seventeenth century. This feverish cultural effort, in turn, drove the near-frenzy of cultural upheaval and change, which marks seventeenth-century England. Yes, as Sarton pungently points out, "Most of the science books (and others as well) were of little or no significant value—the pedestrian remains king."[23] This acute and sardonic assessment remains true since virtually Gutenberg's day. But these many copycat books, more than the widely accepted minority of published books, which are the timber of the historian of ideas, and which have provided the lumber for this history, are a necessary factor in the shaping, contemporary explication, and the ensuing structuring of the culture. It is the second- and third-string books oriented to others in the same or related fields of knowledge, which constantly serve the purpose of interpreting and recasting into more accessible terms the often convoluted, arcane, and always alien thoughts and the usually tortured linguistic constructions frequently required in seeking to convey unique and initially obscure intellectual constructions by the gifted few.

As hardly needs saying, there remains the further, enormous didactic undertaking of bringing these falsifications and new hypotheses to an increasing literate but always more or less indifferent and/or widely varying intellectually capable lay audiences—or the culture goes dead, the plaything only of overly facile minds. While the instruction of lay audiences in the growing esoterica of much of the sciences is unnecessary, substantial social or other cultural consequences are associated with some aspects of every one of the scientific bodies of knowledge. Some knowledge of the esoterica related to these special cases is essential to the ongoing formulation of other more remote bodies of knowledge. For these purposes, well-written and well-informed popularizations have always been needed. The same is roughly true with respect to the other bodies of advanced knowledge.

Having dealt with books of intellectual substance and the role of the authentic publishers in entering them into the public square, it is necessary to point out that the vast bulk of the books, which have been produced, have been and remain geared to the passing entertainment of mass-popular audiences. But that confessed, it must be added that the sole relationship between the producing of this vast body of mass-popular books and the publications of the serious, authentic publisher is that both depend upon the printed codex as their mode of presentation. It is the latter, the authentic publisher, with whom this text has been concerned. And it is these publishers who have been at the center of the creation and maintenance of culture.

Even more questionable than the publishing of mass-popular books has been the role of some publishers in advancing more or less harmful or false or, in some notable instances, positively evil writings. In this connection, the notorious *Protocols of the Elders of Zion*, a nineteenth-century Russian fabrication and its numerous, successive translations and editions, immediately springs to mind. The twentieth century is awash with books, often published in huge quantities, which any authentic publisher would reject out of hand, for they have no purpose other than to raise the basest emotions in humankind and commonly encourage the overt exercise of these malevolent emotions. Examples of nineteenth- and twentieth-century harmful and evil books have been used only because they are more likely to be known to present readers than some of the equally culturally pernicious books of the first two-and-one-half centuries of the printed book. But since the early days of print, a few renegade publishers in every generation have entirely abrogated the canons of not just authentic publishing but entertainment publishing as well.

By contrast, it was the hard-tested band of authentic seventeenth-century English publishers, booksellers, and other book-people, who had stood steadfast through the tempest, which swept that island for much of the century all the while aggressively participating in the falsification, creation, and integration of the enormous body of culture that flowed from that astonishing century and its dissemination across the world. Today's book-people could well and wisely choose to set such predecessors, as well as those of the prior one and a half centuries, before themselves as exemplars of the best the book can be.

In closing this account of the substantial seventeenth-century English contribution to the bodies of knowledge that formed the cultural heritage of the West, the reader must surely be struck by how much of that culture, which shapes the present in large measures, was finally put into place in that place and time. In a very genuine sense, it can be said that the late twentieth, and presumably, at least, the early twenty-first, century is a continued playing out of that cultural paradigm. The still evident structure of the British Empire might be taken as symbolic of the measure of that cultural heritage and the present hegemony of that cultural heritage throughout the larger world. And as has been the argument of this book, that cultural heritage was carried to such a point of ascendancy by the powerful knowledge-generating engine at the core of which is the printed book, the "arte" of Johannes Gutenberg, which had no parallel in the other three great world cultures.

Some readers may question the fundamental thesis of this history or the explanatory approach employed—as have some kind readers of the manuscript in its preparation. To answer these animadversions, I have added a short epilogue by way of responding to them in a responsible fashion.

Notes

1. Van Bath, 1963, 65 and 91.
2. Kamen, 2003, 409.
3. Himmelfarb, 2004.
4. Collinson, 2004, 42.
5. Greenslade, 1963.
6. Hudson, 1948, 55.
7. Among others, these included the German immigrant Samuel Hartlib (1599–1670), the author of one of the more famous utopian writings of the seventeenth century, *A Description of the Famous Kingdome of Macaria*, and the correspondent of most of the leading European lights of the first half of the seventeenth century; John Amos Comenius (1592–1670), a Moravian bishop and the famed reformer and advocate of universal education, who agitated for the overthrow of the Austrian monarchy and the Roman Catholic Church, resident in England for about two years; John Dury, a pacifist who confronted Gustavus Adolphus in 1631, seeking a resolution of the Thirty Years' war; John Rogers (1627–1665), the leading figure among the Fifth Monarchy Men; and others. All were millenarians and strong believers and continuing advocates of both religious and political reform not just in England but across Europe and did much to provide the soil for the upheavals of the mid-seventeenth century. They seem to have been associated in some sort of secret society dedicated to these ends. See Lasky, 2004, 320ff.
8. Himmelfarb, 2004.
9. Lasky, 2004.
10. Ibid., 437.
11. Quoted by Lasky, 2004, 466.
12. Lasky, 2004.
13. Weber, 1930.
14. Kurth, 1998, 223 and 233.

15. Pagel, 1958, 345ff.
16. Ibid.
17. West, 1961, 102.
18. Hunter, 1990, 387ff.
19. Principe, 2000, 216ff.
20. Pagel, 1935, 110.
21. "... Bacon's wise suggestions are merely a rehash of often-repeated alchemical maxims: to make gold one must discover the proper substance to begin with and use only moderate heat with the temperature kept steady for a rather long time, [etc.]" or "... Bacon never tires of praising the Light of Nature and insisting on experiment, experiment, and more experiment—themes worn almost bare by the alchemists from the times of Democritus [ca. 460–370 BC] and the Alexandrian Archelaos, through Arnold of Villanova and Paracelsus ...," West, 1961, 104.
22. Collinson, 216.
23. Sarton, 1938, 84.

5

Epilogue: Closing Remarks and Summary

Invention is a game against nature and to play certain mental conditions have to be satisfied ... if the universe is subject to logical, rational laws, the payoff is a standard of living above subsistence.

—Joel Mokyr

Some kind readers of the first chapters of this writing have questioned the continuing emphasis upon the central place of the book printers/publishers and the booksellers in the formation of the bodies of ideas that collectively constitute the immense and related bodies of knowledge forming and animating Western culture. Their various questions and animadversions can best be summed up in the question one delivered, "Weren't the book people simply the agents who produced and sold the writings of others without any hand in the formulation of those falsifications and/or creation of new hypotheses contained therein?"

There is no question that in substantial measure, publishers have always performed an agency function. That said, the authentic publisher has always brought to every text submitted a foundational belief in assessing every one of them in terms of its truth- or goodness-seeking orientation. That is, authentic publishers have always sought the responsible exercise of the substantial capacity for disseminating knowledge, which they know the book to possess. They have earnestly sought to avoid publishing the carelessly or willfully misguided or misguiding. So they are not neutral advocates but rather active agents of responsible truth- or goodness-seeking ideas. Texts not so oriented are largely turned down, but the best of publishers repeatedly make judgmental errors, so the culturally counterproductive regularly manages to appear.

The serious readers of the books of publishers having the reputation of maintaining high standards of responsible publishing come to trust the values of the books published by those imprints. Such a reputation is a substantial asset both in acquiring meritorious editorial content and in marketing such books, especially in the case of writers possessing no previous track record in writing.

More to the point, the assertion of the active role of the book people in this entire culture–building enterprise rests on several well-understood principles and widely employed practices of book people since virtually the inception of the printed book. The first and simplest role is that of "gatekeeper." In this function, the publisher undertaking the risks, monetary and reputational, of publishing a writing offered to him/her makes a genuine judgment as to the writer's bona fides with respect to both the knowledge content possessed by the writer and the cultural worth of the writing offered. In short, the publisher is in every case faced with making the critical judgment of the cultural worth of the offered writing. This same judgmental imperative must be exercised even in the case of a previously published writer, inasmuch as most writers are notoriously one-book authors. The bookseller of such a title must also make a parallel judgment as to whether or not to take the risk of utilizing capital and shelf-space for any given title.

It is all too easy for those not involved in the book trades to overlook or deprecate this gate-keeping function. The sheer amount of weird and wonderful linguistic trash of which the human mind is forever capable and the towering audacity of many of these "mental disposals" is truly astonishing. These characteristics and problems are as common among academics and "public intellectuals" as they are of the general population. So such "star" status is no substitute for sound bona fides and cultural content. One need not long read book proposals and manuscript submissions to have these facts firmly and indelibly impressed upon one's mind. The reverse face of this coin is that hardly any genuine contributions to the cultural knowledge stores of the West remain unpublished, even if the first print-run must remain in the publisher's warehouse for years.

A more complicated case, now demanding not only the judgments marking the gatekeeper role but also a weightier involvement, turns on the authentic publisher's close knowledge and in-depth understanding of the literature of a specific body of knowledge. In this instance, the publisher may identify a "hole" in the literature or a problem within the received body of knowledge or some unexplored consequences of the ideas intrinsic to the present store of such a body of knowledge. In such, and related, deficiencies, the authentic publisher then turns to some student of, or writer in, the field whose bona fides are known to the publisher. After exposing whatever shortcomings in the literature so identified to the writer together with suggestions for the editorial content of a book to fill that knowledge gap, the publisher seeks the writer's agreement to undertake the compiling of such a book. This quite common practice may be styled a publisher-initiated book. The bookseller's role remains the same in this case as in the previous case.

Then there is the yet more profound intervention of the publisher, oftentimes referred to by the gentle and author-assuaging metaphor of "editing." Here the publisher or the publisher's surrogate, a knowledgeable editor, undertakes the more or less extensive rewriting of the text. This exercise is not limited to the effort to clarify the author's language, and hence meaning, but as frequently to making "suggestions" as to the strengthening of arguments, adducing supporting evidence, developing other logical conclusions and consequences than the writer, checking for plagiarism, and in general preparing a text consistent with the prior understanding of the content to be dealt with and the intellectual objectives to be realized. Lack of clarity in language and overdependence upon professional or academic jargon is usually a good indicator of an underlying shortcoming of understanding and/or intellectual rigor.

Lastly in terms of publisher initiatives, simply the rewriting of the bulk or entirety of the text using the detailed information and sourcing supplied by the nominal author is done, much as a reporter utilizes the material derived from an interview to subsequently formulate the substance of the resulting report. The publisher or editor, like the reporter, provides the structure, arguments, and conclusions as well as language. This way of proceeding is far from an uncommon practice in the book publisher's world. The author of this book has resorted to this approach over the years on a number of books, which have proved, in the event, to be well-reviewed and useful.

One of the same helpful readers of this writing concluded that the above description of the role of the authentic publisher in the active shaping of the culture is all too one-sided or "goody-goody." He pointed out that the publisher is in business in a real world of profit and loss, which will inevitably bias against such robust editorial initiatives. This observation carries some weight. The authentic publisher is indeed faced with the never-ending problem of seeking to balance editorial judgment against the assumed judgment of the marketplace. Publishers have long since learned that he/she can never recover costs on all the titles published. But the number carrying their own financial weight must exceed 60–70 percent of the entire list. The publisher cannot long survive at a failure rate much in excess of this level. Thus the authentic publisher must exercise sufficiently prescient judgment of the market to publish less than 30–40 percent which impose a burden on the remaining resources of the firm. The balance of judgment must heavily weight in favor of the cultural contribution of every manuscript under review.

These editorial judgments and practices have been the case since the early days of the printed book. Johannes Froben in Basel and Aldus Manutius in Venice, printers/publishers working at the turn of the sixteenth century, complained of the never-ending cloud of visitors and others seeking intellectual stimulation and authorial support. Aldus, as is well-known in publishing circles, maintained a substantial corps of translators and editors in his home to prepare the translations he wished to publish. Froben is noted for housing and even hounding such an international celebrity as Erasmus to prepare new editions of his *Adages*. Publishers and booksellers were active partisans, not simply agents, in every one of the "pamphlet wars" adverted to in this history. In short, the best of the houses engaged in the publishing trade have always been active players in the world of ideas and knowledge.

Perhaps the best response to questions respecting the relationship of authentic publishers to the books they publish is to focus on three aspects of the authentic publisher's armamentarium. The first is the extensive knowledge the authentic publisher must routinely bring to bear in the judgment with respect to every submission or book idea as outlined above. These bodies of subject-specific knowledge and information possessed by every authentic publisher/editor with respect to the subject area fields in which he/she publishes are of a high order in terms of extent and currency, compared to that of most specialists in these various fields. The failure to maintain such high levels of subject understanding by neglecting the book and journal literature in the field and losing touch with the specialists at professional meetings, by correspondence, and one-on-one conferences spells the death knell for any authentic publisher. Akin to good horticulturists, publishers/editors are thoroughly familiar with the plants they select for their garden and always attentive to not only the particular garden they cultivate but also the larger cultural environment in which they do so.

The second is the genuinely enormous sense of responsibility to their readers and the knowledge-generating engine of the culture in which they are intimate and active players. The authentic publisher genuinely endeavors to publish and sell only responsible assays at the further discovery of/insight into the true and the good. All of the publishing functions of the authentic publisher outlined above are informed and constrained by this overarching sense of responsibility to present readers

Epilogue

and the future health of the culture. Yes, publishers not uncommonly publish books advancing a particular ideology, but the authentic publisher will always signal this special-interest advocacy, informed by the larger responsibility to the true and/or the good which is under debate in the public square. The authentic publisher has traditionally assumed, and still does assume, a full and overriding responsibility for not only the clarity of what is published but also the legitimacy of the motives being served by each book.

Lastly, a comparison between the cultural place of the scribe may be usefully compared to that of the publisher. The scribe is surely an agent of the author whether transcribing a book for his/her personal use or for a library. However, that transcription serves but limited ends—it can only transmit an idea or body of knowledge to a single or a handful of readers. By contrast, the publisher assumes a far different level of risk and the far larger costs of not only getting a manuscript into print but also establishing and maintaining long and constantly shifting channels of dissemination to distribute a book to as many readers as possible. By investing in these costly undertakings, he/she, together with other publishers, establishes a powerful network of minds all focused on an identical text—hence they are at the controls of a giant epistemological or knowledge-generating engine. Or to offer a different metaphor, the scribe may be likened to a single cultural neuron, the publisher, to a complex cultural network of nerves—in short, a brain. Hence, the contention of this writing that the culture of the West is unimaginable save as the consequence of the knowledge-generating engine of the printed book and the engineers who shape and drive it.

Turning now to a brief summary of the argument of this writing: The controlling principle in its structuring and exposition is that ideas singly and in symbiosis with larger bodies of related ideas initiate, guide, and maintain the human-made environment and govern substantial elements of human behavior, save those hardwired into the human genetic structure. The sum total of the human-made environment clearly includes all the ideas overtly embodied in the obvious physical objects of human manufacture; however, these are but one genera of the human-made environment. The all-encompassing totality of the human-made environment is here labeled culture. Culture includes all the symbolic systems of which the most obvious are language and mathematics. And these symbol systems structure and transmit all the other symbol systems defining people at any time—religion, philosophy, constitutional and political organizations, economic systems, legal systems, and science. To these bodies of abstract knowledge, the bodies of related practical knowledge shape, establishing institutions and structuring their functions, such as churches; families; nurturing the young and provision for education; political activities and the continuous struggle for power; trade, business, and banking and the continuing struggle for wealth: attorneys and courts to resolve the continuing differences between people; other social structures; technology, which largely governs the visible human-built environment; and, of course, the world of ideational reflection, debate, and their distribution are symbiotically attached. This complex of interactive ideas and knowledge are reflected in the making of books and other culture-dissemination instrumentalities.[1] Culture encompasses, in short, all the ideas motivating, shaping, and supporting a self-identifying group of people at any given time.

These ever-evolving bodies of ideas are continuously being formed and reformed along the lines of the epistemological principles articulated by the late twentieth-century philosopher Karl Popper. Throughout this text, Popper's terminology and principles of the evolution of knowledge have been repeatedly employed to form the explanatory skeleton of this history of the role of the book in Western culture. Popper holds that as problems emerge within a body of knowledge, abstract or in practice, the principle(s) evoking that problem is first falsified, i.e., proved to be somehow counterproductive. One or several creative minds thereupon propose new hypotheses that incorporate the values provided by the falsified principle(s) but remedies its (their) shortcoming(s). These hypotheses are debated as to likely outcomes or consequences. The one seeming most likely to resolve the problem is adopted and then tested in the context of the culture. If still unsolved by this new hypothesis, another is placed in its stead. In every case, the new hypotheses must be integrated into the existing bodies of knowledge, which in turn frequently compel the falsification of related ideas and the creation of new hypotheses to accommodate the new idea(s). In short, Popper developed, as he observed, the epistemological foundations of the commonplace "cut and try" methodology—or the venerable English practice of "muddling through." Using this powerful epistemological tool, the present writing seeks to explain the evolution of the bodies of knowledge developed in the West, which led to the cultural inheritance, which framed the culture of the West through the seventeenth century.

This approach was taken to lay bare the crucial hypothesis of the utterly pivotal and necessary role that Gutenberg's invention of printing and the printed book had in the epistemological shaping of the culture of the

West and the rapidity with which this culture was subsequently formed into what might be called the early-modern synthesis. The test cases of this hypothesis were the renascences of the eighth and twelfth centuries, both of which fell back to substantially more primitive cultural levels in the ninth and the fourteenth centuries and the succeeding centuries. The renascence of the fifteenth century was saved by Gutenberg's creation of the printed book. Through this agency, the fifteenth century renascence became the Renaissance, which proved to be the opening chapter in the remarkably culturally prolific period in the West engendered by the powerful knowledge-generating engine that crystallized around the printed book. (It must be noted again that this hypothesis simply follows the groundbreaking work of Elizabeth Eisenstein.) This transformative character was so because for the first time in humankind's history, a large number of trained minds spread widely across a major geographic area of a general cultural allegiance could read and debate an identical text. The result was a vast speeding up of the epistemological processes of culture falsification/creation/integration.

A number of compelling analyses/explanations have been proposed for the comparatively recent preeminence of Western culture and for the cultural hegemony that this Western cultural inheritance has fostered by the slow and commonly reluctant adoption by the other principal cultural groups. These various insightful analyses/explanations have all employed some particular Western cultural factor as the causal basis to account for this outcome. Thus several of these historians have employed factors of geography, natural resources, economics, technology, institutional (usually political) arrangements, private property rights, etc., as the animating cause of this preeminence and hegemony. The analysis/explanation of the preeminence of ideas advanced here does so simply on the basis of the fact that all of the explanatory factors noted above are themselves products of vast bodies of knowledge developed in the West. All were in turn the cultural products emerging out of a veritable sea of ideas all of which have passed through the lengthy, repeated, and difficult evolution of Popper's epistemological falsification/creation/integration paradigm. In short, ideas and the bodies of knowledge that incorporate ideas into interrelated bodies of knowledge are the drivers and shapers of culture. So the present history seeks to identify the principal ideas and briefly trace their emergence and evolution through the seventeenth century to explain the present worldwide preeminence of Western culture.

One of the basic characteristics of the West is a continuing intellectual curiosity about ideas. Associated with this curiosity is a willingness to understand and oftentimes to employ them in the practical business of trying to come to the truth of the nature and the world in which humankind lives. The continuing exercise of this pair encompasses the parallel understanding of the good and the associated ethical precepts. The West seemed never content, for any substantial lengths of time, to stand pat on a received canon of writings and weave convoluted variations on them as were the other three great cultures. Yes, the West always conceived of the Judeo-Christian Bible as a foundational writing, but repeatedly sought to augment or refine its meanings in new or alternative ways in a stochastic effort to finally plumb the mystery of the "why" of the universe, life, and how the latter must be lived. Nor was the West given simply to passively receiving new or alternative ideas from these other cultures but was actively involved in seeking out such concepts and precepts in particular eras—the renascences of the eighth, twelfth, and fifteenth centuries offering particularly apposite examples. It is almost as if concepts and precepts were playthings to the Western mind. But whatever the associated intellectual pleasure and fascination, there was always a serious intent underlying every one of these extrinsic acquisitions as there was in the intrinsic creation of new concepts and precepts. And to relate this epistemological curiosity and cultural experimentation to the principal theme of this history, all of this ideational vitality was worked out in and incorporated into books.

Curiosity, a hardwired characteristic of humankind but in the West raised to a cultural characteristic, was itself the product of a more basic foundational sense of the soundest and most productive way of coming to grips with the world. This basic epistemological axiom was that of ordered freedom—of inquiry, of falsification, of the creation of alternative hypotheses, of the testing of alternative hypotheses, etc. There was always an astonishingly productive impulse in the continuing tension between the absolute dictates with respect to the true and the good ordained by the Judeo–Christian faith-based body of religious knowledge concepts and ethical precepts and the Greek body of reason-based knowledge concepts and ethical precepts. Both of these integrated bodies of knowledge/ethics, of course, were from early in the present era incorporated into the fundamental modes of understanding utilized in the West. This initial job of synthesis was largely the work of the church fathers, most notably St. Augustine. Repeated efforts of synthesis were reiterated by subsequent churchmen or augmented by introductions of Greek philosophical tenets from Islam (St. Thomas Aquinas) and the flood from Constantinople (most notably variant forms of Neoplatonism).

Epilogue

The claims of ordered cultural freedom were repeatedly advanced over the centuries, but with increasing frequency beginning in the fourteenth century, reaching something of a climax in England of the seventeenth century. All of these claims for freedom were coupled with the sincere effort to establish a final resolution or true synthesis of the joint and equal claims of faith and reason. Long windows of opportunity for particularly venturesome individuals to propose or seek out alternative cultural options opened in this continuing, if intermittent, current of freedom. So neither the periodic bursts of culture-making initiatives nor the repeated plumbing of other cultures that set the culture of the West aside from the three other great cultural traditions of the world can be conceived absent a pervasive ambience of ordered freedom incorporating basic ethical and cognitive foundations.

But in these episodes of free, intense culture building, when the knowledge-generating engine was working at a goodly pace, an even more fundamental pair of closely associated factors was constantly correcting the course of free epistemological falsification/creation/integration. These paired functions were, and are, almost visceral or existential factors. The first of these is the continuing thirst for cognitive or conceptual understanding—for getting to the roots of true knowledge. The second is the fully parallel thirst for comprehending true goodness—for getting to the roots of a true ethics. In short, the free culture-building exercise is the primal expression of the eternal search for truth and standards of ethical judgment—ultimately meaning. It is the West that has been, to our times, the foremost exemplar of the search for fully and firmly defensible principles to make whole the twin deficiencies in intellectual understanding and ethical conduct that we all perceive in our primitive, limited beings, but seldom acknowledge. And it was the book people who were the patrons and/or transmission belt that facilitated these outcomes. Freedom in the falsification/generation/integration of ideas is of no avail absent widespread dissemination of ideas generated in that environment.

A Further Note to Publishers, Booksellers, Librarians, and Others Associated with the Book Trade

In seeking to limn out the tremendous culture-building power of the knowledge-generating engine at the heart of which is the printed book, I had the colleagues in my profession very much in mind. I wished to sensitize, perhaps for the first time, those who entered one of the professions involved in the serious and authentic book trade to the remarkable cultural responsibility, which they volunteered to shoulder when so doing. Underlying this exercise is the hope that it will reawaken or fortify their moral commitment to deal only in the ideas, hence books, aimed at advancing the effort to more closely approach the true and the good and to do so in a responsible way. We all, when being fully candid, well recognize the guileful pleading of far too many books pretending to be serious and authentic contributions to the stock of knowledge and the common cultural heritage which are, in point of fact, merely disguised exercises in special-interest pleading. Such publishing/bookselling exercises only disfigure and sully the magnificent cultural heritage, which we have inherited from our responsible and dedicated predecessors. It is hoped that this writing will energize a similar sense of responsibility to the highest standards of truth and goodness seeking among the present-day book people.

Note

1. Greenfield, 2004, 288–99.

Bibliography

Abel, Richard. "IHHBIO: A Response to Rick Anderson in ATG, Nov. 2002." *Against the Grain* 15 (2003): 3.
Allen, Michael J. B. *Plato's Third Eye: Studies in Marsilio Ficino's Metaphysics and Its Sources*. Aldershot: Variorum, 1995.
Arien, Roger, and Marjorie Grene. "Ideas in Before Descartes." *Journal of the History of Ideas* 56 (1995): 87–106.
Artz, Frederick B. *The Mind of the Middle Ages: An Historical Survey, AD 200–1500*, 3rd rev. ed. Chicago, IL: University of Chicago Press, 1980.
Ashtor, Eliyaha. *Technology, Industry, and Trade: The Levant versus Europe, 1250–1500*. London: Ashgate Variorum, 1992.
Ashworth, E. J. "'Do Words Signify Ideas or Things?' The Scholastic Sources of Locke's Theory of Language." *Journal of the History of Philosophy* 19 (1981): 299–326.
Aston, Margaret. *The Fifteenth Century: The Prospect of Europe*. New York: W. W. Norton. Originally published in 1968.
Ault, W. O. *Open-Field Farming in Medieval England: A Study of Village By-Laws*. New York: Barnes & Noble, 1972.
Baron, Hans. *The Crisis of the Early Italian Renaissance: Civic Humanism and Republican Liberty in an Age of Classicism and Tyranny*. Princeton, NJ: Princeton University Press, 1966.
Bartlett, Robert. *The Making of Europe: Conquest, Colonization, and Cultural Change, 950–1350*. Princeton, NJ: Princeton University Press, 1993.
Barzun, Jacques. *From Dawn to Decadence: 500 Years of Western Cultural Life, 1500 to the Present*. New York: Harper/Collins, 2000.
Beddie, James Stuart. "The Ancient Classics in the Medieval Libraries." *Speculum* 5 (1930): 3–20.
Benson, Robert L., and Giles Constable. "Introduction." In *Renaissance and Renewal in the Twelfth Century*, edited by Robert L. Benson and Giles Constable with Carol D. Lanham. Cambridge, MA: Harvard University Press, 1982.
Benson, Robert L., Giles Constable with Carol D. Lanham, eds. *Renaissance and Renewal in the Twelfth Century*. Cambridge, MA: Harvard University Press, 1982.
Berg, Maxine, and Kristine Bruland. "Culture, Institutions, and Technological Transitions." In *Technological Revolutions in Europe: Historical*

Perspectives, edited by Maxine Berg and Kristine Bruland. Cheltenham: Edward Elgar, 1998.
Bloch, Marc. *Feudal Society*, translated by L. A. Manyon. Chicago, IL: University of Chicago Press.
Bolgar, R. R. *The Classical Heritage and Its Beneficiaries: From the Carolingian Age to the Renaissance*, reprint. New York: Harper & Row, 1954.
———. *Classical Influences on European Culture, A.D. 500–1500*. Cambridge: Cambridge University Press, 1971.
———. *Classical Influences on European Culture, A.D. 1500–1700*. Cambridge: Cambridge University Press, 1976.
Bouwsma, William J. *The Waning of the Renaissance, 1550–1640*. New Haven, CT: Yale University Press, 2000.
Braudel, Fernand. *Civilization and Capitalism, 15th–18th Century*, 3 vols. New York: Harper, 1984.
Bredsdorff, Thomas. "Lovejoy's Idea of 'Idea'." *New Literary History* 8 (1977): 195–211.
Breen, Quirius. "Giovanni Pico della Mirandola on the Conflict of Philosophy and Rhetoric." *Journal of the History of Ideas* 12 (1952): 384–416.
Brown, Lloyd A. *The Story of Maps*. Boston, MA: Little, Brown, 1950.
Burke, Peter. *A Social History of Knowledge: From Gutenberg to Diderot*. Cambridge: Cambridge University Press, 2000.
Butler, Pierce. *The Origins of Printing in Europe*. Chicago, IL: University of Chicago Press, 1940.
Cantor, Norman. *Civilization of the Middle Ages*, rev. and exp. ed. New York: HarperCollins, 1993.
Carter, T. F., and C. L. Goodrich. *The Invention of Printing and Its Spread Westward*. New York: Ronald Press, 1955.
Carter, John, and Percy Muir. *Printing and the Mind of Man: A Descriptive Catalogue Illustrating the Impact of Print on the Evolution of Western Civilization During Five Centuries*. London: Cassell, New York: Holt, Rinehart and Winston, 1967.
Cassirer, Ernst. "Giovanni Pico della Mirandola; a Study in the History of Renaissance ideas." *Journal of the History of Ideas* 3, nos. 2 & 3 (1942): 123–44 & 319–46.
———. *The Individual and the Cosmos in Renaissance Philosophy*, translated by Mario Domandi, reprint 2000. Mineola, NY: Dover, 1963.
Cavallo, Guglielmo, and Roger Chartier. *A History of Reading in the West*, translated by Lydia G. Cochrane. Cambridge, UK: Polity Press, 1999.
Christ, Karl. *The Handbook of Medieval Library History*, revised by Anton Kern, translated and edited by Theophile M. Otto from *Handbuch der Bibliothekswesenschaft,* Dritten Band; *Geshicte der Bibliotheken*. Metuchen, NJ: Scarecrow Press, 1984.
Clark, James M. *The Abbey of St. Gall as a Centre of Literature and Art*. Cambridge: Cambridge University Press, 1927.
Clark, Sir George. *Early Modern Europe: From About 1450 to About 1720*, 2nd ed. Oxford: Oxford University Press, 1966.

Clark, Gregory. "The Political Foundations of Modern Economic Growth: England, 1540–1800." *Journal of Interdisciplinary History* 36, no. 4 (1996): 563–88.

———. "Common Sense: Common Property Rights, Efficiency, and Institutional Change." *Journal of Economic History* 58, no. 1 (1998): 73–102.

Clark, Gregory, Michael Huberman, and Peter H. Lindert. "A British Food Puzzle, 1770–1850." *Economic History Review* 48, no. 2 (1995): 215–37.

Colish, Marcia L. *Medieval Foundations of the Western Intellectual Tradition, 400–1400*. New Haven, CT: Yale University Press, 1997.

Collinson, Patrick. *The Reformation: A History*. New York: Modern Library, 2004.

Concannon, R. F. G. "The Third Enemy: The Role of Epidemics in the Thirty Years War." *Journal of World History* 7, no. 10 (1967): 500–11.

Cranz, F. Edward. *Nicholas of Cusa and the Renaissance*, edited by Thomas Izbicke and Gerald Christenson. Aldershot: Ashgate, 2000.

Crosby, Alfred W. *The Measure of Reality: Quantification and Western Society, 1250–1600*. Cambridge: Cambridge University Press, 1997.

De Sola Price, Derek. "The Book as a Scientific Instrument." *Science* 158 (1967): 102–04.

De Sota, Hernando. *The Mystery of Capital: Why Capitalism Triumphs in the West and Fails Everywhere Else*. New York: Basic Books, 2000.

DeMolen, Richard L., ed. *The Meaning of the Renaissance and Reformation*. Boston, MA: Houghton-Mifflin, 1974.

Derry, T. K., and Trevor I. Williams. *A Short History of Technology: From the Earliest Times to A.D. 1900*. Oxford: Oxford University Press, 1961.

DeVries, Kelly. *Guns and Man in Medieval Europe, 1200–1500: Studies in Military History and Technology*. Aldershot: Ashgate Variorum, 2002.

Diamond, Jared. *Guns, Germs, and Steel: The Fates of Human Societies*. New York: W. W. Norton, 1997.

Duckett, Eleanor Shipley. *Alcuin, A Friend of Charlemagne: His World and His Work*. New York: MacMillan, 1951.

———. *The Gateway to the Middle Ages: Monasticism*. Ann Arbor: University of Michigan Press, 1988.

Eisenstein, Elizabeth L. *The Printing Press as an Agent of Change: Communications and Cultural Transformations in Early-Modern Europe*, vols. 1 & 2. Cambridge: Cambridge University Press, 1979.

Elmer, Peter. *The Renaissance in Europe: A Cultural Enquiry: The Challenge to Authority*. New Haven, CT: Yale University Press, 2000.

Fernandez-Armesto, Felipe. *Civilization: Culture, Ambition and the Transformation of Nature*. New York: Free Press, 2001.

Finlay, Robert. "China, the West, and World History in Joseph Needham's *Science and Civilization in China*." *Journal of World History* 11, no. 2 (2000): 265–303.

Fischer, David. "Chronic Inflation: The Long View." *The Journal of the Institute for Socioeconomic Studies* 5 (1980): 82–103.

———. *The Great Wave: Price Revolutions and the Rhythm of History*. New York: Oxford University Press, 1996.

Fischoff, Ephraim. "The Protestant Ethic and the Spirit of Capitalism." *Social Research* 11 (1944): 53–77.
Fletcher, Richard. *Moorish Spain*. New York: Henry Holt, 1992.
Flint, Valerie. *Ideas in the Medieval West: Texts and Their Contexts*. London: Ashgate Variorum Reprints, 1988.
Foster, M. B. "The Christian Doctrine of Creation and the Rise of Modern Natural Science." *Mind* 43 (1934): 446–68.
———. "Christian Theology and Modern Science of Nature." *Mind* 44 (1935): 439–66.
———. "Christian Theology and Modern Science of Nature (II)." *Mind* 45 (1936): 1–27.
Garraty, John A., and Peter Gay. *The Columbia History of the World*. New York: Harper & Row, 1972.
Gatti, Hilary. *Renaissance Drama and Knowledge: Giordano Bruno in England*. London: Routledge, 1989.
———. *Giordano Bruno: Philosopher, Man of the Renaissance*, edited by Hilary Gatti. Aldershot: Ashgate, 2002.
Gilson, Étienne. *History of Christian Philosophy in the Middle Ages*. New York: Random House, 1955.
Girard, René. *Violence and the Sacred*, translated by Patrick Gregory. Baltimore, MD: Johns Hopkins University Press, 1977.
Goldschmitt, E. Ph. *Medieval Texts and Their First Appearance in Print*. London: Bibliographical Society, 1943.
Goldstone, Jack A. "Cultural Orthodoxy, Risk, and Innovation: The Divergence of East and West in the Early Modern World." *Sociological Theory* 5, Fall (1987): 119–35.
Gordon-Bournique, Gladys. "A.O. Lovejoy and the History of Ideas." *Journal of the History of Ideas* 48, no. 2 (1987): 207–10.
Grafton, Anthony T. "Joseph Scaliger and Historical Chronology: The Rise and Fall of a Discipline." *History and Theory* 14 (1975): 156–85.
———. *Bring Out Your Dead: The Past as Revolution*. Cambridge, MA: Harvard University Press, 2001.
———. "Dating History: The Renaissance and the Reformation of Chronology." *Daedalus*, Spring (2003): 74–84.
Grant, Edward. *The Foundations of Modern Science in the Middle Ages*. Cambridge: Cambridge University Press, 1996.
———. *God and Reason in the Middle Ages*. Cambridge: Cambridge University Press, 2001.
Greenfield, Liah. "A New paradigm for the Social Sciences?" *Critical Review* 16, nos. 2 & 3 (2004): 288–322.
Greenslade, S. L. *The Cambridge History of the Bible: The West from the Reformation to the Present Day*. Cambridge: Cambridge University Press, 1963.
Greif, Avner. "Cultural Beliefs and the Organization of Society: A Historical and Theoretical Reflection on Collectivist and Individualist Societies." *The Journal of Political Economy* 102, no. 5 (1994): 912–50.

Grendler, Paul F. *Books and Schools in the Italian Renaissance*. Aldershot: Ashgate Variorum, 1995.

Grousset, René. *The Empire of the Steppes: A History of Central Asia*, translated by Naomi Walford. New Brunswick, NJ: Rutgers University Press, 1970.

Guy, Donna J. "The Morality of Economic History and the Immorality of Imperialism." *American Historical Review* 104 (October 1999): 1247–52.

Hale, John. *The Civilization of Europe in the Renaissance*. New York: Atheneum, 1994.

Hall, A. Rupert. *The Scientific Revolution, 1500–1800: The Formation of the Modern Scientific Attitude*. Boston, MA: Beacon Press, 1966.

Hanson, Victor Davis. *Carnage and Culture: Landmark Battles in the Rise of Western Power*. New York: Doubleday, 2001.

Harbison, E. Harris. *The Christian Scholar in the Age of the Reformation*. New York: Charles Scribner's Sons, 1956.

Haskins, Charles Homer. *Studies in the History of Medieval Science*. Reprint ed. 1960. New York: Frederick Ungar Publishing, 1924.

———. *The Renaissance of the Twelfth Century*. New York: Meridian Books, 1957.

Hendricks, Donald. "Profitless Printing: Publication of the Polyglots." *The Journal of Library History* 2 (1967): 98–116.

Herlihy, David. "The Economy of Traditional Europe" *The Journal of Economic History* 31 (1971): 153–64.

Himmelfarb, Gertrude. *The Roads to Modernity: The British, French, and American Enlightenments*. New York: A.A. Knopf, 2004.

Himmelmans, Nikolas. *Reading Greek Art: Essays by Nikolas Himmelman*, selected by Hugo Meyer, edited by William Childs. Princeton, NJ: Princeton University Press, 1998.

Hirsch, Rudolph. *Printing, Selling and Reading: 1450–1550*. Wiesbaden, Germany: Otto Harrrasowitz, 1967.

Holborn, Louise W. "Printing and the Growth of a Protestant Movement in Germany from 1517 to 1524." *Church History* 11 (1942): 12–137.

Holmes, Urban T. "The Idea of a Twelfth Century Renaissance." *Speculum* 26 (1951): 643–51.

Holmes, George, ed. *Oxford History of Italy*. Oxford: Oxford University Press, 1997.

Hucker, Charles O. *China's Imperial Past: An Introduction to Chinese History and Culture*. Stanford: Stanford University Press, 1975.

Hudson, Winthrop S. "Mystical Religion in the Puritan Commonwealth." *Journal of Religion* 28 (1948): 51–56.

Huizinga, Johan. *The Autumn of the Middle Ages*, translated by Rodney J. Payton and Ulrich Mammitzch. Chicago, IL: University of Chicago Press, 1966.

Hundert, Edward. "D'Alembert's Dream and the Utility of the Humanities." *Critical Review* 15, nos. 3 & 4 (2003): 459–72.

Hunter, Michael. "Alchemy, Magic and Moralism in the Thought of Robert Boyle." *The British Journal for the History of Science* 23, no. 79 (1990): 387–410.
Ing, Janet Thompson. *Johann Gutenberg and His Bible: A Historical Study*. New York: Typophiles, 1998.
Jackson, Sydney L. "Printed Books and the Mass Mind: Some Sixteenth-Century Views." *Libri* 18, no. 1 (1968): 35–50.
Jacob, Margaret C. "The Cultural Foundations of Early Industrialization: A Project." In *Technological Revolutions in Europe: Historical Perspectives*, edited by Maxine Berg and Kristine Bruland. Cheltenham, UK: Edward Elgar, 1998.
Jones, Leslie W. "The Influence of Cassiodorus on Medieval Culture." *Speculum* 20 (1945): 433–42.
———. "Further Notes Concerning Cassiodorus' Influence on Medieval Culture." *Speculum* 22 (1947): 254–56.
Kamen, Henry. *Empire: How Spain Became a World Power, 1492–1763*. New York: HarperCollins, 2003.
Kantorowicz, Ernest H. *The King's Two Bodies: A Study in Mediaeval Political Theology*. Princeton, NJ: Princeton University Press, 1957.
Kapr, Albert. *Johann Gutenberg: The Man and His Invention*, translated by Douglas Martin. Aldershot: Scolar Press, 1996.
Kearney, Hugh F. "Puritanism, Capitalism, and the Scientific Revolution. *Past and Present* 28 (1964), 81–101.
Keegan, John. *A History of Warfare*. New York: A.A. Knopf, 1994.
Kekevich, Lucille, ed. *Impact of Humanism*. In *The Renaissance in Europe: A Cultural Inquiry*, series. New Haven, CT: Yale University Press, 2000.
Kelley, Donald R. "What is Happening to the History of Ideas." *Journal of the History of Ideas* 51, no. 1 (1990): 3–25.
———. "The Old Cultural History." *History of the Human Sciences* 9, no. 3 (1996): 101–26.
———. "Eclecticism and the History of Ideas." *Journal of the History of Ideas* 62, no. 4 (2001): 577–92.
———. *The Descent of Ideas: The History of Intellectual History*. Aldershot: Ashgate, 2002a.
———. "Intellectual History and Cultural History: The Inside and Outside." *History of the Human Sciences* 1115, no. 2 (2002b): 1–19.
Kelly, Davis R. *Foundations of Modern Historical Scholarship*. New York: Columbia University Press, 1970.
Kenney, F. J. *The Classical Text: Aspects of Editing in the Age of the Printed Book*. Berkeley: University of California Press, 1974.
Kibre, Pearl. "The Intellectual Interests Reflected in Libraries of the Fourteenth and Fifteenth Centuries." *Journal of the History of Ideas* 7, no. 3 (1946): 257–97.
Kline, Morris. *Mathematical Thought from Ancient to Modern Times*. New York: Oxford University Press, 1972.
Knowles, David. *The Evolution of Medieval Thought*. New York: Oxford University Press, 1962.

Bibliography 177

Kristeller, Paul Oscar. *Renaissance Thought: The Classic, Scholastic, and Humanist Strains*. New York: Harper Torchbooks, 1961.

Kuhn, Thomas S. *The Copernican Revolution: Planetary Astronomy in the Development of Western Thought*. Cambridge, MA: Harvard University Press, 1957.

Kurth, James. "The Protestant Deformation and American Foreign Policy." *Orbis* 42, no. 2 (1998): 221–39.

Ladurie, Emmanuel LeRoy. *Times of Feast, Times of Famine: A History of Climate Since the Year 1000*. New York: Doubleday, 1971.

Laistner, M. L. W. *Thought and Letters in Western Europe, AD 500–900*, rev. ed. Ithaca, NY: Cornell University Press, 1957.

Lal, Deepak. *Unintended Consequences: The Impact of Factor Endowments, Culture, and Politics on Long-Run Economic Performance*. Cambridge: Cambridge University Press, 1998.

Lampe, G. W. H., ed. *The Cambridge History of the Bible: Volume II; The Wets from the Fathers to the Reformation*. Cambridge: Cambridge University Press, 1969.

Landes, David S. "East is East and West is West." In *Technological Revolutions in Europe: Historical Perspectives*, edited by Maxine Berg and Kristine Bruland. Cheltenham, UK: Edward Elgar, 1998.

———. *The Wealth and Poverty of Nations: Why Some Are So Rich and Some So Poor*. New York: W. W. Norton, 1999.

Lang, Paul Henry. *Music in Western Civilization*. New York: W. W. Norton, 1941.

Langdon, John. *Horses, Oxen and Technological Innovation: The Using of Draught Animals in English Farming, 1066 to 1570*. Cambridge: Cambridge University Press, 1986.

Lasky, Melvin J. *Utopia and Revolution: On the Origins of a Metaphor*, reprint ed. New Brunswick, NJ: Transaction Publishers, 1976.

Lerner, Fred. *The Story of Libraries: From the Invention of Writing to the Computer Age*. New York: Continuum, 1998.

Levi, Anthony. *Renaissance and Reformation: The Intellectual Genesis*. New Haven, CT: Yale University Press, 2002.

Lindberg, David C. *The Beginnings of Western Science: The European Scientific Tradition in Philosophy, Religion, and Institutional Context, 600BC to AD 1450*. Chicago, IL: University of Chicago Press, 1992.

Lindberg, David C., and Robert S. Westerman. *Reappraisals of the Scientific Revolution*. Cambridge: Cambridge University Press, 1990.

Lovejoy, Arthur O. "Reflections on the History of Ideas." *Journal of the History of Ideas* 1, no. 1 (1940): 3–23.

———. *The Great Chain of Being: A Study of the History of an Idea*. Cambridge, MA: Harvard University Press, 1964.

Lynch, Joseph H. *The Medieval Church: A Brief History*. New York: Longman, 1992.

MacMullen, Ramsay. *Christianity and Paganism in the Forth to Eighth Centuries*. New Haven, CT: Yale University Press, 1997.

Maenchen-Helfen, Otto J. *The World of the Huns: Studies in Their History and Culture*. Berkeley: University of California Press, 1973.

Mahorney, Edward P. "Lovejoy and the Hierarchy of Being." *Journal of the History of Ideas* 48, no. 2 (1987): 211–30.
Man, John. *Gutenberg: How One Man Remade the World of Words*. New York: John Wiley & Sons, 2002.
Mandelbaum, Maurice. "The History of Ideas, Intellectual History and the History of Philosophy." *History and Theory* 5 (1965): 33–66.
Manuel, Frank E. "Lovejoy Revisited." *Daedalus* 116, no. 2 (1987): 126–31.
Manuel, Frank E., and Fritzie P. Manuel. *Utopian Thought in the Western World*. Cambridge, MA: Harvard University Press, 1979.
Marcham, Frederick George. *A History of England*. New York: MacMillan, 1937.
Mattingly, Garrett. "Machiavelli's Prince: Political Science or Political Satire?" *American Scholar* 27 (1958): 482–91.
McGuire, J. E., and P. M. Rattansi. "Newton and the Pipes of Pan." *Notes and Records of the Royal Society of London* 21 (1966): 108–43.
McKitterick, Rosamund. *The Carolingians and the Written Word*. Cambridge: Cambridge University Press, 1989.
McLean, Antonia. *Humanism and the Rise of Science in Tudor England*. New York: Neale Watson, Academic, 1972.
McNeill, William H. *The Rise of the West: A History of the Human Community*. Chicago, IL: University of Chicago Press, 1963.
———. *Plagues and People*. New York: Anchor Books, 1977.
McNeill, J. R., and William H. McNeill. *The Human Web: A Bird's-Eye View of World History*. New York: W. W. Norton, 2003.
Mokyr, Joel. *The Lever of Riches: Technological Creativity and Economic Progress*. New York: Oxford University Press, 1990.
———. "Cardwell's Law and the Political Economy of Technological Progress." *Research Policy* 23 (1994): 561–74.
———. "Induced Technical Innovation and Medical History: An Evolutionary Approach." *Journal of Evolutionary Economics* 8 (1998a): 119–37.
———. "The Political Economy of Technological Change: Resistance and Innovation in Economic History." In *Technological Revolutions in Europe: Historical Perspectives*, edited by Maxine Berg and Kristine Bruland. Cheltenham, UK: Edward Elgar, 1998b.
———. "Editor's Introduction: The New Economic History and the Industrial Revolution." In *The British Industrial Revolution: An Economic Perspective*, edited by Joel Mokyr, 2nd ed. Boulder, CO: Westview Press, 1999a.
———. "Eurocentricity Triumphant." *American Historical Review* 104 (October 1999b): 1241–46.
———. "Evolutionary Phenomena in Technology Change." In *Technological Innovation as an Evolutionary Process*, edited by John Ziman. Cambridge: Cambridge University Press, 2000a.
———. "Knowledge, Technology, and Economic Growth during the Industrial Revolution." In *Productivity, Technology, and Economic Growth*, edited by Bart van Ark, Simmel K. Kuipers, and Gerard H. Kuper. Boston, MA: Kluwer Academic Publishers, 2000b.

---. *The Gifts of Athena: Historical Origins of the Knowledge Economy.* Princeton, NJ: Princeton University Press, 2002.

Momigliano, Arnoldo. "Ancient History and the Antiquarian." *Journal of the Warburg and Courtauld Institutes* 13 (1950): 285–315.

Mooney, Michael. *Vico in the Tradition of Rhetoric.* Princeton, NJ: Princeton University Press, 1985.

More, Louis Trenchard. "Boyle as Alchemist." *Journal of the History of Ideas* 2, no. 1 (1941): 61–76.

Nauert, Charles G., Jr. "The Clash of Humanists and Scholastics: An Approach to Pre-Reformation Controversies." *Sixteenth Century Journal* 4, no. 1 (1973): 1–18.

Needham, Joseph. *Science and Civilization in China*, vols. 1–7, pt. 1. Cambridge: Cambridge University Press, 1954–1998.

Nelson, Richard. "Selection Criteria and Selection Processes in Cultural Evolution Theories." In *Technological Innovation as an Evolutionary Process*, edited by John Ziman. Cambridge: Cambridge University Press, 2000.

North, Douglas C., and Barry R. Weingast. "Constitutions and Commitments: The Evolution of Institutions Governing Public Choice in Seventeenth-Century England." *Journal of Economic History* 49, no. 4 (1989): 803–31.

Oakley, Francis. "Lovejoy's Unexplored Option." *Journal of the History of Ideas* 48, no. 2 (1987): 231–45.

O'Leary, De Lacy. *Arabic Thought and Its Place in History.* London: Routledge & Kegan Paul, 1939.

Olsen, Mancur. *The Rise and Decline of Nations: Economic Growth, Stagflation, and Social Rigidities.* New Haven, CT: Yale University Press, 1982.

Olsen, Margaret J., ed. *Rethinking the Scientific Revolution.* Cambridge: Cambridge University Press, 2000.

Ovitt, George, Jr. *The Restoration of Perfection: Labor and Technology in Medieval Culture.* New Brunswick, NJ: Rutgers University Press, 1987.

Pagel, Walter. "Religious Motives in the Medical Biology of the XVIIth Century." *Bulletin of the Institute of the History of Medicine* 3, no. 2 (1935): 97–128.

---. *Paracelsus: An Introduction to Philosophical Medicine in the Era of the Renaissance.* Basel: S. Karger, 1958.

Panofsky, Erwin, and Fritz Saxl. "Classical Mythology in Medieval Art." *Metropolitan Museum Studies* 4 (1932–1933): 228–80.

Piaia, Gregorio. "Brucker versus Rorty? On the Models of the Historiography of Philosophy." *British Journal for the History of Philosophy* 9, no. 1 (2001): 69–81.

Pirenne, Henri. *Economic and Social History of Medieval Europe*, translated by I. E. Clegg. New York: Harcourt, Brace, 1937.

---. *Mohammed and Charlemagne.* London: George Allen & Unwin, 1939.

---. *A History of Europe from the Invasions to the XVI Century*, translated by Bernard Miall. New York: University Books, 1956.

Popper, Karl. *The Poverty of Historicism*, corr. ed. New York: Harper & Row, 1944.
——. *The Open Society and Its Enemies*, 5th ed. Princeton, NJ: Princeton University Press, 1966.
——. *Objective Knowledge: An Evolutionary Approach*, rev. ed. Oxford, UK: Clarendon Press, 1979.
——. *The Logic of Scientific Discovery*, 10th ed. London: Hutchinson, 1980.
——. *Conjectures and Refutations: The Growth of Scientific Knowledge*, 5th ed. London: Routledge, 1989.
Previté-Orton, C. W. *The Shorter Cambridge Medieval History*, 2 vols. Cambridge: Cambridge University Press, 1952.
Principe, Lawrence M. "The Alchemies of Robert Boyle and Isaac Newton: Alternative Approaches and Divergent Deployments." In *Rethinking the Scientific Revolution*, edited by Margaret J. Osler. Cambridge: Cambridge University Press, 2000.
Procacci, Giuliano. *History of the Italian People*. New York: Harper & Row, 1970.
Rachun, Ilan. "The Meaning of 'Revolution' in the English Revolution (1648–1660)." *Journal of the History of Ideas* 56, no. 2 (1995): 195–215.
Randles, W. G. L. *Geography, Cartography, and Nautical Science in the Renaissance: The Impact of the Great Discoveries*. Aldershot: Ashgate Variorum, 2000.
Rattansi, P. M. "Paracelsus and the Puritan Revolution." *Ambix; The Journal of the Society for the Study of Alchemy and Early Chemistry*, 11 (1963): 24–32.
Reynolds, Robert L. *Europe Emerges: Transition Toward an Industrial World-Wide Society, 600–1750*. Madison: University of Wisconsin Press, 1961.
Reynolds, L. D., and N. G. Wilson. *Scribes and Scholars: A Guide to the Transmission of Greek and Latin Literature*. Oxford: Oxford University Press, 1975.
Robb, Theodore K. "Religion and the Rise of Science." *Past and Present* 31 (1965): 110–26.
Roll, Johannes. "A Crayfish in Subiaco: A Hint of Nicholas of Cusa's Involvement in Early Printing." *The Library* 16, no. 2 (1994): 135–40.
Rose, Paul Lawrence. "Humanist Culture and Renaissance Mathematics." *Studies in the Renaissance* 20 (1973): 46–105.
Rosenberg, Nathan, Ralph Landau, and David Mowrey, eds. *Technology and the Wealth of Nations*. Stanford: Stanford University Press, 1992.
Rossi, Paolo. *Philosophy, Technology, and the Arts in the Early Modern Era*. New York: Harper, 1970.
Rostenberg, Leona. *Literary, Political, Scientific, and Legal Publishing, Printing, and Bookselling in England, 1551–1700*. New York: Burt Franklin, 1965.
Rowland, Ingrid D. *The Culture of the High Renaissance: Ancients and Moderns in Sixteenth Century Rome*. Cambridge: Cambridge University Press, 1999.

Bibliography

Runciman, Steven. *The Medieval Manichee: A Study of the Christian Dualist Heresy.* Cambridge: Cambridge University Press, 1947.

Sarton, George. "The Scientific Literature Transmitted through the Incunables." *Osiris* 5 (1938): 43–227.

———. *The Appreciation of Ancient and Medieval Science During the Renaissance (1450–1600)*, 2nd printing. Philadelphia: University of Pennsylvania Press, 1955.

Scammel, G. V. "The New Worlds and Europe in the Sixteenth Century." *The Historical Journal* 12, no. 3 (1969): 389–412.

———. *Ships, Oceans and Empire: Studies in European Maritime and Colonial History, 1400–1730.* Aldershot: Ashgate Variorum, 1995.

Schlipp, Paul Arthur, ed. *The Philosophy of Karl Popper*, 2 vols. LaSalle, IL: Opencourt Publisher, 1974.

Schmitt, Charles B. "Perennial Philosophy from Agostino to Leibniz." *The Journal of the History of Ideas* 27 (1966): 505–32.

Schottenloher, Karl. *Books and the Western World: A Cultural History.* Jefferson, NC: McFarland, 1989. Translation of *Bücher bewegten die Welt: Eine Kulturgeschichte des Buches*, German ed., by William Douglas and Irmgard H. Wolfe. Stuttgart: Hiersemann, 1968.

Schrecker, Paul. *Work and History: An Essay on the Structure of Civilization.* Princeton, NJ: Princeton University Press, 1948.

Southern, R. W. *The Making of the Middle Ages.* New Haven, CT: Yale University Press, 1953.

Sowell, Thomas. *Conquests and Cultures: An International History.* New York: Basic Books, 1998.

Sprenger, Kai-Michael. "Voluntus tamen quod expressio fiat ante finem mensis Maii presentiis: Sollte Gutenberg 1452 im Auftrag Nicholas von Kues' Ablassbriefe drucken?" *Gutenberg Jahrbuch*, Mainz (2000): 42–57.

Steele, Robert. 1903–07, "What Fifteenth Century Books Are About." *The Library* 4 (October 1903): 337–54; 5 (October 1904): 337–58; 6 (January 1905):137–55; 8 (July 1907): 225–38.

Stokes, Gale. "The Fates if Human Societies: A Review of Recent Macrohistories." *American Historical Review* 106 (April 2001): 508–25.

Stoye, John. *Europe Unfolding: 1648–1688*, 2nd ed. Oxford, UK: Blackwell Publishing, 2000.

Strayer, Joseph R. *Western Europe in the Middle Ages.* New York: Appleton-Century-Crofts, 1955.

———. *On the Medieval Origins of the Modern State.* Princeton, NJ: Princeton University Press, 1970.

Temin, Peter. "Is It Kosher to Talk About Culture?" *The Journal of Economic History* 57, no. 2 (1997): 267–87.

Thomas, Keith. *Religion and the Decline of Magic: Studies of Magic and Popular Beliefs in Sixteenth and Seventeenth Century England.* London: Weidenfeld & Nicholson, 1971.

Thompson, James Westfall. *The Medieval Library.* New York: Hafner Publishing, 1957. Reprint of 1939 ed., Chicago: University of Chicago Graduate Library School.

Tilley, Charles. "A Grand Tour of Exotic Lands." *American Historical Review* 104 (October 1999): 1253–57.
Tuchman, Barbara W. *A Distant Mirror: The Calamitous 14th Century*. New York: Ballantine Books, 1978.
van Ark, Bart, Simon K. Kuipers, and Gerard H. Kuper. "Introduction." In *Productivity, Technology, and Economic Growth*, edited by Bart van Ark, Simon K. Kuipers, and Gerard H. Kuper. Boston, MA: Kluwer Academic Publishers, 2000.
van Bath, B. H. Slicher. *The Agrarian History of Western Europe: A.D. 500–1850*. Translation of *De agarische gescheidenis van West-Europa (500–1850)*, by Olive Ordish. London: Edward Arnold, 1963.
van Gelder, H. A. Enno. *The Two Reformations in the Sixteenth Century: A Study of the Religious Aspects and Consequences of the Renaissance and Humanism*. The Hague, The Netherlands: Nijhoff, 1964.
Veitch, John M. "Repudiations and Confiscations by the Medieval State." *Journal of Economic History* 46, no. 1 (1986): 31–36.
Walker, D. P. "The Prisca Theologia in France." *Journal of the Warburg and Courtauld Institutes* 17, no. 3 & 4 (1954): 204–59.
Watanabe, Morimichi. *Concord and Reform: Nicholas of Cusa and Legal and Political Thought in the Fifteenth Century*, edited by Thomas M. Isbicki and Gerald Christianson. Aldershot: Ashgate, 2001.
Weaver, Richard M. *Ideas Have Consequences*. Chicago, IL: University of Chicago Press, 1948.
Weber, David J. *The Spanish Frontier in North America*. New Have, CT: Yale University Press, 1992.
Weber, Max. *The Spirit of Capitalism and the Protestant Ethic*. New York: Unwin Hyman, 1930.
Weinberg, Philip P. *Dictionary of the History of Ideas*, 4 vols. New York: Charles Scribner's Sons, 1973.
Weitzman, Martin L. "Hybridizing Growth Theory." *The American Economic Review* 86, no. 2 (1996): 207–12.
West, Andrew Fleming. *Alcuin and the Rise of the Christian Schools*. New York: Charles Scribner's Sons, 1892.
West, Muriel. "Notes on the Importance of Alchemy to Modern Science in the Writings of Francis Bacon and Robert Boyle." *Ambix: The Journal of the Society for the Study of Alchemy and Early Chemistry* 9 (1961): 102–14.
White, Lynn, Jr. *Medieval Technology and Social Change*. New York: Oxford University Press, 1967.
———. *Medieval Religion and Technology: Collected Essays*. Berkeley: University of California Press, 1978.
Willison, Ian R. *On the History of Libraries and Scholarship*. Washington, DC: Library of Congress, 1980.
Wilson, Daniel J. "Lovejoy's Great Chain of Being After Fifty Years." *Journal of the History of Ideas* 48, no. 2 (1987): 187–206.
Windelband, W. *A History of Philosophy: With Special Reference to the Formation and Development of Its Problems and Conceptions*, translated by James Tuft, 2nd rev. ed. New York: MacMillan, 1901.

Bibliography

Witte, John, Jr. *Law and Protestantism The Legal Foundations of the Lutheran Reformation*. Cambridge: Cambridge University Press, 2002.

Wittkower, Rudolph. "Individualism in Art and Artists: A Renaissance Problem." *Journal of the History of Ideas* 22, no. 2 (1961): 291–302.

Witty, Francis J. "Early Indexing Techniques: A Study of Several Book Indexes of the Fourteenth, Fifteenth, and Early Sixteenth Centuries." *The Library Quarterly* 35, no. 3 (1965): 141–48.

Wolff, Phillipe. *The Awakening of Europe; The Pelican History of European Thought, Volume I*, translated by Anne Carter. Hammondsworth, UK: Penguin Books, 1968.

Yamey, B. S. "Scientific Bookkeeping and the Rise of Capitalism." *The Economic History Review*, 2nd ser., I, no. 2 & 3 (1949): 99–114.

Yates, Frances A. "The Art of Ramon Lull; An Approach to It Through Lull's Theory of the Elements." *Journal of the Warburg and Courtauld Institutes* 17, no. 1 & 2 (1954): 115–73.

———. *Giordano Bruno and the Hermetic Tradition*. Chicago, IL: University of Chicago Press, 1964.

Zilsel, Edgar. "The Sociological Roots of Science." *American Journal of Sociology* 47 (1942): 544–62.

———. "The Genesis of the Concept of Scientific Progress." *Journal of the History of Ideas* 6 (1945): 325–49.

Ziman, John. "Evolutionary Models for Technological Change." In *Technological Innovation as an Evolutionary Process*, edited by John Ziman. Cambridge: Cambridge University Press, 2000.

Index

Act of Settlement, English (1701), 142
Agricola, Georgius, 117
   De Re Metallica, 117
Alberti, Leon Battista, 49
   De re aedificatoria, 49
Albertus Magnus, 15, 17, 43
Alcuin, 8-9
Ambrosian Library (Milan), 130
Anne I (queen of England), 142
Anthropology, 69, 95
Antiquarians, antiquities, 61-62
Aquinas, Thomas, 15, 17
Aristotle, 33, 43, 51, 55, 63
   On the Heavens, 51
"Artificial writing," 47
Avicenna, 54
   Canon, 54

Bacon, Francis, 127, 153, 156
   The Advancement of Learning, 153
   De Augmentis Scientiarum, 153
   Novum Organum, 153
Bacon, Roger, 68, 151
Bede, the Venerable, 7-8
Bessarion (cardinal), 34, 44
Bible, 4, 134, 137
   King James Version, 137, 150
   Tyndale translation, 137, 150
   Vulgate, 4
Bill of Rights, English (1689), 141
Biringuccio, Vannocio, 117
   De la Pirotechnia, 117
Biscop (bishop), 7
Black Death, 20
Boccaccio, 32, 37
Bodin, Jean, 106
Bodleian Library (Oxford), 130
Boethius, 6
Boniface VIII (pope), 18

Boyle, Robert, 152, 153, 156
Brahe, Tycho, 114, 130
   Commentaries on the Motions of Mars, 114
   Harmonica Mundi, 114
Bruno, Giordano, 109, 110, 111, 112, 119-120, 128, 152
   Spaccio de la Bestia Trionfante, 119
Buchanan, George, 120
Budé, Guillaume
Burckhardt, Jacob, 49
   The Culture of the Rennaisance
Byzantine Empire/Byzantium, 10, 11, 14, 19

Calvin, John, 79, 82, 134
Cassidorus, 6
Charlemagne (king of France), 8-10, 11
Charles I (king of England), 138, 139
Charles II (king of England), 139, 140, 145, 153
Charles VIII (king of France), 46
Cicero, 42, 48
Civil War, English, 142, 145
Clement VII (pope), 18
Cluniac Reform, 12-13
Coke, Edward, 144
Columbus, Christopher, 68, 75, 93, 94-95
Common law, 143-146
Copernicus, Nicholas, 114, 115, 130
   De Revolutionibus Orbium Coelestium, 114
Coronation Oath of Office, English (1689), 141
Cosmology, Copernican-Galilean, 111
Council of Basel, 18
Council of Constance, 18
Council of Pisa, 18

Council of Trent, 79
Counter-Reformation, 79, 84, 94, 102, 111, 138
Cowley, Abraham, 153
Croce, Benedetto, quoted, 23
Cromwell, Oliver, 139, 140, 143

D'Ailly, Pierre, 68
  Imago Mundi, 68
D'Étaples, Jacques Lefèvre, 105
Dante Alighieri, 42, 118
  De Monarchia, 118
  The Divine Comedy, 98
De Beauvais, Vincent, 54
  Speculum maius, 54
De Medici Library (Florence), 130
De' Medici, Cosimo, 32, 107
Dee, John, 111
Dionysus the Areopagite, 39
Dioscorides, 43, 109, 113
  Materia Medica, 43, 55, 109, 113
Dolet, Etienne, 106
Donatus, 6
  Ars Grammatica Grammatica
Duns Scotus, 105

East India Company, 148
Eisenstein, Elizabeth, ix, x, 167
  The Printing Press as an Agent of Change, ix
Elizabeth I (queen of England), 134-135, 136
English Revolution (1640-1660), 133, 145
Erasmus, Desiderius, 27, 39, 44, 103
  Adagia, 39, 103
  Apophthegemata, 39
  In Praise of Folly, 105
Euclid, 51, 57
  Elements, 51
Evelyn, John, 153

Faulkner, William, 38
Ficino, Marsilio, 27, 32, 39, 107, 130, 152
  Theologia Platonica, 39
Foreign trade, 147, 150
French Revolution, 145-146
Froben, Johannes, 103, 164

Galen, 54, 109, 152
Galileo, viii, 33

Gesner, Conrad, 113
  Historia Animalium, 113
Glorious Revolution (England), 133, 142
Gunpowder revolution, 63
Gutenberg, Johannes, vii, viii, ix, x, 28-30, 31, 55, 56, 75-76, 77, 86, 92, 123, 166-167

Hahn, Ulrich, 43
Hegel, G.F.W., vii
  Philosophy of History, vii
Henry the Navigator, 95
Henry VIII (king of England), 82-83, 134
Hermes Trismegistus, 32, 104, 107
  Corpus Hermeticum, 104, 107
  Liber de potestate et sapientia Dei, 32
Hildegard of Bingen, 55
Hippocrates, 54, 55
Hirsch, Rudolf, 41
Hoarders of classical texts, 3-7
Hobbes, Thomas, 156-157
  Leviathan, 156
Holy Roman Empire, 8
Hotman, François, 120
Hundred Years War, 18, 31
Hus, Jan, Hussites, 17, 46

Index librorum prohitorim, 80-81
Isidore (bishop of Seville), 7
  De viris illustibus, 7
  Etymologies, 7

James I (king of England), 137
James II (king of England), 140, 141
Joachim of Fiore, 97
Julius II (pope), 76
Julius III (pope), 79
Justinian, 1, 12
Justinian law (*Corpus Juris Civilis*), 84-85

Kaballah, 108
Kepler, Johannes, 114, 115
Knox, John, 120, 135

Leibniz, 155
Leo X (pope), 76, 80
Licensing Act, discontinuation of, in England (1695), 142
Locke, John, 144

Index

Lollard movement, 17, 46
Long Parliament, 138, 145
Louis XIV (king of France), 140, 141
Loyola, Ignatius, 80
Luther, Martin, 76, 80, 81, 82, 93, 105-106, 134

Machiavelli, Niccolò, 119, 130
   Discourses, 119
   History of Florence, 119
   The Prince, 119
Maimonides, 54
   Aphorismi, 54
Manutius, Aldus, 79, 164
Marlowe, Christopher, 106, 111
   Doctor Faustus, 111
Marsilio of Padua, 64-65, 105, 118
   Defensor Pacis, 64, 118
Martianus Capella, 6
   De Nuptis Mercurii Et Philologiae
Matthias Corvinus (king of Hungary), 27, 34
MacKintosh, James, quoted, 23
Medicine, 54-56, 109
Melanchthon, Philip, 111
Milton, John, vii, viii, x, 143
   The Areopagitica, vii, 143
   Paradise Lost, 143
Mokyr, Joel, quoted, 162
Montaigne, Michel de, 106
More, Thomas, 98-99
   Utopia, 98-99
Münzer, Thomas, 87
Music, 53-54

Newton, Isaac, 152
   Philosophiae naturalis principia mathematica, 155
Nicholas of Cusa, viii, 32, 103-104, 109, 119
   De Docta ignorata, 105

Paracelsus, Philipus, 109, 110, 112, 114, 128, 152
Paul III (pope), 79
Petrarch, 32, 37, 40, 42
Pico Della Mirandola, 33, 119
Pius II (pope), 33
Pius IV (pope), 79
Plato, 14, 33, 63
   Timaeus, 6
   Republic, 98

Pliny the Elder, 55, 113
   Historia naturalis, 55
Plotinus, 48
Popper, Karl, 166
Porphyry, 6
   Isagoge, 6
Printing, 40-47, 79-81, 82-90, 138, 93-102 et passim
Proclus, 39, 48
Protectorate (Cromwell), 145
Ptolemy, 51, 93
   Almagest, 51
   Cosmographia, 51
Purbach, Georg von, 53

Rabelais, 99
   Gargantua, 99
Reformation, 79, 84, 92, 138
Regiomontanus of Nurnberg, 53, 115
   Ephemerides, 53
   Theoricae planetarum, 53
Renaissance (Carolingian), x, 9-10, 23, 25-26, 47, 77
Renaissance (fifteenth century), vii, 21, 24-25, 38, 40, 48, 49-50, 62-63, 70-71, 77, 90-93
Renaissance (twelfth century), x, 10-16
Roman Empire, vii, 1, 17, 23, 84
Royal Society (England), 154-155
   The Philosophical Transactions, 154

Scaliger, Joseph, 156
Shorey, P., 6
St. Augustine, 4, 98
   City of God, 98
St. Benedict of Nursia, 4
St. Jerome, 4
Steel, Robert, 41
Stevin, Simon, 115

Theophrastus, 55, 113
Thirty Years' War, 131
Thomas à Kempis, 28
   Imitatio Christi, 28
Toleration Act, English (1689), 141
Treaty of Westphalia, 143
Triennial Act, English (1694), 142
Tuchman, Barbara, 16
   A Distant Mirror, 18
Tyndale, William, 134

Urban, VI (pope), 18

BAKER COLLEGE LIBRARY

3 3504 00560 2778

```
Z 124  .A519 2011
Abel, Richard, 1925-
The Gutenberg revolution
```

DATE DUE

PROPERTY OF
BAKER COLLEGE
Owosso Campus

Index

Lollard movement, 17, 46
Long Parliament, 138, 145
Louis XIV (king of France), 140, 141
Loyola, Ignatius, 80
Luther, Martin, 76, 80, 81, 82, 93, 105-106, 134

Machiavelli, Niccolò, 119, 130
   Discourses, 119
   History of Florence, 119
   The Prince, 119
Maimonides, 54
   Aphorismi, 54
Manutius, Aldus, 79, 164
Marlowe, Christopher, 106, 111
   Doctor Faustus, 111
Marsilio of Padua, 64-65, 105, 118
   Defensor Pacis, 64, 118
Martianus Capella, 6
   De Nuptis Mercurii Et Philologiae
Matthias Corvinus (king of Hungary), 27, 34
MacKintosh, James, quoted, 23
Medicine, 54-56, 109
Melanchthon, Philip, 111
Milton, John, vii, viii, x, 143
   The Areopagitica, vii, 143
   Paradise Lost, 143
Mokyr, Joel, quoted, 162
Montaigne, Michel de, 106
More, Thomas, 98-99
   Utopia, 98-99
Münzer, Thomas, 87
Music, 53-54

Newton, Isaac, 152
   Philosophiae naturalis principia mathematica, 155
Nicholas of Cusa, viii, 32, 103-104, 109, 119
   De Docta ignorata, 105

Paracelsus, Philipus, 109, 110, 112, 114, 128, 152
Paul III (pope), 79
Petrarch, 32, 37, 40, 42
Pico Della Mirandola, 33, 119
Pius II (pope), 33
Pius IV (pope), 79
Plato, 14, 33, 63
   Timaeus, 6
   Republic, 98

Pliny the Elder, 55, 113
   Historia naturalis, 55
Plotinus, 48
Popper, Karl, 166
Porphyry, 6
   Isagoge, 6
Printing, 40-47, 79-81, 82-90, 138, 93-102 et passim
Proclus, 39, 48
Protectorate (Cromwell), 145
Ptolemy, 51, 93
   Almagest, 51
   Cosmographia, 51
Purbach, Georg von, 53

Rabelais, 99
   Gargantua, 99
Reformation, 79, 84, 92, 138
Regiomontanus of Nurnberg, 53, 115
   Ephemerides, 53
   Theoricae planetarum, 53
Renaissance (Carolingian), x, 9-10, 23, 25-26, 47, 77
Renaissance (fifteenth century), vii, 21, 24-25, 38, 40, 48, 49-50, 62-63, 70-71, 77, 90-93
Renaissance (twelfth century), x, 10-16
Roman Empire, vii, 1, 17, 23, 84
Royal Society (England), 154-155
   The Philosophical Transactions, 154

Scaliger, Joseph, 156
Shorey, P., 6
St. Augustine, 4, 98
   City of God, 98
St. Benedict of Nursia, 4
St. Jerome, 4
Steel, Robert, 41
Stevin, Simon, 115

Theophrastus, 55, 113
Thirty Years' War, 131
Thomas à Kempis, 28
   Imitatio Christi, 28
Toleration Act, English (1689), 141
Treaty of Westphalia, 143
Triennial Act, English (1694), 142
Tuchman, Barbara, 16
   A Distant Mirror, 18
Tyndale, William, 134

Urban, VI (pope), 18

Vatican Library, 33
Vesalius, Andreas, 113-114
   De humani corporis fabrico, 113-114
Vespucci, Amerigo, 68, 97
Viète, François, 115
Virginia Company, 148

Waldseemüller, Martin, 68
Weber, Max, 147

William III/of Orange (king of England), 140, 142
William of Ockham, 103-104, 105, 151, 152
Winthrop, John, 149
Wordsworth, William, 145-146
   The Convention of Cintra, 146
Wyclif, John, 46

Yarrow (library), 7-8

BAKER COLLEGE LIBRARY

3 3504 00560 2778

Z 124 .A519 2011
Abel, Richard, 1925-
The Gutenberg revolution

DATE DUE

PROPERTY OF
BAKER COLLEGE
Owosso Campus